Praise for *Hidden Blessings*

This wise book will guide you through the greatest challenge of middle age—dissolving and expanding your ego into love.
— **Andrew Harvey,** author of *The Hope: A G̶u̶i̶*

Without formulaic prescriptions, Jett ̶̶̶̶̶̶ ̶k of meeting the ordeals of midlife, allowin̶ ̶̶̶̶̶̶ ̶o come forward. This is a generous book, suffus̶ ̶̶̶̶ ̶. and an unmistakable kindness.
— **Francis Weller,** author of *The Wild Edge of Sorrow*

Jett Psaris' compassionate (but not sugarcoated) book speaks to the importance of submitting yourself to the process of change—to know there's a profound difference between getting older and *growing* older.
— **Gregg Levoy,** author of *Callings* and *Vital Signs*

Hidden Blessings will help anyone find purpose, meaning, and fulfillment in life's second half.
— **Larry Dossey, MD,** author of *Prayer Is Good Medicine* and *One Mind*

Hidden Blessings combines orthodox and innovative practices of spiritual development, never forgetting that the goal is not to transcend but to fully embody our humanity: to walk in shoes neither too big nor too small, but just right for us.
— **Marlena Lyons, PhD,** coauthor of *Undefended Love*

What happens when everything you know and do loses its significance, and you feel you're too "old" to start life all over again? You jump. Jett Psaris is that precise spiritual guide who brings understanding to the cliffs of our lives.
— **Zenju Earthlyn Manuel, PhD,** ordained Zen Buddhist priest and author of *The Way of Tenderness*

Jett Psaris stunningly describes life's process of disillusionment, not only an essential phase but a vital constituent in the alchemy of awakening.
— **Rashani Réa,** author of *Beyond Brokenness*

I trust Jett Psaris—with my confusion, my wounds, the whole of my spiritual journey. She's a wonderful writer with infinite knowledge.
— **Raphael Cushnir,** author of *The One Thing Holding You Back*

Accompanying us as a wise and loving friend, Jett Psaris leads us into the soulful work of embracing our humanity, one step at a time.
— **John Amodeo, PhD,** author of *Dancing with Fire*

Challenging us to face the humbling and inspiring truths of each moment, *Hidden Blessings* is an indispensable companion as we move through the currents, rapids, and tide pools of middle age.
— **James Flaherty,** founder of New Ventures West, Integral Coaching

Jett Psaris encourages us to fully embrace the confusion, the uncertainty, and even the despair that is necessary to shake our ego structure to its core. When we "experience the thing we fear the most if we are to evolve," as she writes, we come out with a new foundation, fresh and authentic, inclusive and fluid.
— **Paul Jaffe,** co-owner and founder of Copperfield's Books

Jett Psaris' heartful, soulful writing offers diamonds of insight: what many view as a period of breakdown or crisis is really a metamorphosis.
— **Gay Hendricks, PhD,** coauthor of *Conscious Loving* and *Conscious Loving Ever After*

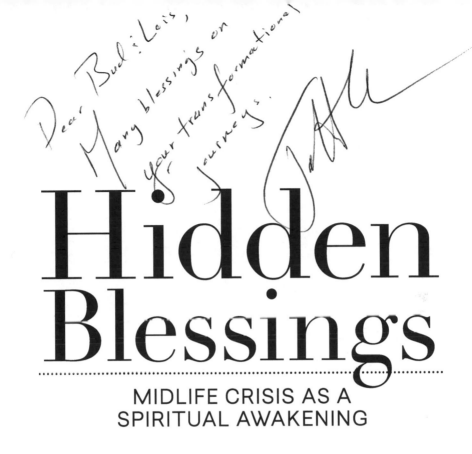

Dear Bud & Lois,
Many blessings on
your transformational
journeys.

Hidden Blessings

MIDLIFE CRISIS AS A
SPIRITUAL AWAKENING

JETT PSARIS, PhD

SACRED
RIVER PRESS

Sacred River Press
Oakland, California

ISBN: 978-0-9982935-2-3 (softcover)
ISBN: 978-0-9982935-1-6 (ebook)

Cover and interior design: Vicky Vaughn Shea, Ponderosa Pine Design
Author photo: Rod Searcey
Cover photo: Bill Frymire

Other books by this author:
Undefended Love, by Jett Psaris and Marlena S. Lyons

For more information, or for permission to excerpt:

Sacred River Press
Oakland, CA
info@sacredriverpress.com

This work is lovingly dedicated to
Marlena Lyons and Jonathan Tenney.

Thank you for teaching me to wonder about myself
and for adding your fascination to my own.
While I might have made it to the other side without you,
I would surely not be all of who I am today.
I am eternally grateful for your love, clarity, support,
wisdom, skillful means, generosity, and kindness.

My boat struck something deep.
Nothing happened.
Sound, silence, waves.
Nothing happened?
Or perhaps, everything happened
And I'm sitting in the middle of my new life.
—Juan Ramon Jimenez

Contents

Foreword

❧

When I first studied adult developmental psychology as a graduate student in the early 1970s, the emerging field was in much the same state as the field of biology before the invention of the microscope. We knew there were changes that took place at midlife, but we didn't understand much about the details. One of the earliest truisms I heard about midlife was an example of our woefully thin understanding of the middle period of adult life: *In your Thirties, you find your life; in your Forties, you build your life; in your Fifties, you enjoy your life.*

I recall thinking at the time, "Why can't we enjoy the whole process?" Now, with the microscope provided by Jett Psaris in *Hidden Blessings*, our chances of understanding and appreciating the depth and complexity of midlife's changes – and, yes, even enjoying them – are greatly enhanced.

There are many things to recommend about this book, but let me focus on just a few that I think you will appreciate most about it. First, the journey that Dr. Psaris takes us on is carefully mapped out. From her exploration of her own midlife journey, as well as the midlife paths taken by clients she has guided, she clearly knows the territory well. The map she provides takes us through 12 stages of the process, illuminating each stage as a potential work of art that we can create by engaging with the positive choices she outlines. I found her analysis of the 12 stages remarkably useful in understanding the shifting dynamics of midlife.

Second, and perhaps even more important, is the voice that comes through the text. Although it is a deep and thorough exploration of midlife, this book is no dry, academic textbook. Because Dr. Psaris has obviously gone through the myriad changes of midlife herself as well as with her clients, she speaks to us in the voice of the wise coach or companion that I would wish for all people going through those changes. Indeed, I found myself wishing her counsel had been available to me during my own slips, falls, and recoveries as I rode the sine-wave ups and downs of midlife.

Now, thanks to the work of Dr. Psaris and others who offer us rich detail about midlife rites of passage, we have access to a new level of understanding about the journey. What sets Dr. Psaris' work apart is the way she combines psychological insight with a spiritual perspective, taking us further than many books about the midlife passage go. My personal experience has shown me that the journey, if taken fully, is ultimately a spiritual one, leading us to an encounter with our divine essence and deepest potential. Those navigating this profound transformation that is available in midlife will benefit from the practical, spiritually based tools that Dr. Psaris shares with us. Through the generosity of her wisdom, I found that not only were my eyes opened but also my heart.

I urge you to read this book and let its deep counsel reveal the same hidden blessings to you.

Gay Hendricks, PhD

Preface

❧❀❧

Dear Friend,

If you have picked up this book, chances are that you or someone you know is in the age range of 40-65 and is struggling in some way with what is often popularly called a "midlife crisis." Maybe a divorce, job loss, affair, or illness has precipitated the crisis; or a restlessness or longing that feels uncontrollable; or maybe the experience has been more gradual, a loss of interest in what used to be meaningful. Whatever the challenge, it is taking place against the backdrop of aging or a feeling of time running out.

At midlife, a major sea change in our lives is, in fact, taking place. This sea change goes beyond anything former generations have experienced or defined. I wrote this book as I took the midlife journey myself, keenly feeling the absence of a comprehensive and contemporary map. This is, therefore, one part guidebook and one part scrapbook, both professional and confessional. I include my own story alongside the stories of friends, clients, family members, colleagues, and others I have met along the way.

In these pages, I walk beside you. I felt so disoriented and buffeted about during my midlife passage that writing was, first and foremost, my way of trying to get a grip. The great gift for me now, on the other side of my own journey through midlife, is the opportunity to share what I've learned in the hopes that the map I created for myself will help guide you, especially when the way grows dark and you might feel lost and confused as I did. In addition to inspiring and guiding you, I hope this book will let you know that you are not alone in this journey even though you may, at times, deeply believe you are.

The book's perspective is, overall, hopeful: the experience of crisis at midlife invites us into a process of psychological and spiritual metamorphosis. If we accept the invitation, then, at the end of that metamorphosis, we emerge from the cocoon of the first half of our adult lives to manifest freely the deepest creative contributions of our individual souls, unfettered by the ambitions and social contracts that directed us prior to midlife.

As you begin reading, it is helpful to bear in mind that *your soul will move in purposeful ways, forcing you to stretch beyond where you believe you can go by taking you to places you do not care to visit.* Although during the first half of this journey – Stages 1 through 6 – you might feel laid low, confused, or even scared, I pray that simply knowing that midlife is a shared human passage will lift your spirits. The second half of the journey – Stages 7 through 12 – offers new horizons and meaning as the hidden blessings of the process begin to emerge. The midlife transition is, after all is said and done, about the miracle of rebirth.

So, as we step into this midlife curriculum together, let's do our best to leave what has been with grace, and turn toward what is to come with awe and wonder. And let's move toward that newness holding each other's hands with compassion, courage, and love.

I welcome you as a fellow pilgrim navigating your way into the second half of your life and look forward to our journey, discovering together the hidden blessings awaiting each of us there.

In loving companionship,
Jett Psaris, PhD

Introduction

❦

If you are reading this book, chances are that you are in your forties, fifties, or sixties and finding yourself slowed down, stopped, or thwarted in a disturbing way. For some of us, this experience is abrupt; for others, it is a gradual erosion of energy or interest. Something has happened. We have run into a barrier. We have lost our way.

The precise nature of our distress might not be clear at first. It might feel like a vague sense of dissatisfaction or an irrepressible uprising of seemingly irrational or impractical urges. Or it might be crystal clear: a stark reality imposed by a disturbing medical condition or the loss of a steady paycheck or partner. One way or another, we sense that something significant has changed. *Without our consent or consideration, we have been ushered out of the first half of our adult lives into the midlife passage, the turbulent stretch that separates the life we have lived from the possibilities going forward.* We are at the threshold of an unexpected journey for which none of us is prepared.

Many words have been written about this period of life sometimes called middle age. What makes *Hidden Blessings* different is its unique blend of psychological and spiritual guidance. This guidance, which comes from my own midlife experience and that of others, draws on many traditions and schools of thought to help us respond fully to the transformative invitation of midlife. That invitation is to step away from taking life literally – and, perhaps, superficially – to discover a deep and profound underlying existence. Midlife invites us to surrender the narrowly defined view of ourselves and others that prevails during the first half of life, so that we can become more complex and multi-dimensional beings, capable of living the largest lives possible going forward.

To take full advantage of the unprecedented opportunity for transformation during this period, we need to understand the process that is unfolding beneath the surface. This is true whether we are experiencing midlife as a crisis or a quieter but no less desperate shift in our most basic ground. The transformation that is possible during midlife is more than just a continuation of the developmental arc of the first half of our lives; midlife offers the possibility of metamorphosis into an entirely new life with a vaster perspective than we have enjoyed until now.

Understanding midlife as a metamorphosis enables us to see the full measure of the possibility opening up during this period of our lives. *The midlife passage invites the death of who we have known ourselves to be and promises the birth of our authentic, soul-infused self, long suppressed under years of outward obligations.* The more we view midlife as a spiritual rebirth rather than something to get over or simply endure, the less likely we are to settle for trying to repackage what we have lived during the first half of our adult lives – and the more likely we are to discover the full range of the blessings that await us if we surrender to the challenging process of unraveling and being transformed.

A rebirth within life is not simple; it entails profound uncertainty and destabilization. Most of us are familiar – from our own experience or that of friends and family members – with the confusion, insecurity, and extended periods of grief that many feel in response to the losses experienced during the middle adult years. A central message of this book is that these experiences, which disrupt the predictability of our lives, are *necessary*. They realign us to a new order of living, a shift most of us would be unwilling or unable to make if we were not forcibly dislodged from our familiar comfort zones.

"Midway along the journey of our life," we are *supposed to* find ourselves "lost in a dark and treacherous wood," as Dante wrote. We are meant to feel shaken to our roots. It is supposed to feel hard. We are supposed to wonder why we are here and whether we are on the right track. We are meant to experience boredom, anger, unhappiness, fear, and even despair over our lives as well as confusion about what to do about it.

Most of us are familiar with Jesus' teaching, "seek and ye shall find." But many are not familiar with the version from the Gospel of Thomas: "If you are searching, you must not stop until you find. When you find, however, you will become troubled."

The gospel affirms the troubled state we might be feeling as the potential for new insight and expanded perspective rattle the cage of our familiar paradigms. In midlife, no matter how our lives have been lived up to this point – no matter what level of success we have achieved – *we are destined to arrive at the shocking realization that we have outlived the agendas of the first half of our lives.* We never imagined or anticipated that these agendas would come to an end. The realization that the old guidelines have expired often produces bewilderment, unexpected aimlessness, anxiety, or desperation.

We may be surprised at the extent of the shift that midlife calls on us to make: during the midlife passage, our *entire shape* undergoes metamorphosis. We are transformed on every level – physical, emotional, psychological, and spiritual – and a new life awaits us on the other side of this transformation. That new life is often entirely unplanned and different from the one we have been living even if its outer appearance might in some cases seem similar to what it was before midlife. In Thomas' words, "Your confusion will give way to wonder. In wonder you will reign over all things. Your sovereignty will be your rest." Thomas offers us a vision of a new universe resting on an unshakeable foundation that emerges during midlife.

This new foundation is the part of our nature that is continuously creative, uniquely alive, and able to imbue life with newness and freshness. We can call this part of our nature the soul. It is where the life force that unites all beings resides and moves in and through us. The midlife passage is all about contacting and shifting our center of gravity toward our souls' aims, increasingly discovering and living from the authentic core of who we are.

This can happen in an infinite number of different ways, and the results can take an infinite number of forms. Each of us must ultimately find his or her own way through the midlife journey. Therefore, the map offered in this book is not meant to create a midlife formula but rather to provide navigational tools for our individual passages. What is most important is that we make our journeys our own so that we can each discover the heart and soul of who we are.

Even though each person's midlife journey is unique, some elements of the path are widely shared. *Hidden Blessings* lays out those shared elements of the journey as I have personally experienced them, observed them in clients and friends, and understood them with the help of colleagues. Although the book offers a map to help make the terrain knowable, the midlife journey requires long periods during which we must surrender the comfortable coordinates of the known and experience the wildness of the unknown. Midlife is not a boilerplate experience. It opens doorways that allow each of us to have our own singular experiences and to discover and develop our own personal properties.

At midlife we are not trying to be like other people. Unlike during the first half of our adult lives, we are not seeking to fulfill a preordained pattern or accomplish another goal. Instead, in midlife, space opens up for something entirely different to happen. Thus, the stories recounted within this book are only a guide; they offer a flashlight and a compass to help us explore the truth of our own unmaking and rebirth in midlife as those processes unfold in an individual way for each of us.

The stages presented here are designed to create a holding environment – a context – within which each of our unique states of consciousness can expand and our personal gifts and qualities can find expression. This holding environment can support us in cooperating with, rather than resisting, the powerful currents of change at this time of life.

Psychological and Spiritual Guidance

Understanding the psychological and spiritual currents underlying the disorienting realities of midlife will help us participate fully in our own transformation. These currents flow in what we can call the invisible world, "that which transpires behind that which appears," in the words of the Sufis. To help us develop the ability to see what lies behind the visible world, *Hidden Blessings'* approach to midlife draws on both psychological and spiritual perspectives.

Although psychological and spiritual work might appear to be separate prior to midlife, these two domains become harder to tell apart during midlife as our psychological work brings us in touch with our spiritual nature, and our experience of spiritual states of consciousness expands our psychological understanding and depth. Engagement in both dimensions is part of the process of spiritual awakening that begins when we are born and takes a large leap forward during the middle of our lives.

The Psychological Lens

The *psychological* lens gives us insight into the structures of our psyche that obstruct awareness of our deep, soulful nature. When we look through the psychological lens, we discover a host of unconscious beliefs, unresolved issues, and hidden agendas that rule our lives without our consent or conscious participation. Our psychological work in this book focuses mainly on gaining an understanding of our ego, the part of our psyche that corresponds to our sense of our identity and its survival and coping patterns.

Psychology helps us understand that, for the most part, when we use the word "I," it is the ego speaking. Our egos are built from our infancy in response to the ways our needs are and are not met as well as other forms of family and social conditioning. Unless we have engaged in psychological work, most of us remain unknowingly hypnotized into believing the ego's rendition of "me and my story," which is a composite of recurring thoughts and emotional patterns entirely conditioned by the past.

Familiarizing ourselves with our psychological patterning includes understanding the degree to which our early family environments continue to animate our thoughts and feelings in our current lives. Understanding our psychological patterning also requires an exploration of cultural, religious, racial, and other beliefs acquired and encoded in us through experience and education. The combined effect of family environment and cultural and other beliefs that shape us is broadly called "conditioning."

Once we begin to identify our conditioning, we can recognize the role this training has played in separating us from the more genuine qualities and energies of our deepest and truest nature. The first half of the midlife journey (Stages 1–6) is, in large part, about liberating ourselves from this conditioning, which has solidified into the form of our ego and creates a thick veil over a more authentic and spontaneous experience of who we can be and truly are.

The Spiritual Lens

Through the *spiritual* lens, we gain access to our souls, enabling us to perceive the world as it really is, unfiltered by our conditioning. Some people reach for contact with their souls through organized religion. Others find the soul through intimate partnership, nature, contemplative practices, or creative exploration and expression. We experience this spiritual part of ourselves when we are in the presence of something larger than ourselves, such as a breathtaking natural sight or an awe-inspiring event. Before midlife, conscious contact with our souls is usually intermittent.

It is important to understand that the soul, our unconditioned self, is *within* us, not outside of us, and is connected to our ego in very complex and intricate ways. Many authors pit the ego against the soul as if these two were separate and embattled. Rather than viewing the ego as an obstacle, we will see that the ego's transformation at midlife prepares us for the next stage in our evolution. As long-time Buddhist Jack Engler has written: "You have to be somebody before you can be nobody." *Rather than an opponent of the soul on the battlefield of life, the ego has been a reflection all along of the more spontaneous, authentic possibility of who we can be when we are soul-centered; in fact, as we will discover, the ego is the soul in a primitive, undeveloped state.*

Although the ego is disassembled in the course of the midlife journey, it is not discarded. It transforms into a more transparent and malleable vehicle for our soul's aims, a means of allowing our soul full expression.

To describe this in a different way, ego is to the soul as coal is to the diamond. The ego and the soul share the same existence – or "suchness" as the Buddhists might say – just as coal and diamonds are both pure carbon. But coal must go through a tremendous transformation, during which time it is subjected to high temperatures and incredible pressure, before its atomic structure is reordered into the pattern of the crystal that we know as a diamond. During midlife, our egos are similarly placed under tremendous stress that realigns them into the full brilliance of the soul.

During midlife, conditions become optimal for us to reverse the process of ego (or identity) formation that began in our infancy and has continued during the first half of our lives. Our midlife experiences facilitate the process, creating an urgency to liberate ourselves from the conditioned rigidity, predictability, and density of our ego identities; we shift toward being lighter, more transparent, and conscious, as we come to realize that our souls are the true, essential part of us, lying beneath who we have believed ourselves to be. *The success of our midlife transformation depends on our ability to allow the soul to evolve beyond the ego structure encasing it.*

Becoming Mature Adults

In our first adult lives, the ego helps us fulfill what philosopher Jean-Jacques Rousseau calls "the social contract": to be good citizens, have families, go to work, and contribute to the building of society, all of which are adult versions of patterns of behavior and accommodation learned in childhood. Some elements of the social contract – such as paying bills, restraining ourselves from harming others, and obeying traffic signs – maintain their validity throughout our lives. But, in the second half of our lives, our emphasis will shift away from meeting the obligations of the social contract. Now, the assignment is to become something more than the social selves we created in childhood and maintained and renovated during the first half of our adult lives.

The ego is destined to dissolve in the face of an inner urgency to grow up – not just grow old – and become mature adults. I am not talking about the ability to move out of our parents' homes, become financially self-sufficient, and create families of our own. These are first-half-of-life indicators of adulthood as defined by the social contract. The maturity developed in the second half of our adult lives means something entirely different.

At midlife, the journey is no longer about adapting and adjusting to the needs of others or society at large. Instead, midlife maturity is about discovering and becoming *unique* human beings not bound by social and personality contracts. At midlife, we have the opportunity to realize the mystery that we have covered over with thoughts, beliefs, conditioning, and obligations. We have a chance to reorient and ask what our lives are truly about.

This does not mean we stop contributing to society. Paradoxically, after midlife, we enroll ourselves into a higher order of the social contract, this time fulfilling the obligations of our souls for the good of the whole of life rather than meeting obligations, attempting to avoid consequences, or trying to feel safe, which are legacies from childhood.

For us to become mature adults, the emphasis of the first half of our lives on ego formation must give way to the midlife rigors of ego deconstruction. That is, midlife is the time to emotionally detach from, and psychologically disassemble, the ego. During the first stages of our midlife transformation, this detachment and disassembly occur very much against our will. The good news is that, as our ego disintegrates, we become aware of our essential or true nature: we come into contact with our soul.

Mapping Midlife

The 12 midlife stages I have mapped in *Hidden Blessings* encourage us to experience the process as a developmental path. Each stage delineates the various experiences we can expect during one leg of the journey. Although I present the stages linearly, as if they are discrete and chronological, they will not take place in any everyone's life as neatly as they are laid out here. Nevertheless, most people will traverse most of the territory I have outlined, and the vast majority will recognize the overall pattern or sequence of the 12 stages as presented. It might take a full 10 to 12 years to traverse them, or, the process might be more pronounced during three or four tumultuous years.

Here are the 12 stages:

Stage 1   Shock When the Center Cannot Hold
Stage 2   The Unraveling
Stage 3   The Uprising

Presenting the stages in a linear order offers an overall lay of the midlife landscape and an understanding of the cycle of transformation. The danger of this linear map lies in our tendency to become frustrated or confused when our individual processes do not match the succession of stages outlined. Lived reality exceeds and evades logic; the linear order outlined here may very well differ from what unfolds during each individual's journey.

In reality, we can expect to simultaneously experience more than one stage at a time rather than neatly progressing through the stages one by one. We might also experience the stages out of order, for example finding ourselves in Stage 7 experiencing expansion into our newly unified fields and then suddenly returning to Stage 1 when we are shocked by another life challenge. For most people, the stages run parallel and overlap throughout the midlife passage, not once but many times.

The overall movement of the 12 stages as presented in this book is a repeating cycle of failure, depression, refinement, and realignment that conducts our consciousness across progressive thresholds until our ego identity expands into our soul identity. The outcome is neither exclusively spiritual nor exclusively worldly but a unique synthesis of the two. The culmination is that each of us becomes a profoundly human individual whose character is grounded in the universal while remaining very personal. We become undefended: deeply loving, wise, vulnerable, imperfect, and kind. This is not a conceptual leap but a structural change in awareness that allows each of us to know ourselves as both an individual consciousness (our individual identity) and a universal consciousness, separate from nothing and connected to everything.

A Common Misunderstanding

In my mind, the midlife passage has been largely misunderstood and miscategorized. As a result, many people do not take the journey that is possible at this stage of life, which diminishes their opportunity to live the full potential of the second half of their adult lives.

Perhaps the most common misunderstanding about the midlife passage is how long it takes. Although there are notable deviations, a preponderance of people experience the passage between the ages of 40 and 65 years old, and, for the majority, the journey takes about 12 years from start to finish.

Bracketing off a dozen years for the midlife passage helps us recognize the long-term nature of the changes that take place during this period. When we are engaged in personal and spiritual evolution, *a long-term view is essential*, enabling us to acknowledge the length of time that true transformation takes and reminding us that we might not be able to measure our progress on a day-to-day scale. This is a helpful perspective when our experience feels stagnant or unbearably dark. Recognizing the length of time involved also allows us to understand the commitment necessary to learn a new rhythm and fully enter a new field of experience. The length of the midlife passage serves a purpose. It gives us much-needed context and time to identify lifelong patterns – an important activity, as we will see – in what might otherwise appear to be a string of isolated experiences.

A Vertical Leap

The type of deep spiritual transformation that is for many of us most accessible at midlife is potentially available in smaller doses in any life experience that suddenly and drastically alters the trajectory of our lives and challenges us to break out of our conditioned ego selves. Midlife opens this door for many of us because of the direct collision that happens when midlife's imperative for change meets the ongoing weight of social and cultural expectations, against the backdrop of our sense of dwindling time.

Major life dislocations – births, deaths, disabilities, serious illnesses, profound childhood traumas, spiritual emergencies – take us outside patterns of ego and conditioning and open the possibility for what Ken Wilber calls "vertical development." Wilber defines vertical development as "an actual transformation or an actual shift in one's level of consciousness. If you imagine a 10-story building, vertical transformation is moving from one floor to a higher floor" in contrast to the horizontal activity of "moving furniture around on the same floor."

Relatively few of us make the vertical leap that Wilber describes when we are confronted with potentially transformative experiences during the first half of our lives. Instead, most of us respond to these experiences horizontally: we rearrange the furniture of our egos by making changes in jobs, careers, partners, or geographic locations. Although these changes can be significant, most of us are, until midlife, able to reconstitute our core identities after powerful life events and to move forward with our conditioned egos intact. By contrast, the midlife passage exerts such force on our egos that eventually their centers can no longer hold, as we will see in Stage 1. This forces us into true vertical change, the process of rebirth.

We can delay the midlife passage, as we will discuss in a moment, and, as mentioned above, we can have life-altering experiences at any age that thrust us into the process of rebirth, but generally we cannot take the midlife journey before midlife. It takes actual life experience for our constructed self, our ego, to mature. And, paradoxically, it takes ego strength to go through ego dissolution. We have to have the strong ego built during the first half of our lives in order to make the midlife transformation because *the ego must involve itself in its own metamorphosis by failing to take us into the next stage of life.*

Evolve or Die

Far too many people die in their fifties but are not buried until their eighties; their bodies may keep going, but, because they do not take the full journey possible at midlife, their potential for self-realization withers. Some of these people manage to avoid the inevitable process of midlife disintegration; others are caught in earlier life stages, unable to move forward. In either case, the outcome is similar. We've all met these people. In their old age, they cannot cover up their misery, resentment, and bitterness. They are demanding, insensitive, and ungrateful; they complain endlessly. *Their inner lives have withered away along with their outer capacities.*

It's never too late to be who you might have been.
—George Eliot

Those who resist the call to transform during their middle adult years lose the connection with the source of their vitality, the soul, which lies deep below the surface realities of existence. They ignore or have become deaf to the inner imperative to enlarge their lives in a new, never-before-experienced way. As a result, instead of stepping into the great adventure of midlife, they are haunted by unlived potentialities and life is reduced to a repetition instead of a fresh unfolding and endless discovery.

The impulse to avoid the journey is understandable; especially in the opening stages, our fear of what will be lost can obstruct our commitment to what is yearning to be lived. Many of us will cling to our old lives while looking for a guarantee that new lives are possible and will be better. Even as the old well is drying up – often felt most acutely in the beginning of the journey as a loss of energy, motivation, and purpose – we try to maintain our lives until the passage disables us altogether. Or we rearrange the furniture of our lives to try to make things better: we trade in an old spouse for a fresher model or scurry out of our own lives into someone else's in hopes of reviving the selves we have known up until this point.

We might try to turn back the hands of time, reinforcing insecurities that are rooted in what we have been taught are the places where we have value: women may over-commit to hormone replacement therapies; men may over-commit to sexual enhancement drugs. We might become weekend sports warriors or redouble our efforts to make money. We might consider anti-depressants, anti-pain, and anti-anxiety medications to try to pull back from the midlife emotional challenges of discomfort and lack of safety. Some might dive further into a host of well-worn addictions – food, work, sex, alcohol, gambling, pornography – or less widely recognized dependencies like over-exercising, over-reading, or over-socializing.

However, *the whole point of midlife is to allow the construct of who we are and the lives we have created to fail.* The way we have coped and dealt with our emotional needs in the past is not working anymore; the lives we are living are coming to a close.

Many try to straddle what has been while reaching for what might be. One client attempted to live in two worlds at the same time by attending to her husband just enough to keep him invested in their marriage, all the while looking for someone "better." A group member maintained his grip on his old world by investing all of his energy into rebuilding his failing company while privately dreaming of walking the Appalachian Trail. A woman in the same group turned to a host of cosmetic surgeries and anti-aging treatments to extend the time she could remain in the more comfortable seductress role of her youth while at the same time wanting someone to really see the real her, below the image she portrays. A workshop attendee shared that while he was straining to be a good husband and father on the outside, he secretly wanted to retreat to a cabin in the woods and live alone for a while.

Even though we might know how precarious straddling two lives can be, at various times throughout midlife we will find ourselves unavoidably stretched between the known and the unknown, between what has been and what may be. In this position all we can do is try to balance with one foot in each world – ideally in the most conscious manner possible, as this book helps us learn to do.

When we arrive at midlife torn, confused, desperate, burned out, unmotivated, or fearful, what we don't yet understand is that there isn't any more life force in our old habits and patterns because we have used it all up! A new direction is needed.

It is unimaginable to us that the old system is actually not reparable. But at midlife we undergo radical change; our old way of being is not something we can tweak and rejuvenate. We need to start over from the ground up. *It is not an opportunity for a fresh start; it is a mandate for one.*

Carl Jung wrote, "we walk in shoes too small for us." If we resist the call to transform at midlife, all the makeup, money, and medications in the world won't stem our grief over having aborted the possibility of living the authentic, soul-centered life that belongs uniquely to us.

This is not to ignore the fact that many people live outstanding lives before they reach midlife. But in my experience, it is generally true that on the other side of midlife we have a greater opportunity to live a less conditioned and conditional life. Once we have completed the midlife passage, we can manifest the creativity and expression that were hidden by our egos during the first half of our lives. By the grace of the midlife mandate to transform, we begin to fulfill our souls' destinies for the first time.

A session with a 47-year-old woman who had been diagnosed with cancer comes to mind. In the middle of her first course of chemotherapy treatments, she said hopefully: "I can't wait until I am through this and can get back to my life."

"This is your life now," I responded quietly; "there is no going back." At midlife we all receive the same stark diagnosis: evolve or die.

As is true with all developmental passages, there is no right or wrong way to experience midlife, and all generalizations in this book are meant as guidelines, not prescriptions. It is more important that we strive to become conscious of the deeper processes particular to our own journeys than it is to fit into the generalities offered here.

Those who successfully navigate the developmental transitions from childhood into adulthood and then through midlife realize that our personal development continues throughout life. This enables us to live lives that become increasingly more fulfilling, authentic, and aligned with our souls. If we successfully traverse the midlife passage, we become more conscious, alive, and loving, free of the stress of having to *become* someone because we already *are* someone.

Shock When the Center Cannot Hold

❧⸰⸱⸰❧

Now we begin, as Elizabeth Bell says to her groups on conscious aging, "the journey of 10,000 surprises along a road never traveled before." For most of us, arriving at midlife comes in the form of encountering a situation that is too big or unfamiliar for us to respond to using our familiar resources. It's as if we are driving along in our car, living our life as usual, and we arrive at an immense body of water. In the past we have been temporarily stopped by challenges, but never before have we been confronted with what appears to be the end of the road.

We might feel scared, excited, or cautious. Our minds might tell us to circle back because we must have taken a wrong turn. Before this, we did not know – directly and deeply know – that the road would end, other than having the distant understanding that we will all die one day. But an ending within life: what does that mean?

At the outset of our midlife journeys, we stand at the edge of this sea. It soon becomes clear that the vehicle that got us to this point, our ego, cannot transport us across the vast, unknown body of water stretching out before us. *We have come to the end of our first adult life.*

The ego is the part of ourselves that has been focused on self-preservation and adaptation. For decades we have identified with our egos, and through our egos we have gained experience, acquired knowledge (and often approval), and fulfilled the social contract. For many of us, the result has been good lives. Now we enter what is popularly called a midlife "crisis" because we have exhausted the ego's resources and agendas. *What we don't know yet is that, all along, our egos have housed the germ of new life – the part of us that is equipped to enter the vast ocean before us and take us into the second half of our adult lives.*

For most of us, the lives we have created and their associated satisfactions are not destroyed in one fell swoop. Instead, we encounter multiple midlife entry points that chip away at us over time. That is, most people don't experience a single cataclysmic event but a series of midlife entry experiences, large and small "crises." These crises are meant to enlarge us, initiating us into larger, wider, and more inclusive frames of reference. Although we shrink back from each confrontation at first because no one enjoys the pain, confusion, or suffering that these experiences elicit, our future lives depend on the degree to which we can work with and see these challenges as transformative and necessary, moving us toward a clearer and more encompassing worldview of ourselves, others, and life itself.

The poet W. B. Yeats describes the experience of consciousness being enlarged in his poem "The Second Coming." He writes, "Things fall apart; the centre cannot hold." *Midlife is a process in which the ego, which has been our center, cannot hold in the face of the crises that confront it.*

Self-Inquiry

* Are you experiencing anything in your life as a crisis? What is it, and in what way does it challenge you?

* Each life crisis or struggle can lead to an expansion of consciousness or barrier to life. Can you imagine an increased capacity, understanding, or larger perspective that the above challenging experience could reveal to you? Don't worry if you don't have a clear insight about a larger frame of reference that a challenge might be pointing to. The goal here is simply to wonder what the experience might reveal that is outside the envelope of how you usually react to or view challenging events.

The End of Our First Adult Life

As we will see in more detail later in this chapter, the ego's failure to deal with experiences that show up during the middle years of our lives – and the feelings evoked in us by the ego's failure to manage life and control outcomes – are what initiate our midlife journey. Before looking at different types of midlife entry experiences, let's understand a little bit more from the world of psychology about our egos and how they develop and function during the first half of our lives.

The purpose of life is to be defeated by greater and greater things.
—Rainer Maria Rilke

When we are born, the inability of the environment to meet our every infant need creates frustration and fear in us. We develop an ego (this is our psychological birth) to protect us from these feelings as well as other, more complex emotions that we experience over time, such as disappointment, jealousy, and shame.

A little later in life, when we are toddlers and beyond, the ego expands its function to help us adapt and adjust to those around us so that we can get our needs met, feel safe, and fit in. The ego's development is a natural part of our development, and the ego serves us well for a long while. Over time, this emotional coping and defense system becomes very elaborate – and, until midlife, the ego thinks of itself as who we are, now and forever.

We can glimpse an aspect of our egos through the habitual roles we play, which are often not fully conscious. Some common roles are: the perfectionist, the helper, the super-achiever, the know-it-all, the boss, and the mediator. There are many more. One client identifies his role in his family and in life as the guy who "makes things work." Another says she is "where the buck stops," the "ultra-responsible one" in her family.

We take on different roles with different people in different situations. For example, we might act like a good little girl with our father and play the role of hero with our mother; we might be a joker with friends and a worrywart with our primary partner. Even if we rebelled against what was asked of us as a child, that rebellion was a reaction to our family of origin, not a native movement coming from our intrinsic self. As we repeat and reinforce our roles, we eventually lose sight of who we are without them.

We take on these roles because we want something from others around us, and we believe we have to play a role to get it. As children, we want to get approval and avoid disapproval. The truth is, all we ever wanted was love, but, over time, we gave up on trying to get love and began pursuing a host of love substitutes, such as approval, recognition, fame, respect, power, admiration, adoration – whatever would make us feel safe, noticed, or valued. If the capacity to play one of our roles is compromised, the ego begins to break down.

We rely on our egos to operate smoothly and unimpeded. When the functioning of these coping patterns breaks down, is compromised, or impaired, our first experience is shock. The more rigid our ego identities are, the more shocked we feel when they fail us.

The title of Stage 1 is "Shock When the Center Cannot Hold." We experience shock when who we are at a given moment is too small to "handle" whatever has come up; our being places us in shock to give us the time to adjust to an experience that feels too big for us to address or respond to. Not all experiences of shock are the same; we can experience large and small shocks, as I will explain shortly. But, for now, an example of a big shock might be a cancer diagnosis, and a small shock feels more like being thrown off track or blindsided.

Our midlife entry points are shocking and can initiate an experience of crisis in us because they deeply challenge our primary ego identities and therefore compromise our sense of security. For example, the stability of a friend's sense of self is dependent on her ability to maintain a strong social structure; her capacity to sustain strong connections with family and friends is what makes her feel safe and okay. Her entry into midlife came in the form of divorce and the subsequent disassembly of her nuclear family, which directly challenged her primary identity. Who is she if she is no longer Mrs. Jones, the mother, matriarch, and center of her circle of friends?

To name some other examples, a colleague whose ego identity was wrapped around being sexually appealing to men faced breast cancer as her entry into midlife. A former Silicon Valley co-worker based his self-worth on his net worth; his entry into midlife came in the form of bankruptcy. A chiropractor who sees himself as a healer entered midlife when he developed a muscular disease that shifted him from being the caretaker to the one in need of care.

For most of us, the first response to this experience of shock is to try to put the pieces of our egos back together. For example, if our identity has solidified around being the one who has the answers, when successive challenges at midlife reveal that we don't have the answers, or that the ones we are coming up with are lame, we might become fiercely determined to find those answers by going back to school to pick up a fifth degree, perhaps in psychology this time. That response would be an attempt to reinforce our ego identity of being the one in the know.

Discovering that we don't have all the answers exposes us to the uncomfortable feelings that we used the know-it-all identity to suppress in the first place. If we don't know, then we don't know what will happen or whether we will be able to deal with what will happen. That's why our first response will be to try to figure it out so we can once again feel safely wrapped up in knowledge; however, unbeknownst to us, we will be further away from the truth. Although we will try to repair and rebalance our egos more than once during our midlife journey, ultimately the integrity of the ego's structure is permanently compromised; in Yeats' words, the center cannot hold.

Moreover, the shock we feel over our midlife entry point is simply the opening act. We will experience a series of losses during the first six stages of midlife.

Over time, we will realize that these obstacles or crises have a beneficent outcome and serve a higher purpose: they stop us or slow us down considerably while life strips away the social and psychological constructs we have been living in up to this point (to be discussed in Stage 2, The Unraveling).

Our entry points or crises are deep and true summons to evolve beyond our egos into something larger that can inspire us for the rest of our lives. These calls initiate the passage that, if we navigate it fully, will allow each of us to pass through necessary periods of darkness and emerge to live a fulfilling and rich second half of our adult life.

In the next section of this chapter, we'll take a look at the types of crisis experiences that can initiate us into midlife, inviting us to give birth to the greater selves that are buried within the egos that have carried us through the first half of our adult life.

Entering Midlife

For some, a dramatic crisis initiates midlife. Illness, divorce, the death of a spouse or parents, or the loss of a career are common dramatic initiating events. On the less common but decidedly dramatic side, a client literally fell out of the sky when the engine of her Cessna failed and the plane plummeted to Earth, crushing many of the bones in her body. Another woke up one morning to learn his home had burned to the ground in the Oakland Hills Firestorm of 1991. A woman I met in my mother's nursing home in Virginia entered midlife when her 22-year-old daughter became a paraplegic in a near-fatal car accident.

Dramatic midlife entries can also come from a collective crisis: the stock market might crash, a war might be declared, or an ecological disaster or terrorist attack might disturb our fragile illusion of safety and control.

A dramatic midlife entry point usually feels like a shocking, instantaneous change in circumstances after which nothing is the same.

Gradual Entries

Midlife entry points are not always dramatic. Instead, we might gradually develop a sense that the horizon ahead feels limited. The lives we have been living can begin to feel increasingly narrow, restricted, and uninspiring.

A common phrase I hear when people enter midlife slowly is that they feel like they are trapped or in a box. They want to break out but cannot. They feel unable to affect what is happening, and they are unhappy about this condition. In the words of one client: "I feel like a wild stallion in a corral; it is too confining, and the energy inside me is exploding in reaction to feeling so restricted and restrained." In the words of another client: "I feel stuck. Nothing is working. I can't get out of this place I'm in. It feels oppressive, suffocating, deadening."

Gradual entries might bring us to an intense awareness of life choices no longer available to us, such as having children, becoming professional athletes, or pursuing new endeavors that require years of preparation. We begin to realize that desires and interests once placed on a back burner must now be moved off the stovetop entirely. Lost dreams, neglected capacities, and atrophied skills can activate fears of a wasted life and self-condemnation that we allowed this to happen. The lost opportunities stimulate fear as we anticipate that our options for the future may continue to narrow.

Physical challenges and the awareness that we are aging might also elicit a growing sense of limitation or of feeling trapped. Development of intermittent or chronic physical pain or feelings of weakness or fatigue might force us to modify our lives in unfamiliar ways. We might notice a slowing down in our reflexes while driving or playing sports, or we might confront disturbing lapses in memory. We might experience changes in eating and sleeping patterns. We find ourselves needing to adapt and accommodate to various bodily changes in a multitude of small and large ways. Weight gain often becomes a disturbing factor. Self-care and self-maintenance require increasing amounts of time, attention, and resources if we are to maintain the highest quality of life possible.

Some enter midlife through the gradual dawning of a sense of diminishing returns. Activities and relationships that once held value and interest might deliver less and less satisfaction. The thrill of shopping or the latest promotion no longer provide the emotional boost they once did. Children move away from home, leaving parents feeling alone and disoriented. Or a parent might be gradually overtaken by a desire to leave the kids and spouse behind. Tried and true ways of relaxing, like watching sports or playing games, can begin to feel less pleasurable, more like killing time than passing time. They don't cease to offer fulfillment altogether; they just deliver less than they once did.

We might experience a gradual loss of energy, a loss of interest in life, or uncomfortable levels of anxiety. We might feel as though we are slowly dying on the vine as the vitality drains out of us, emotionally and physically. A "been-there-done-that" malaise might creep in, leaving us apathetic, depressed, or bored.

The Common Thread in Midlife Entry Points

Whatever the nature of a midlife entry point, it communicates the message that our current life streams are drying up. Poet Mary Oliver captures the feeling of this narrowing of life experience in her query, "Listen, are you breathing just a little, and calling it a life?"

In his journal Michael, a 44-year-old client, describes this sense of increasing limitation in this way:

> My life could go on this way until I die. It's not a bad life but something is missing: a spark, some juice. I have moments when I really feel alive, expressive, and strong like when I'm drumming, while making love, and when I'm riding my mountain bike. There is not enough of that in my life. Mostly there is a shrinking back from life, a lack of the spark, aliveness, happiness, and joy I want so much. In between these moments of flow I feel bored or lifeless. I feel trapped by my outer life and disabled in my inner life.

Michael's old self – and the life belonging to that self – is drying up. He experiences a deflation when he thinks about his life continuing to proceed along the same lines that it has been; much of the life force has been exhausted from his old existence, so it lacks vitality and joy. At the same time, his new self and new life are not yet born. In the absence of something to go to, Michael clings to his old ways even though he feels suffocated and disabled.

When we enter midlife, which always includes some form of slowing down or stopping, many of us panic. Those of us living in Western, industrialized societies have been indoctrinated with the cultural mandate to move forward and succeed – to "do" rather than to "be." In these cultures, stopping is equated with moving backward. If we stop making money, stop accumulating things, or are no longer achieving increasing levels of recognition or productivity, we conclude that we are stagnating or backsliding.

Everything has a point beyond which it cannot travel without completely letting go. Our body is the main teacher of this. As capacities we've relied on begin to weaken, our sense of security is endangered. Our bodies can only go on for so long, and then, at some point, they cannot sustain themselves anymore. They have to die. This is the nature of all living things. But the same is true of our psychological bodies; they too must pass. Michael is beginning to die, psychologically. Whether the initiating crisis comes through loss, involuntary changes in health and lifestyle, or other events that we feel helpless to address and repair, midlife's changes and challenges are our first direct experience that the temporary nature of life includes us. Letting go is necessary before something new can be born, but without a *guarantee* of rebirth it is frightening to Michael, as it will be for all of us.

For now, it is enough to remember that midlife entry points can take many forms, some slow, others fast, some dramatic, others less so. Some affect the external structures in our lives and are therefore visible; others are more internal and therefore less visible. In almost all cases, we will feel helpless to change what is happening even though most of us will expend effort to right our ships and get back on course. Whatever form our entry takes, we will eventually get the message: *our lives are no longer business as usual.*

Self-Inquiry

Can you name a midlife entry point? In what ways did, or does, it feel shocking?

Our Initial Response to Midlife

Some experience their entry points into midlife as maximally disturbing, with overwhelming levels of stress and fear. They cannot believe this is happening to them; they feel incredulous. Sometimes they notice impaired judgment, confusion, and agitation. Those familiar with post-traumatic stress disorder will recognize these as the mind and body's response to feelings of intense helplessness.

Not knowing what the midlife passage is about, most of us redouble our efforts to get back on track, resume our lives, move past the obstacle at hand, and do something – anything – to return to the predictability, control, and pleasures of normal life. Many of us resist the invitation to step away from our familiar lives because we don't appreciate that the challenges we are facing are a call to transform. Instead, we search for ways to overcome each challenge as we have in the past so that we can resume traveling on a familiar track at familiar speeds.

But the midlife passage will not be dismissed. *We do not overcome it; it overcomes us.*

In response, some of us become radical and decide our entire lives have been a lie. We sell our businesses and become artists. We join the Peace Corps. We move to Italy. We try to create our own version of Walden Pond. We get divorced and marry someone 20 years our junior. We take up extreme sports like skydiving or car racing.

Although a sudden change in relationship, landscape, or adrenaline might provide a temporary reprieve or an imagined new life, we eventually discover, as a client of mine who chose skydiving observed, that it's impossible to jump out of one's life. At some point we have to confront the futility of our efforts to change the reality that all things decline and pass away, and so will we.

Most of us fight this stopping, slowing down, or letting go in part because we don't know that it is a process and is pointing us toward something bigger than we have lived so far. *We are caught unaware because we are uninformed.* Instead of tearfully slipping out of our ordinary lives and grieving our losses as any initiate entering a convent or monastery might do, we fight the losses every step of the way. And, although some fighting is required (because our egos will not slip quietly into the night), we might cooperate more with the process if we knew why we were going through what appears to be our demise.

Sadly, because of widespread ignorance about the meaning and purpose of midlife, health care providers unwittingly conspire to prolong our suffering as they attempt to enhance our short-term functioning. Rather than directing us toward discovery of the hidden aspects of ourselves, they prescribe hormones, erectile drugs, anti-depressants, and other treatments that suppress the symptoms that are arising to support our transformation, as we will see most clearly in Stage 10.

Similarly, family and friends will try to get us back to who they knew us to be. They will try to make us feel *better* instead of encouraging us to feel *more* of whatever it is we are feeling. In fact, feeling more of what we are feeling (rather than "getting over it" and moving on) will foster the deepening of our experience that is necessary for our transformation. Just as most of us lack understanding of the profound role that the midlife passage plays in our ultimate ability to live more authentic lives, so too do most of our loved ones.

Self-Inquiry

* How are you working hard, or being encouraged by others, to get back to life as you knew it?

* In what ways do you feel resistant to change?

A Midlife Entry Point or Just Another Life Challenge?

I am often asked how to determine when a challenging life event — a setback or psychological trauma of some kind — is a midlife entry point and when is it just another challenging life event. The truth is, if we lived in a culture where death and impermanence were widely acknowledged and accepted, each profound challenge throughout our lives would be a confrontation with the reality of mortality and would propel us to expand our consciousness, as the midlife passage does, beyond the ego-driven illusion of our own immortality.

But we do not live in such a culture. For the most part, westernized societies are insulated against direct confrontations with death. In the United States, especially, we live in a culture that ardently favors youth, and we are encouraged to maintain our youthful appearances, preferences, and pursuits far beyond our actual youth. We are not encouraged to learn how to ripen as human beings, grow old, and become wise. As a result, in Western societies, the passing of our youth and the glimpses of death, either anticipating our own or directly experiencing our parents' and friends' passings when their turns come, are experienced as shocks to our perception of reality.

Take the story of Siddhartha, widely known as the Buddha. When Siddhartha's father, King Shuddhodana, consulted a well-known soothsayer about his son's future, he was told that his son would be either a great emperor or a great sage. The king wanted Siddhartha to become a ruler like himself, so he shielded Siddhartha from any experiences that might result in spiritual transformation. To accomplish this, his father surrounded Siddhartha with vibrant, young, healthy, and happy servants. Siddhartha was kept in one of three palaces at all times until his demands to see his people and his lands finally forced the king's hand. The king agreed but secretly continued his plan of protecting his son from anything that might invite spiritual growth, by arranging that Siddhartha would only see young and healthy people on his tour of the kingdom.

The king's plan was not successful. A couple of old men crossed the parade route, and Siddhartha ran after them to learn what they were. In the course of his pursuit, Siddhartha came across some people who were severely ill. Then, at the riverbank, he saw a funeral under way; for the first time, he saw death. He discovered the simple truths of life: we all get old, become sick, and eventually die. He realized that he could not be happy living in luxury, shielded from the truth of life.

If we lived in a culture where suffering, old age, sickness, and death were an integrated part of life, the stages of transformation outlined in this book would still take place, but we would enter the experience in a less bewildering and abrupt way. Theoretically, our spiritual metamorphosis from an ego-centered consciousness to a soul-centered consciousness would be more of an ongoing process throughout our lives instead of condensed into a deeply disturbing dozen years during which we are repeatedly forced out of our ego palaces.

Our palaces are just as luxurious as King Shuddhodana's, by the way. We have the same window treatments, consisting of ego-formed beliefs that block out rather than let in the light and fullness of our humanity. We have the same contrived allegiance to youth, fashioned by a cultural king-father. Our palaces are surrounded by alligator-filled moats, in the form of our emotional reactivity, geared to control those around us and protect us from emotional discomfort.

All the illusions that collapsed for Siddhartha in one day will collapse for us as well. For many of us, this will occur at midlife.

The Backdrop of Aging

As long as Western societies favor youth, aging will be a key backdrop to many of the entry points we have been discussing.

At 41 years old, when Olympic medalist Dara Torres attended her fifth Olympics, she had a different experience than her considerably younger opponents. One of the differences is that it would likely be her *last* Olympics – and possibly her *last* competition. This fact alone brought gravity to the event. The last time we do anything is a powerful reality check, ushering in meaningful, and sometimes troubling, life questions.

After I turned 50, I began to count the number of times I might see a lifelong friend who lives in Boston. I live in the San Francisco Bay Area, so, I reasoned, if I am able to travel to the East Coast once a year until I am 80 years old, I would only see her 30 more times. This felt very sobering. For a handful of years, every time I flew east, I would continue the countdown: 29 more times, 28 times, 27, 26. Everything after 50 becomes a countable event.

In terms of worldly pursuits, at midlife everything is happening against the backdrop of last chances and endings. The horizon is finite now. We no longer have the buffer of time to fix what isn't working, try harder, retool, or start over. At 20 years old, we had not been there or done that; we were just starting out, with a sense of limitless possibility. At 45, 55, or 65 years old, we have been there and been doing that for decades, and our possibilities feel increasingly limited.

All midlife entry points unfold against the backdrop of aging and its psychological, emotional, and physical implications. The fact that we are aging is, in and of itself, a shock. When we find ourselves confronted with a midlife entry point, the aging factor tends to intensify or aggravate the issue. For example, if our midlife entry point is divorce, the loss of the relationship can feel annihilating, and the backdrop of aging intensifies the experience: Who will want me at 50? How will I attract another mate? (This can be especially disturbing for women because of the cultural expectation of older men seeking younger women, although it is noteworthy that, at midlife, the majority of divorces are initiated by women.)

If we lose or end our careers or jobs at midlife, the disorientation and anxiety from the loss of what might have been our primary identity is hard to manage. But when we add the age factor, we might panic: Who will hire me at 55 years old? If I find a new position, how will I keep up with the 35-year-olds? Do I have the time to retrain and master a new craft?

Speaking more broadly, when our new, two-year-old car breaks down on the road, it's different than when our well-used, 20-year-old car breaks down. Both are inconvenient. With the two-year-old car, we don't have a lot of decisions to face; we get it fixed even if we have to borrow the money, and we get back on the road as quickly as possible.

The older car's breakdown is more complex and has more profound implications. Can it be fixed in the first place? Is it worth further investment? Are we tired of driving it? Are there more mechanical problems than the part that failed this time? Do we have the energy and interest to deal with it? During the first half of our adult lives, we rush around with agendas and goals and things to do. At midlife, many of the first-half-of-life's activities subside; our interest declines, our abilities decline, and our tolerance for activity declines. We ask ourselves if we even want or need a car any longer.

Our aging body is not the car in this metaphor; that is the conventional misunderstanding. The 20-year-old car we are driving is our ego, and our larger self is the driver of the car. As with the car, when it breaks down – when our ego fails us – we try to trade it in for a new one or repair the old one. If we were two years into our ego's journey – i.e., if we were still in the first half of our adult lives – that's what would be expected of us. But now, if we try to repair or revise the ego, we will increasingly experience its inability to take us further, and we will repeatedly be exposed to its limitations and inevitably more frequent breakdowns. Just like the 20-year-old car, the ego has a built-in obsolescence. Although it can fall apart in response to any transformative life experience, for most of us, midlife is the ego's time to come undone, as we will see in Stage 2.

At midlife we need to shift our attention to something deeper, truer, and ultimately more real and satisfying than the obsessions such as youth and ambition that have compelled us in the past. We are being guided below these concerns to a less accessible realm of our being. But we cannot know this – deeply know it in the marrow of our bones – at the start of the journey.

The summary answer to the title of this subsection – how do we know the difference between "just another" life challenge and a midlife entry point? – is that *a midlife entry point puts us irretrievably on a path toward dissolution of the ego and is set against, and informed by, an awareness of a finite amount of time left.* If an event is just another life challenge, we will find a way to get our lives back on track. In contrast, a midlife entry point leaves us unable to reconstitute our past selves, past interests, and past motivations in a way that is fulfilling and energizing. A midlife entry point shows us that the vehicle of the ego has worn out and cannot be resuscitated in the form we have known it.

Self-Inquiry

* Are you counting the number of years left to engage in an activity you love or to spend time with people you care about?

* What disturbing signs of aging are you noticing, and how is this affecting you?

Fundamental Faith

Fleets of fishing trawlers sling miles of netting into the ocean to haul in huge schools of tuna. Sometimes dolphins get tangled in the nets and are drawn, along with the tuna, into holding pens aboard the ships.

The mother dolphins can easily jump out of the nets; their young cannot. The baby dolphins become disoriented and helpless to escape. When the mother dolphins see that the babies cannot free themselves, the mothers jump back into the nets and companion their young.

A colleague told me about this dolphin behavior; he learned of it from a student who works with the International Marine Mammal Project. Although I cannot verify the facts, I think of the story as a parable. It illustrates the quality of shock we experience when we are unexpectedly pulled away from our lives – caught in the nets – with no control and no conceivable way out. It brings to life the helpless, overwhelmed, and disoriented states we experience when snatched away from what's familiar and dragged into something we don't feel we've chosen. Faced with big and small shocks at the outset of midlife, we become like the baby dolphins: confused and frightened, we thrash about as we feel familiar sources of energy and inspiration drain out or watch helplessly as we are swept away from the external, safe structures of the lives we have known.

The parable also illustrates the possibility of a higher response than the resistance that our egos are accustomed to mounting. *The mother dolphins surrender to the nets – to an uncertain future that might include both their deaths and the deaths of their young. They allow themselves to be drawn into whatever is to come.*

Even as our egos are feeling caught in the nets, a part of us is sending out the call to transform with an intelligence and love similar to that exhibited by the mother dolphins. This part of us wants us to lay our lives down instead of trying to get on with them in the old way. This is a deeper consciousness, of which the ego is just the palest reflection. Our future life is calling on us to step away from what has been and to cooperate with what is unfolding. We might not be able to do this wholeheartedly at the outset. We need regular doses of distress and fear, which act like solvents helping to break down the ego's familiar ways of behaving and enable its metamorphosis. Over time, we develop a greater capacity to choose to dive into the nets when we feel them closing in, rather than seeking to escape and continue living the ego-circumscribed existence that we have been calling home.

To make the choice to dive back into the nets to companion our shocked and startled selves, we must develop the fundamental faith that, whatever happens, the outcome will be beneficial. This kind of faith ultimately comes from a deep confidence that life is good and trustworthy and that what happens is what needs to happen whether we understand it or not. When we have a fundamental faith in a kind and loving universe – and know ourselves to be an interwoven thread in this goodness – we experience a sense of well-being no matter what is happening. With a fundamental orientation to life as "good" – "good" not in the sense of reinforcing what our egos want but in fulfilling life's purpose – we can respond with a resounding *yes* to whatever arises, no matter how challenging.

Needless to say, at the start of this journey few of us experience an unquestioned belief in the goodness, wisdom, and benevolence of life. During the course of our lives so far, most of us have, at best, developed conditional faith instead: if certain conditions for safety, control, and comfort are met, then we trust that we are going to be okay, and, by extension, that life is intelligent and good. Our midlife entry points expose these conditions we place on life. Midlife entry points are crises in the sense that they reveal our lack of faith and expose the narrow frame that prevents us from perceiving the larger picture of life and its purpose.

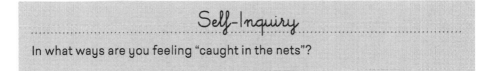

Self-Inquiry

In what ways are you feeling "caught in the nets"?

Under Every Deep a Lower Deep Opens

In the words of Ralph Waldo Emerson, "Our life is an apprenticeship to the truth that around every circle another can be drawn; that there is no end in nature, but every end is a beginning, and under every deep a lower deep opens." Although we are focusing in this opening stage on the visible crises that appear to initiate our midlife transformation process, we might eventually come to recognize that what starts the midlife ball rolling is not the crises we can identify but something more subtle that precedes them. Because our ego self-definitions are basically constrictive – self-constrictive – and because the ego is a shell obscuring the soul that is encased within it, an increase in pressure from the soul against the container that has confined it for the first half of life is the true initiating force at midlife. *The seeds of our soul within us call specific life events to us to initiate our opening to new life forms and options.*

An organic movement, an uncontrollable drive toward wholeness and greater self-expression, brings crises to us, forcing us to reflect on, rather than react to, our circumstances. The deep faith we cultivate during the midlife passage is in the rightness of this organic movement and the benevolence of the universe that guides us toward greater wholeness.

Over the course of meeting crisis after crisis, we develop faith that, as uncomfortable as it is, the midlife passage is refining our humanity and offering us a new life. *If our courage holds, and our intention to surrender is sincere, we will die and be brought back to life as surely as the sun will set tonight and rise tomorrow morning.*

At the outset of our journeys, we begin to build this faith by identifying each entry event and affirming that it is inviting us to expand our consciousness or to transform in some way. Over time, we learn that life events that shock us are ushering us toward a dramatic reordering of consciousness. Our next step after *shock* is *unraveling*, as we will see in Stage 2.

Self-Inquiry

Honoring what has been before letting go is important:

* What have you accomplished?

* Where have you succeeded?

* In what ways do you feel satisfied with your life thus far?

STAGE 2

The Unraveling

෴

As we are brought to the threshold of midlife, it's common to feel insecure, angry, confused, and not at all ready for the journey ahead. The shock of each entry event may leave us afraid that we won't be able to make sense of life again or to succeed in remaking ourselves. The hands of self-doubt and anxiety press firmly at our backs, pushing us into the unknown. We might feel despair in the face of all that cannot be understood or reversed at this time.

If we were 5, 10, or 15 years younger, our response to challenges to our identities would likely be renewed effort or a move toward new goals and directions. We would craft new values, visions, and action plans. That's not going to work now because we – our egos – cannot address what is happening in our old ways: some part of us knows that the solution lies beyond the strategies we've developed thus far in our lives. We are being carried into new territory where what is familiar to us has to unravel if we are to transform in the way that midlife demands.

To understand what is actually breaking down, let's return to our conversation from Stage 1 about how our *ego identity* forms, beginning in infancy. Object relations theory, a school of thought within psychology, explains that we have an inborn capacity to transform our day-to-day experience into mental pictures.

Over time, these mental pictures form an inner world, parts of which are fixed, and parts of which are fluid. This inner world has both conscious and unconscious aspects (the unconscious aspects are the subject of Stage 3, The Uprising). The key feature for us to recognize to understand what happens to the ego at midlife is that our ego gradually took shape out of *unrelated fragments of raw experience* as we will see below. These fragments eventually cohere into an internal latticework through which we view the external world.

Let's break this process down into some basic steps.

At birth, a newborn has no sense of self or self-consciousness because it has no real mental functioning. An infant uses her inborn capacity to sense the world around her: she comes in contact with other people – referred to as "objects" in object relations theory – who make an impression. She forms an internal picture or mental image of each object. As long as the infant is looking at the object, she is relating to that object alone. The moment she turns away from the object, she gives up the object itself but takes the image with her.

The infant has a pain or pleasure response to each object, and the image of the object that she takes away is charged with that associated emotion. The image and the associated emotion are collected together in memory. Our ego structures develop as we internalize and formalize these inner images of others as well as of ourselves in relation to others, and our emotional reactions to both. When an experience is too painful or overwhelming – too much for us to handle – we avoid (or dissociate from) it. This habit of avoidance also becomes part of the ego's self-defense structure. (We will look more closely at the process of disassociation in Stage 6.)

The images we have internalized about who we think we are, plus the ideas we have about who others are, plus the emotional relationship between the two, form our self-image or ego. Thus, object relations theory helps us understand that the ego is an *acquired* sense of self that is constructed out of internalized experiences from the past. *Once this sense of self has taken shape, we begin to act according to the needs of the self-image instead of in alignment with our real-time experience.* In Stage 1, I mentioned that we adopt roles and behaviors, largely unconsciously, to uphold and protect this self-image; for example, we try to feel safe by acting in ways that we have learned often get us what we want (approval, recognition, etc.)

and that enable us to avoid the emotional experiences that our young selves found overwhelming and intolerable (disapproval, rejection, etc.). Because we relate to the world through the lens of this acquired sense of self, we are able to interact only indirectly with others and to know ourselves only in limited ways. It's as if we were wearing tinted glasses that let in the shape but not the actual color of things.

Breaking Down the Self-Image

During the unraveling portion of our midlife passage, our internalized mental constructs start to come apart. Here are two examples of how our midlife unraveling might challenge the aspects of our identities that we hold to most strongly.

The first one is from my personal experience. One of my ego identities (the person I believed I was supposed to be) was to be an emotionally strong and stable person. My entry into midlife came in the form of a month-long trip to India to participate in the Maha Kumbh Mela, a huge Hindu religious festival that is held every 144 years. On this trip, I had hoped to meditate and relax after the publication of my first book, *Undefended Love*, but instead found myself trapped in a camp surrounded by armed guards and run by a group with questionable motives. At the same time, I was experiencing extreme physical challenges from heat, cold, and being in a crowded gathering of 70 million people.

After my stay in India, I felt anxious all the time and found myself crying regularly although I couldn't connect the sudden flow of tears to anything in particular in the moment. The anxiety and tears began to dissolve my lifelong self-definition as the emotionally strong one. I couldn't exactly hold together a self-image as emotionally sturdy when I was so emotionally unsettled. I no longer knew who I was. The more I couldn't recognize myself, the more I thought something was terribly wrong.

Not only were the feelings themselves uncomfortable, but I also could not depend on myself to maintain my composure in public. At first I tried to keep up the appearance of being stable, but sometimes I was not able to carry on the charade; the slightest things could agitate me or bring me to tears. Because my actual experience of myself no longer matched my internalized self-image, I withdrew from social settings to avoid exposure and further unraveling.

While I was going through my own undoing, a high school friend was also going through his. I had my experience in India as an apparent cause; initially, he had nothing to point to. All he knew was that he woke up one morning, and his passion for work was gone. At first he thought he was sick. Later he tried to reassure himself it was a passing phase.

Before this, he had always looked forward to the workday ahead. His primary identity throughout adulthood had been tied to his professional life; work had reliably been his greatest source of satisfaction. He told me that, after that fateful morning when he woke up without his usual drive and ambition, he tried for a year or more to find ways to start new projects and come to his work with fresh eyes. He kept reminding himself that, through his work, he was contributing to the world, helping others, and making a difference. But nothing he told himself helped. His passion for the work had dried up. Unmotivated at work, he felt a gaping hole open in his identity. Who was he if he was not working? Without work as an organizing principle, his daily routines began to break down, and his relationships with co-workers began to weaken. The integrity of his familiar sense of self was compromised and threatened.

Interrupting the Continuity of Our Mental Constructs

The stability of our ego relies on the *continuity* of experience that the ego achieves by bringing our past into our present. This means we come into every situation with a set of expectations. It's like we are always living inside a movie where we know what is going to happen and, even if what is going to happen is unpleasant, we feel secure because we know the script. For example, if someone has a self-image as a victim, even though this role is uncomfortable, it is predictable and therefore that person feels some sense of safety as he repeatedly experiences himself as being at the mercy of larger forces.

As long as a percentage of our expectations – about what will happen and how we will feel about it – are met, the ego identity believes it is safe. If our expectations for continuity are not met in an area of primary identity – such as being emotionally strong in my case or identifying with an ongoing passion for work in the case of my friend – the ego is compromised and begins to lose control. When the ego can no longer rely on the present and future to be the same as the past, it begins to *unravel*.

In Stage 1, Shock When the Center Cannot Hold, we looked at a range of experiences that could be midlife entry points. Now, in Stage 2, it is time to ask which of our familiar roles might be challenged by those experiences. Perhaps we are being called on to relax or relinquish the role of mother or father, caretaker, boss, or provider for the family, to name a few possibilities.

Let's say that a primary self-image is as a "competent" person. And let's assume that we have begun to feel an erosion of energy and interest in areas where we have been supremely competent up to this point (along with feeling some emotional concerns over signs of aging). We notice that we are not throwing ourselves into our projects as usual. It feels harder to do our taxes or balance our checkbooks; numbers just aren't making as much sense for us. We find ourselves forgetting appointments, friends' birthdays, or items we meant to pick up at the store. We feel confused and irritated when trying to figure out why we can't get on the Internet.

With these changes, our faith in our competence begins to erode. We notice the shift and feel a lack of energy or capacity to do anything about it. Maybe we care and don't care at the same time. Every day we face the choice to force ourselves to do more or relax our identification with our competence and allow ourselves to be less capable.

It is important to notice our response to the loss of identity cohesion and try to relax the reflex to pull ourselves back together. What would it be like to allow the identity that is under pressure to unravel further?

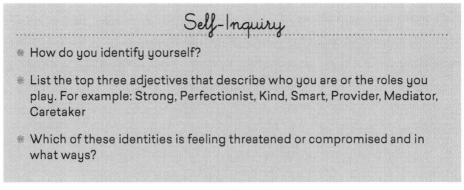

Self-Inquiry

* How do you identify yourself?

* List the top three adjectives that describe who you are or the roles you play. For example: Strong, Perfectionist, Kind, Smart, Provider, Mediator, Caretaker

* Which of these identities is feeling threatened or compromised and in what ways?

What has been must be destroyed before something new can be created. It's the brutal truth. During the unraveling stage, we face a series of losses that level us. It is also extremely helpful to remember that *what is unraveling is an acquired construct*, not the sum total of who we are. With this perspective, we can see the breakdown of our egos as messy but necessary to help break apart a box we have outgrown. The known self is the container that is being shattered into a million pieces, which will free up seed possibilities waiting deep within us.

The good news is that the moment we begin to observe our egos, we are beginning to go beyond them. The bad news is that going beyond the ego is frightening because built into the very structure of the ego is the compulsion to prop up, enhance, and reinforce itself. The ego believes – and wants us to believe – that *its* survival is equated to *our* survival.

Blame Points

As our egos (and, seemingly, our lives) begin to unravel, some of us will invest our energy in focusing on an external issue or person that we see as responsible for our condition. This is our "blame point." "Of course I feel anxious, I've been diagnosed with cancer." Or: "Of course I am unhappy, my wife is having an affair." The external situation becomes the point of reference around which our unraveling takes shape.

Having a blame point gives us ground to stand on, false though it may be. If we can identify the reason we are in pain, this helps us make sense of our despair and distress. However, focusing on a blame point limits our understanding of what is going on because, by doing so, we avoid looking at the ways that our experiences are deconstructing who we think we are and thus our sense of control and ability to make sense of our life. Directing our attention to a blame point prevents us from recognizing that what is being undermined is a *false* image, the way we imagine ourselves to be, rather than who we actually and fundamentally are.

Some of us will have so many blame points that it will feel like an avalanche. Over a six-month period, Maura, a 49-year-old woman, ended her marriage, left her company because she could not face seeing her ex-husband and business partner every day, gave up the home she could no longer afford, moved to another part of the state, and lost her teenage son who chose to live with his father.

She sat in my office deeply shaken. After telling her story for 30 minutes, she looked up and said, "It seems as though I lost everything while my friends seem to have their lives on track. If midlife is about the loss of everything, why don't I see other people losing it all as I have? What am I doing wrong?"

Figuratively or realistically, midlife requires the loss of everything even if sometimes we can only see one reference point at a time. Whether we have a satisfying marriage or a marriage mired in struggle, it is likely that our primary relationship – if we are in one at the time – will feel the impact of midlife during the course of the 12-year journey. Whether we have always been passionate about our work or have never found a compelling career, it is likely that our professional life will feel the impact of our midlife passage as well. Whether we have always enjoyed a healthy body or suffered from illnesses, it is likely we will feel the impact of our midlife passage physically at some point in the journey. The fact that we cannot see other people's lives unraveling doesn't mean they are holding it together.

If we are not working with an obvious external blame point during the unraveling portion of the midlife journey's second stage, then *we* can become our own blame point. Even if it looks like everything is fine on the outside, inside we may feel volatile, anxious, disinterested, or depressed without any identifiable reason. Although this experience is destabilizing, we must resist the temptation to judge and condemn ourselves, as Maura did, for not keeping it together. We are being subjected to experiences over which we have no control and for which we have no explanation, other than a general understanding that we are in the midlife muddle. For the time being, there is nothing to do but be here and watch (but not indulge) the impulse to pass judgment on ourselves, others, or life.

The thing for Maura – and us – to remember is that we are not meant to *resolve* our midlife crises; we are meant to be *dissolved* by them. We have not done anything wrong and we are not being punished even though it may feel as though our life is coming apart at the seams.

During the unraveling stage, the self-images we cling to, the ideas about who we are and who we should be, are the baggage we can either let go of or carry around for the rest of our lives. *To be emancipated later, we must unravel now.* The self-concepts and stories we perpetuate will trip us up as we try to move toward a life that can be more open, soulful, and satisfying than we have experienced previously. Thankfully, although we may be suffering in Dante's inferno now, *The Divine Comedy* ends in paradise. The truth is, the entire story takes place in paradise, but we cannot know that – deeply, truly, and permanently – until we have reached the other side.

Self-Inquiry

Are you unraveling with a blame point? (For example, I'm unraveling because my relationship is ending; I'm unraveling because I have been diagnosed with colitis; I'm unraveling because my work is no longer fulfilling.) What is your blame point if you have one?

Disillusionment

The unraveling process not only challenges aspects of our identity and destabilizes our sense of ourselves, but it also breaks down illusions, destabilizing our perception of others and the world around us. We unexpectedly experience things that once held so much promise as dull, flat, monotonous, or tedious. A relationship that at one time was thought to be perfect might fail to meet our expectations now. Work that once held so much meaning might no longer excite us. Hobbies we looked forward to each weekend might now feel like a chore. Our passion for raising children might begin to wane. The loss of our interests, dreams, hopes, and expectations can feel deflating in the absence of new ones to take their place.

If we responded to our midlife entry point in a radical way, the dramatic actions we took at that time will likely also be experienced as lackluster now: the affair we started might begin to feel like a big mistake; the college degree program we enrolled in might begin to feel onerous instead of enlivening; the initial pleasure of owning a new car might start to be dulled by the burden of the monthly payments.

To be "disillusioned" is to be no longer deceived by illusion. We tend to guard and defend our illusions. We want to believe that there can be effort-free accomplishments or problem-free relationships, that we will never grow old, and that we will leave a casino with more money in our pockets than when we walked in. As we pierce our illusions, what we once thought to be gold is revealed to be false glitter. "Is that all there is? I thought there was more here than that." "You are not who I thought you were." "I assumed the legal system was here to protect me." Although we might have experienced some portion of the potential that we envisioned, at some point our experience has fallen short. We feel angry and deceived when we discover that, despite our best efforts, we are not able to ensure safe passage for ourselves. This is arguably the greatest betrayal of all. We thought that if we were good, did the right things, and followed the rules, life would turn out the way we wanted it to.

When we were young and became disillusioned with something, we traded it in for a new hope or vision of how things are or could be. By now we've done enough of these exchanges to know that none of the new trades are "it." Nonetheless, we still keep looking for the thing that will fulfill us and will not break down over time.

In reaction to our disillusionment, we might seek escape, diving more deeply into addiction – overworking, gambling, porn, shopping, substance abuse – or compulsively turning to romance novels, sitcoms, murder mysteries, or science fiction thrillers in search of another world to which we can retreat. Some of us find ourselves mired in anger, bitterness, and resentment. Others of us take to our beds and hope the storm blows over soon. All the while, the process of unraveling continues like the steady beat of the dirge drum.

Ultimately, we are being "dis-illusioned" – experiencing the stripping away of the beliefs and worldviews according to which we have lived our lives and the conditioned selves that created these illusions. The assumptions we lived by are giving way along with our value structures and even the apparent rules of society. Although disillusionment like this might have happened before to some degree in our lives, at midlife it is comprehensive.

Before midlife, our egos cannot accept the true nature of life and of being human. In our youth, we needed to glamorize life and fill it with unrealistic hope and expectation. There was always the promise that tomorrow life would turn around and meet our vision of it. Seeing life through the rose-colored glasses of our egos – imagining that we could make life turn out in our favor – was part of a necessary building of illusion that goes with the development and maturation of the ego. The loss of those illusions is the necessary precursor to becoming more authentic and human during the second half of our adult lives.

When the bubbles of our illusion burst, we are left in the present rather than in a glamorous possibility for the future. We become simpler: more right here, right now, meeting life as it truly is. As our journey continues, the true size of our actual presence will eventually fill the space once occupied by illusions and false hopes. But it will be a long while yet before we directly experience the comfort of this fullness.

Self-Inquiry

In what ways are you feeling disillusioned? What illusions about how life could or should be are being stripped away from you?

Stirring Compulsions

As we are coming undone, some of us begin to experience unusual compulsions or repetitive behaviors. I'm not referring to a medical disorder here but to compelling and demanding impulses rising from the unconscious, over which we feel little control.

In the movie *Close Encounters of the Third Kind*, Richard Dreyfuss plays a character, Roy Neary, who fixes electrical lines for a living. One turbulent night while on the job, he and other people in the area experience a "close encounter" with an alien life form. After that evening he is haunted by a vision he doesn't understand, one that drives him to repeatedly create mountain-like forms out of mounds of earth in his back yard. He doesn't have a clue why he is doing this, but he has to do it. Viewed from the outside, Richard Dreyfuss' character is acting in ways that are irrational, bizarre, and incomprehensible to him and others. But he is not crazy, as the movie goes on to reveal. His compulsive activity is revealing something that his psyche demands be made conscious.

As we increasingly unravel, we might feel overtaken by energetic forces we don't recognize or understand. These might come in the form of repeating impulses that appear unusual or inappropriate. Perhaps they are wild parts of our nature that we don't know or have forgotten. If so, their action will be wild: they will resist being domesticated.

Often these compulsions don't make sense. During my midlife passage, all I could think about were goats, sheep, and, later on, chickens. I read books about people leaving conventional city lives to raise farm animals. I rented movies with rural themes. I attended classes on raising goats and sheep in urban settings. I learned how to raise fowl and rabbits. Although I loved animals as a child just as I love them today, my compulsion didn't make sense in the context of my current life.

A client found herself walking in circles in the middle of her morning walks in Central Park. At first she thought she was losing her balance; before long she realized that some part of her seemed to *want* to walk in circles for some unexplained reason. Another client spent much of her spare time over several years rocking in a rocking chair. A third played one song on his guitar compulsively until his girlfriend threatened to leave him (at which point he continued to play the song when alone). Another obsessively counted the spiders around her house.

We should not try to make sense of these repetitive behaviors; it's best not to even wonder about them at this point. But it is important to notice them and allow them expression. What is happening is that we are having an internal experience that has sufficient energy to take shape but only enough to show up in the form of a repetitive action that appears meaningless. It is like being awake in the middle of a dream that we don't quite yet comprehend. The way to respond to this phenomenon is to open to it, not to contain, suppress, or deny it. It is part of the process of unraveling. Opening to the expression of these movements now will assist us later on in the midlife process when these or other fresh energetic movements – often seeming to come out of nowhere – turn into something sustainable and surprising that opens the way forward for us.

On the topic of acting on or allowing compulsions during the midlife process, I want to mention two compulsions that must be treated differently: love interests and addictions. Acting out the compulsion to have an affair has potential consequences, for ourselves and others, that are much more significant than acting out the need to walk in circles or the desire to hang out around goats. Therefore, the urge to have an affair must be evaluated much more carefully than other types of compulsions. A detailed discussion of this topic is beyond the scope of this book, but a few guidelines when we have the urge to engage in an affair are to slow everything down and try to understand what part of us is engaged by the attraction and to what end. Red flags include: a pre-existing pattern of infidelity; lies, secrecy, or danger as part of the attraction; extreme fluctuations in self-esteem or emotional balance around the attraction; violations of boundaries such as sexually transmitted diseases. If these or other similar factors are present, it is important to seek professional guidance.

As for addictions, they are not an expression of new energy trying to find its way to freedom; they are a continued involvement in an uncontrollable habit (e.g., hoarding, overeating, overdrinking, overexercising, etc.). Addictions are ways of avoiding what we cannot tolerate or allow ourselves to know about our lives and ourselves. The addictive process doesn't allow for renewal. The constant grasping and lack of ability to let go that characterize an addiction stand in the way of the spontaneous arising of life's unfolding nature. In contrast, the compulsions that arise during the unraveling phase of the midlife journey are about giving expression to something fresh and new, albeit strange and unexplainable.

During the unraveling period, allowing these compulsions, regardless of how irrational they appear, subtly produces a shift in our psyches. When we are anxious or frustrated, we do not think it strange if we begin pacing. Pacing is a natural response to feeling disquieted. During midlife, we need to *allow* the pacing – i.e., the repetitive behavior that is arising – even if it appears to be meaningless and to not lead anywhere. The key is to simply let the experience be there in whatever way it shows up as long as it will not cause us or others harm.

Something is waking up in us. We feel a stirring deep within. Maybe it's a part of us that has not yet had room to express itself. Maybe it feels restless or restricted and is pacing in its cage. A suppressed energy finds no peace in confinement. Our task is to open the door to the cage and free the parts of us that have been imprisoned, to let those parts of ourselves have some space, time, and attention without trying to package them up in another box by making sense out of them. These midlife stirrings are inner, primordial urgings that will not tolerate captivity much longer.

Tugging at Our Own Threads

The main guideline for the unraveling portion of the midlife journey is to pull at our own threads when we can. Instead of asking ourselves and others how we can put the fabric of our lives (our egos) back together or get the unraveling to stop, we develop a practice of asking questions about each difficulty that arises during the unraveling process (and, ultimately, each difficulty that arises in the rest of our lives).

Some questions we can ask that will pull on the threads to help unravel our egos are:

- What aspect of me is this challenge pointing to, and how can I look at or investigate this part of myself intentionally?
- What is this situation trying to teach or show me?
- In what ways might this challenge offer a new direction, even if that direction includes less control and feels a little unsafe?

By asking these kinds of questions and turning our attention to exploring the answers (rather than resisting, trying to solve, or denying the problem), we loosen the knots in ourselves that were formed in response to childhood conditioning and trauma, and we open the way for our authentic selves to emerge.

Questions like those above are not meant to be answered at once. Like most deeper questions in life, they invite contemplation and revisiting. In the process of contemplating them, we are walking a gentle path toward letting go of our ego constructs. When we try to eliminate, solve, or deny problems, we harden the ego's structure, and we eventually shrivel, suffocate, and die. At midlife, our task is to do something different: to cooperate with the softening and dismantling of our ego identities and resist the habits and patterns that reaffirm those identities, beliefs, and strategies.

When we are being unraveled by life acting on us – or are actively tugging at our own threads by asking questions like the ones above – the experience is usually scary. We feel vulnerable as the fabric of who we are comes apart. We can companion ourselves in this process by remembering that we are trying to contact something that is central to who we are and what our mission is in this lifetime.

We've reached for that contact over and over in various conscious and unconscious ways during our lives up until now – perhaps by repeating certain experiences that lead to failure or left us empty; or by being drawn to certain people, situations, or relationships; or by a host of other gestures. Until midlife, the impulse to come home to our authentic selves has been obscured by the ego's fairy tales about how the world works and our place in it. Now, however, as the ego breaks down, we have another opportunity, a chance of breaking through the obscuring fog and seeing the truth that the ego has been masking. *As our ego dissolves, who we truly are evolves.* Every time we let go of the ego's resistance to a problem or life circumstance and dive – or step slowly and gently – into the heart of the circumstance to see what it is teaching us, we are enabling our own rebirths.

Self-Inquiry

Identify a limitation you are currently experiencing (a limitation is an interruption or obstacle to how we want things to be and feel):

* What is the limitation? (For example, "A swollen knee.")

* What or who are you still trying to be? (For example, "Young; vital; physically strong; a player.")

* What part of you needs to maintain this self-concept so desperately? (For example, "The part of me that wants to believe he is invincible.")

* What or who would you be if you were not that? (For example, "Weak, ineffective, defective, and replaceable.")

* Can you experience the end of trying to hold that identity together, even for a moment? What is that like?

Avoiding the Void

One thing we will discover through the process of sitting with our own unraveling is a deep well of compassion. Compassion literally means "feeling with." We cannot experience compassion unless we are first willing to feel what we feel. When we allow ourselves to feel what we feel — no matter what other voices might be telling us about whether the feelings are okay or not, and no matter what distractions (such as addictive behaviors) might tempt us to avoid our feelings — we are brought to a place of rawness, tenderness, and vulnerability. If we can acknowledge this vulnerability, we become intimately acquainted with ourselves in ways that are both connected to our soul *and* grounded in our humanness.

But why do we spend so much of our time avoiding our direct experience in the first place? Why do we try so hard to stitch ourselves back together as soon as we feel we are unraveling? *What we are really avoiding is not the discomfort of the unraveling itself. We are avoiding what we are afraid the unraveling will lead to: our own annihilation, or the void.* Fear of the void is the fear of non-existence. Because we are, at this stage in our journeys, completely attached to the belief that the ego is all there is to us, the process of the ego's dissolution can feel like the end of us.

We need to experience the thing we fear the most if we are to evolve. Experience of the void is an essential part of making the transition beyond the ego to a larger sense of self. As the unraveling of our egos continues, usually aided by more and more experiences that remind us we cannot count on our old ways of putting our lives back together, we find ourselves confronting the awareness that we no longer exist as who we once thought we were. This process enables us to make a leap in consciousness. That leap takes us from a space that is limited by the ego's blinders to a space that is open, boundless, and spacious. We discover that the void is nothing more than the absence of the ego and all of its fabrications and distortions of reality.

Another way to say this is that, as we unravel, our inner space is emptied of our personality patterns and images. This leaves not a void so much as a space of great potential in which we can be larger than who we thought we were: more compassionate, connected to and in the service of all of life, yet still having the intimate experience of the world as our individual and unique human selves. In case this explanation is unclear, here is a quick story to clarify what I mean:

The Tibetans say that when we are born, each of us is like a singing bowl. A singing bowl is made of brass and, when struck, produces sounds that invoke a deep state of relaxation. As we grow, we stuff our bowls with ideas, images, feelings, coping strategies, and the ego's fabrications. By midlife, our bowls are so stuffed that when we metaphorically strike them, all we hear is a dull thud.

The unraveling I am describing in Stage 2 could also be understood as the jettisoning of this accumulated contents of our bowls. The more we let go of what is unnecessary baggage for the life stages ahead of us, the closer we get to our original, pure sound, and the emptier the bowl feels to us. Initially, this emptiness can feel like a void. That is, we feel empty in comparison to the overstuffed feeling of ourselves that we have been living with all these years. Over time, however, we discover that the process of emptying, or unraveling, creates the "original" space that gives us back our "original" sound, which is the song that we are yearning for when we reach midlife. The overstuffed feeling is replaced by a deep resonance, the fullness of the true sound of us.

At this point in our journey, most of us are still holding tightly to the familiar contents of our bowls and feeling more resistance and suffering than anything else. As a result, we may be wondering about the blessings portion of the title of this book, *Hidden Blessings*. During the first half of our journey, the blessings remain very much hidden and often hard to believe; this will remain mostly so until we arrive at Stage 6. Further along in the book, we will be discussing in more detail the metamorphosis of consciousness to which the emptying of our bowl contributes, and we'll look at how we feel more connected to and moved to serve all of life as a result of these changes. For now, it is helpful to know that these losses create the space for our blessings to flower; they bring in new capacities that will bloom once we learn to tolerate the experience of the void that comes as our egos fall away. These capacities include deepened intuition and expanded awareness, and with them come new and as-yet unimaginable perception, vitality, and meaning. But before we can experience this flowering of self, we have more destabilization ahead of us as disowned parts of ourselves flood through the cracks in our crumbling egos, which is the topic of the next stage.

STAGE 3

The Uprising

❧❧❧

As our fabricated ego self repeatedly fails us, propelling the ongoing unraveling of our identities, our midlife journey confronts us with the next challenge: the suppressed, repressed, and unrealized qualities of ourselves, long hidden from view, come out of hiding. Many of the parts of us that did not fit the social circumstances into which we were born are released during this stage of the journey.

As children, we were conditioned to behave in certain ways. For many of us, that meant being well-mannered, sharing our toys, and eating with our knives and forks instead of our fingers. It was often safer to be seen and not heard. The human traits considered objectionable within our family homes and the social environment of our extended families and communities had to be buried so that we could fit in, get along, and belong. This meant hiding or suppressing a range of natural tendencies such as the urge to touch the world around us, explore sexual impulses, put our own needs first, and express anger. Where did these unacceptable ways of being go?

The complex fortress of our ego has been *suppressing* and *repressing* the aspects of ourselves that we were conditioned to view as undesirable or risky. When we *suppress* a character trait, we make a conscious choice to not express it. In the uprising stage of our midlife journeys, those parts of ourselves that we've kept hidden will no longer be denied expression.

We will also meet aspects of ourselves that were *repressed*. Repressed aspects of being are more deeply hidden; they are parts of ourselves that we don't know are there because we deny their very existence. As our egos unravel, both suppressed and repressed aspects of being break through the ego's failing defense structures in a variety of ways.

The relationship between our ego identities as we have known them and the suppressed and repressed aspects of ourselves that emerge during the uprising stage of the journey can be illustrated simply with a graphic. In the diagram below, we see a circle with an upper hemisphere labeled "The Upper World" and a lower hemisphere labeled "The Underworld." We will return to this basic diagram periodically, expanding it as we move through our discussion of the stages of midlife.

The Upper World

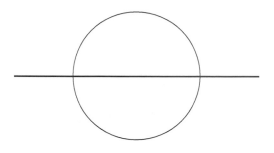

The Underworld

The upper world refers to our lives as we have consciously known them until the midlife passage. The contents of this hemisphere primarily include our ego's ideas of who we are. We can call this the "I am" hemisphere because this is the place where we find the character traits we call our own: I am kind, I am curious, I am serious, I am smart, I am moody, etc.

Below the hemisphere containing the traits with which we identify lies the underworld, containing aspects of the human experience that our ego identities deny, resist, reject, suppress, and repress. These are the traits that would make us feel insecure or out of control if they were conscious or expressed. Generally speaking, the underworld contains the elements of our humanity that would have gotten us into trouble as children. It also includes gifts and talents that we suppressed in order to not challenge our parents. We can call this the "I am not" hemisphere; it contains all the characteristics we believe we are not: I am not mean, I am not selfish, I am not weak, I am not irresponsible, I am not more talented at music than my mother, etc. For now, we will refer to everything in our underworld as our *shadow*, a term coined by Carl Jung.

The more our upper world comes undone as our egos unravel, the more the parts we have subdued, controlled, and abandoned begin to show up at our doorstep. And they arrive not with begging bowls but with battering rams, or like a horde of angry peasants with pitchforks, storming the eroding castle walls of our ideas of what is and is not acceptable for us to be and do. We will explore these undeveloped and suppressed aspects of our beings in a later subsection of this chapter, *Taking Responsibility for Our Shadows*.

The onslaught of uncomfortable encounters with our shadow further loosens our grip on who we have known ourselves to be. As we are exposed to the parts of us that have been locked in the basement, we often feel surprised and overwhelmed. But meeting the underworld or "other half" of us is an absolutely essential part of our midlife experience if we are to survive the passage and emerge transformed. In the words of Jesus of Nazareth, "If you bring forth what is within you, what you bring forth will save you. If you do not bring forth what is within you, what you do not bring forth will destroy you."

Self-Inquiry

* In your family of origin, what were the unacceptable ways of being (loud, not willing to share, unkind, etc.)?

* List 10 "I am nots." The "I am nots" are characteristics that you believe are not who you are (I am not demanding, I am not selfish, I am not mean-spirited, etc.).

* In what ways are the two lists above similar?

Roads Not Taken

In addition to disowned identities rising up and rebelling, choices that we passed over earlier in our lives often reassert themselves during the uprising period of midlife.

We might have turned away from these choices for many reasons, perhaps because we believed that we couldn't financially support ourselves if we pursued them or that we weren't gifted enough to make a mark in that area. Roads not taken might include following an early love of a creative pursuit such as dance or photography. Or a desire to be a parent, set aside in the first half of adult life, might resurface in our middle adult years.

A contractor I know loved horses in her youth. "Horses were my life," she told me. A year or two before her fiftieth birthday, she began to feel regret that horses were no longer a part of her life. At first she resisted the impulse to renew her connection with these noble animals. Internalized adult messages repeated in her mind: "It's too expensive. I'm too old. It's too dangerous."

Over time, however, her interest and love won out. She began attending horse shows and spending time at stables. Before long she was taking lessons and riding. Although she regularly questioned the time and money she was spending on something promising no monetary return, the pull was too strong for her to disregard. Years later, she credits the horse she adopted with saving her life. Her love for this horse, and the relationship they developed, gave her the emotional support she needed to endure treatment during two successive bouts of cancer.

As a young boy, my lawyer used to love to erect forts, kingdoms, and other structures. As he grew older, he moved away from his love of building things and put his energy into pursuits more acceptable to his parents: sports and school-work. Today he is an intellectual property rights attorney.

Around the time of his fifty-first birthday, he began thinking about building things again. "I don't even own a table saw, let alone all the other tools I'd need to really create something from scratch," he tells me. He can't see investing the time and money it would take to pursue his love of woodworking because it might be a passing interest or "just a midlife crisis." He adds, "At 51, I can't afford to make a mistake. I'll go to sleep one night and wake up the next morning and this insanity will be gone." The disappointment in his voice is clear despite his firm dismissal of his desire to build things again.

At the urging of parents and other adult authority figures who undoubtedly believed they were looking out for our best interests, most of us chose the road *more* traveled, not less. We were directed away from what we loved toward what might provide the best chance of monetary success or security. Or we were talked into a parallel path, like the daughter who wanted to be an artist but became an architect for the steady paycheck or the son who wanted to be a pilot but wound up in an air traffic control booth instead of a plane's cockpit.

At midlife our perspectives change. We realize that we are soon to be obsolete (a feeling that changes drastically further along in the journey but in the beginning helps to catalyze our transformation). We keenly feel that time is no longer on our side. Inevitably, the question from the Talmud arises for each of us, not as an idle thought but as a pressing, personal concern: *"If not you, who? If not now, when?"* Our untraveled paths rise up to give us an opportunity to investigate callings once passed over in favor of paths deemed safer or more acceptable. But, most important, they give us an opportunity to engage with intrinsic energies from which we turned away in order to pursue more conventional life choices that aligned with the obligations spelled out in the social contract. As we will see shortly, engaging with the energy of these unexplored options is vital even if pursuing the activities themselves is not something we ultimately choose to do.

I must mention an irony of ironies here. In midlife, those who chose a creative pursuit like music or art – the path less traveled – in the first half of their adult lives sometimes look with envy at those who made conventional choices. In workshops it is always helpful for those who made the safe and socially acceptable choices to hear the artists express their wondering about what their lives might have been like had they chosen a path more traveled.

Self-Inquiry

* What paths or pursuits from your past did you turn away from and why?
* What have you been putting off in your life and why?

Investigating the Roads Not Taken

If nothing comes to mind right away while exploring the questions immediately above, we can make a note to consider these questions over time. If some answers do come to mind, and along with them feelings of nostalgia or regret, we must pause and give these feelings and sensations space and time. It's important not to argue with ourselves about whether these feelings and sensations are appropriate to feel. Once we have allowed space for the feelings, we must notice whether we still feel some energy or "juice" around the path not taken. If so, it is best to allow ourselves to revisit our unlived lives with the *attitude of a dilettante.*

For example, if an unlived life as a dancer begins to rise up, we give ourselves permission to take a dance class. If we don't enjoy the class, we give ourselves permission to drop out and not finish the series for which we signed up. Then we might notice an interest in authentic movement or contact improvisation, and, again, we follow the impulse until it is no longer interesting or appealing. What's important at this stage is that *we only respond when there is energy and interest,* in the same way that a child at Christmas might move from one toy to another with total fascination for each in turn, and without another thought given to the toy left behind moments ago. We do this consciously and with full awareness of what we are doing and why we are doing it; we are loosening the reins of the internalized parent and allowing our spontaneous beings to explore, experience, and express themselves.

Remember: the goal is not to take the path that we passed over years ago. Though some of us might end up ultimately taking a previously rejected path, *our goal right now is only to open up to our impulses.* These impulses are resurfacing for a reason, and our job is to engage with each possibility, for however long it has "juice" for us, to explore whether it is something worth a deeper revisiting. We must try to postpone deciding whether or not the activity or possibility fits into our lives until we have engaged with the energy directly. In other words, we don't just sit and think our way through it; we actively follow the energy until it runs out of steam for us.

Words Unspoken, Feelings Unfelt

The uprush from the underworld might also come in the form of feelings that have been repressed because they fall outside the limits of what is considered appropriate or laudable. Involuntary emotional outbursts can become everyday occurrences during the uprising stage as unexpressed feelings push their way to the surface. We might experience flare-ups of feelings that we have learned are not "acceptable," such as lust, greed, envy, aggression, or hate. Feelings that we find uncomfortable and therefore avoid or reject, such as insecurity, dependency, and powerlessness, might also erupt.

A client was walking her dog at Ocean Beach in San Francisco one morning when she saw a man uncontrollably beating his dog. She ran up to the man fully intending to stop him even if she had to resort to physical intervention. "When I reached him," she told me, "I froze. I looked at him and his poor dog and felt my heart snap in half. I began to cry. I dropped to my knees and begged the man to come to his senses." The man looked at her for a moment and quietly walked away with his dog.

This client rarely cried, let alone in public. This eruption of feeling initiated several months of episodic emotional outbursts the likes of which she had never experienced before. Although these were scary for her, she readily acknowledges feeling deeply moved by the force of her own emotions and believes that these uprisings are part of a powerful inner transformation that is under way.

In addition to suppressed feelings, previously unspoken words might demand expression. So much unexpressed life lies backed up in most of our throats that we can feel like caved-in mine shafts by our middle adult years. Without sufficient ventilation, we might expire beneath the rubble. Our psyches will sometimes forcibly erupt to clear the clogged air passageways and free our original, natural voices.

Most of us are afraid of what will come out if we release the torrent of words dammed up inside. We believe our outpouring will create conflict and pain. It might. Anything that has been suppressed will likely come out in a primitive form at first; the feelings and words that break through can feel toxic, primal, or embarrassing. *We have to allow room for the undeveloped parts of ourselves to emerge in their undeveloped forms at first*; being choked into silence by the accumulation of unspoken words caught in our throats will be more harmful over the long haul than a flash flood of uncensored words now. As we clear out the debris, opening the pathways left unused for so long, at some point we will access a cleaner and truer stream of words and passions.

Most of the time, the unrealized parts of ourselves – the roads not taken, the feelings unfelt, the words unspoken – push their way to the surface on their own. We only need to notice and encourage them when they appear. They are meant to open the flow between the underworld and the upper world.

As we remove the floorboards covering the neglected and censored parts of ourselves and our pasts, we might be flooded with insights and connections. *Our task is to attend to these insights, especially if they appear to seriously undermine a structure – often a self-image – that we might currently value.* Doing this might appear insane or impossibly difficult, but *unless we shed these self-images, we will be buried in them.* There is an entire world lying under the one we are inhabiting. What seem like monsters arising from that underworld now will soon be revealed to be mother dolphins guiding us toward tomorrow's rebirth.

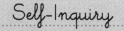

Self-Inquiry

❋ What feelings are you not allowed to feel?

❋ What truths are you not allowed to acknowledge?

❋ What thoughts are you not allowed to think?

❋ What parts of the human experience are you not allowed to experience and express?

Taking Responsibility for Our Shadows

Returning specifically to our suppressed and repressed traits, our task in Stage 3 and beyond is to uncover what has been covered over. The dark, rejected aspects of our being hold positive, unevolved potentials. *Each aspect of our humanity that might appear to be negative evolves into a positive capacity if its developmental curve is fully completed.* Selfishness can be a starting point for self-awareness. Aggression can refine into skillful assertiveness. An inflated self-regard can be the first gesture in our longing to expand and evolve.

Our starting point is to take 100 percent responsibility for what we are experiencing. What this means, in short, is that we recognize that *we* are the source of our perceived reality. The Talmud reminds us: "We don't see things as *they* are, we see them as *we* are." That is, we see everything through our ego filters. Although accepting responsibility for what we experience can be difficult at times, we will not harvest the nourishment available in our midlife journeys if we do not master this basic prerequisite to further human development. Even though it might appear that someone or something outside of us causes the experiences we are having – i.e., it might seem like it is someone else's fault that we are feeling a certain way – we have to summon our courage to move from blame to responsibility by accepting and cultivating the awareness that what happens *to* us is a reflection of what is happening *within* us.

An ancient maxim of alchemists teaches taking responsibility this way: "As above, so below, as within, so without, so that the miracle of the one can be established." In other words, seeing that our inner state of consciousness is reflected back to us through outer situations and events, leads to oneness – both wholeness within ourselves and wholeness of the fabric of life into which we are woven. We will look in more depth at the idea of wholeness in the stages ahead; for now, as we are learning how to take responsibility for our shadows, the first part of this principle bears repeating: *Our inner state of consciousness will be reflected back to us through outer situations and events.* The more we use outer events to draw our attention to our unconscious or less conscious hemisphere (the underworld), the more integrated we become. *Through the activity of compassionately embracing the dark side of our being, we repossess ourselves.*

Remember, as mentioned earlier, anything stuffed away for decades is going to come out in a crude or primitive form at first. While the rest of us was evolving, these lost and disowned aspects of self have been "de-evolving." While other parts of us were progressing, those relegated to the underworld were regressing. As a result, when outer events bring us face to face with our shadows, we will often shift quickly to cover or deny our shadow urges and feelings, to try to manage our overpowering feelings of shame and anger at their unexpected eruption. The task now is not to deny our shadow urges and feelings but to notice them, and then to begin an inquiry to help us discover even more about them.

There are many ways to inquire into our shadows, the unconscious or less conscious parts of our psyches. Here, I outline a basic practice called "Taking Responsibility for Our Shadows" as one method of exploring what rises from the underworld.

The Practice

To begin, think of a person who evokes a strong emotional reaction, negative or positive. Really feel the reaction to this person in your body; allow yourself to be stimulated and disturbed for the purpose of this exploration. When you can actually experience a touch of your reactivity, ask yourself why this person evokes such a strong emotional reaction. In Ken Wilber's words, "...if we are overly attached to somebody (or something) on the one hand, or if we emotionally avoid or hate someone on the other, then we are respectively either shadow-hugging or shadow-boxing." The more charged the feelings of attraction or repulsion, the more we can be sure we are feeling the reverberations of a part of our own shadow.

All of us have qualities, tendencies, and traits that we refuse to see in ourselves. These are our shadows, which show up outside us because it feels unacceptable to see them in ourselves. In psychological terms, we "project" them onto another or others around us and then blame, judge, and criticize the other person for the very qualities that hide in us, instead of turning our attention toward those disowned qualities in ourselves.

Returning to the person you brought to mind at the beginning of this subsection, the first step is taking responsibility for what you see outside yourself as being a reflection of what you deny inside yourself. For example, let's say you experience your brother as critical. The first step is to acknowledge to yourself that you are projecting your shadow onto your brother and this projection is revealing something about yourself that you are not fully conscious of.

The next step is to experiment with your perspective. You might begin to explore ways in which *you* are critical, using the premise laid out above that what we see and judge outside us is often what we are not looking at inside us. This investigation must not be perfunctory. If the exploration does not produce a shift in your original complaint, you have not gone far enough. You must ask yourself to examine the ways in which your complaint about the other – your brother in this example – is true about you. If you deeply open to the truth that you are critical – which should be easy to acknowledge in this case because calling someone else "critical" is itself a criticism – you will experience compassion for the person you are judging as well as for yourself. In that moment, all emotional tension relaxes.

Another way to play with your perspective in this example might be to assume that the critical feedback you are getting is correct. If you see your brother as critical, examine what he is saying to you and whether you can discover what is true about it. For example, if he criticizes you for not listening well, you could acknowledge the truth of that. In fact, your willingness to listen to his criticism or complaint would be a start at addressing his complaint. What the world is telling you can be meaningful and interesting if you choose to embrace the message. Then sift out which parts are true and which do not match your experience. If you do this in an undefended way, you will know yourself better over time.

To use an example that came up in a group I facilitate, a group member I'll call Thomas sees a fellow member, Andrea, as sullen and disengaged. Although Thomas tries to hide his dislike of her, his feelings leak out through small jabs of off-the-mark humor. To add salt to his wound, Thomas' attempts to get others to dislike Andrea are not as successful as he wishes; this infuriates him even more. Shortly, we will look at what Thomas' charged feelings about what he sees in Andrea reveal about Thomas' disowned qualities.

Thomas begins his investigation by rewriting his complaint about Andrea from "I don't like Andrea because she is sullen and disengaged" to "I don't like myself because I am sullen and disengaged."

Let me make it clear that no one who knows Thomas would experience him as sullen and disengaged; quite the contrary. What Thomas discovers by mixing up the way he views the world and owning the qualities he attributes to Andrea is this: he had very little permission to be sullen or disengaged in his family of origin. In fact, the pressure to be engaged and engaging was so high that he can barely accept that anyone could give themselves the permission to behave the way Andrea does. His conditioning taught him that this was self-indulgent and wrong. Thomas discovers a part of him that is envious of Andrea's freedom to be however she feels like being instead of putting on a front to make those around her feel comfortable, which was Thomas' childhood defensive strategy. This up-ends his one-dimensional ego identity as an engaged person. As he discovers this disowned part of himself, he can reclaim it and become more wholly human.

The human qualities that we believe are too negative to accept or express will come back to us in the world many times over. Unconsciously, we will attract who we need to mirror back to us the things we cannot see in ourselves and, in this way, to help us become whole. And while a person who draws our attention might, in fact, possess the quality we are judging, the only thing we gain by reinforcing that observation is further hardening of our emotional and psychological defense system.

As we explore our shadows, we begin to notice that what we project contains within it a dangerous opportunity; there is some fascination and some risk. For example, if we feel an emotional charge about our partner not listening to us, and we reverse the direction and explore the ways in which we are not listening to ourselves, we will discover that listening to ourselves is risky. If we listen to ourselves and know what we want, then we might feel more compelled to do something about that. However, taking action on our own behalf might feel dangerous. If there was no risk, we would not have relegated this material to the underworld in the first place.

To explore our dark side means exploring the parts of ourselves that would have gotten us evicted from the nest as children. How would it be for us to explore the part of us that wants to harm others, act maliciously, or be unkind? Until we have explored these native and natural defense instincts through self-inquiry (not through acting out in a harmful way), we will continue to read about them in the paper, watch them on the evening news, and join the chorus about how messed up other people are.

The Law of Reverse Effect

The Greek philosopher Heraclitus first used the word "enantiodromia"; it literally means "running counter to." Enantiodromia is often called "the law of reverse effect" because it refers to the point when the unconscious opposite of something suddenly bursts into consciousness or out into the world.

Carl Jung appropriated the term to refer to his theory that an overabundance of any force will inevitably produce its opposite. Jung explains that a one-sided tendency that dominates our conscious lives causes a counter-position to build up. What he means by this is that if we live long enough in one life hemisphere populated with personality traits and behaviors, we will inevitably flip upside down and land in the opposite hemisphere. This is another way many of us will experience the uprising stage of midlife.

To give an example of the law of reverse effect, let's say that, for years, a woman has been a dedicated mother and wife; her life has been devoted to the care and well-being of her mate and children. Then, all of a sudden, she does not want to take care of anyone but herself. She has walked the devoted mother and primary partner path all the way to its end, and she cannot do it for one more second. She has flipped into the opposite hemisphere.

"I have zero tolerance for Spencer and the kids right now," a client told me. "I am finished with all the 'attaboys,' bagged lunches, dueling calendars, soccer games, cooking, PTA meetings, cleaning, and the rest of it. I am finished. I want to do what I want to do, when I want to do it, with whomever I want to do it... and for however long I want to do it."

Similarly, a close friend in midlife left a message on my voice mail. "We have to talk. I need help." Desmond is a wonderfully kind, dedicated, skillful, and openhearted psychotherapist. Over the years we have often discussed a question we are frequently asked: how can we endure listening to clients complain about their lives day in and day out? We have agreed that this is a baffling question because what our clients tell us rarely sounds like complaining to us; on the contrary, we experience them as people struggling to wake up, to be more present, to open their hearts, to love more deeply, and to discover who they are.

Desmond's message continued: "I can't stand listening to my clients anymore.

All I hear is complaining. I want to grab their shoulders and shake them. I want to tell them to get a grip and get a life – and I want to fix their problems so I don't have to listen anymore. I've been a therapist for 24 years; I can't just walk away." Desmond had finally reached the limit of his ability to listen compassionately and flipped into an opposite state.

The phenomenon of enantiodromia can be experienced in all kinds of ways, such as the movement from being overly self-involved to discovering an interest in others, or vice versa, or moving from a focus on making money to an intense interest in relationship, or vice versa. A lifetime pursuit of pleasure can overturn, revealing a fierce inner discipline and unwavering pursuit of goals, or vice versa.

The reverse effect strikes in places both big and small. We might find ourselves flipping from always balancing our checkbooks to barely balancing them; from spending lots of time talking on the phone to never answering when friends call; from loving to read to never picking up a book; from being social to becoming asocial. Whether it's a role we've played, a career we've enjoyed, a relationship we're committed to, or a way of being we identify with, when we feel "finished" with it, we have probably crossed into the other hemisphere. Sometimes the flip is immediate and sudden, from white to black, and sometimes we experience the reversal more slowly. Either way, we end up strangers in a strange land.

To understand why it's best to cooperate with this midlife process of enantiodromia, let's return to the diagram introduced earlier.

The Upper World

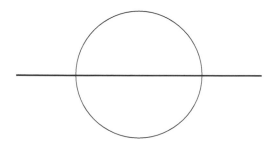

The Underworld

The stability and feeling of security that come from the ego-based worldview rest upon our ability to keep our upper world on top and to keep everything else in the underworld, out of sight. Invariably, during midlife, despite our best efforts, our worlds will turn upside down. Our midlife task is to cooperate with this up-ending by resisting as best we can our ego's sense of urgency to right our capsized worlds. Allowing the collapse of our *assumptions* about who we are and how the world works invites the underworld aspects to come into view more gently.

To illustrate the law of reverse effect in terms of an identity flip – the place where most of us will feel it the most acutely – look at the same diagram now filled in with example identity labels for the upper and underworlds. This example is of someone who has lived most of his life as a "can-do" person, meaning that his basic attitude has been that he is able to do what is necessary in life.

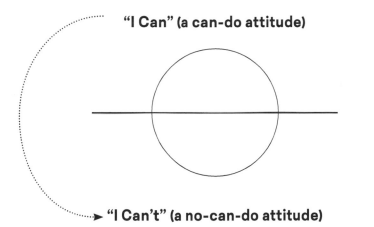

"I Can" (a can-do attitude)

"I Can't" (a no-can-do attitude)

This person identifies as competent and responsible. At some point in the midlife passage, he will therefore probably experience himself as a "no-can-do" person for a while. Things he would normally undertake effortlessly might begin to require more energy and might not work out as well as they had in the past. His task is not to fight this blooming incompetence but to allow himself to experience the other side when it emerges.

Conversely, if he had lived much of his life as a "no-can-doer," he might find himself being more intentional, directed, and competent. He might be surprised to find that this is equally unsettling even though it is often considered, by those in Western cultures, to be the preferred way of being.

Many personal growth teachers suggest that we seek balance when the law of reverse effect strikes. This guidance misses the mark. Generally speaking, seeking balance prematurely will stop a transformational process; in the uprising portion of our midlife journeys, seeking balance is particularly ill advised. Most of us have spent too much time in our lives trying to manage outcomes and control directions. With respect to the law of reverse effect, the objective is not balance but wholeness and integration. *Balance is a byproduct, not the goal.*

Instead of stabilizing our worlds by prematurely seeking balance, we must allow ourselves to capsize. *To know the whole world of who we are, we need to feel equally comfortable in both hemispheres.* Fully experiencing the disowned, underworld aspects or ourselves is a prerequisite for achieving an organic integration of all parts of ourselves. Without that integration, the best we can hope for is chronic tension between two competing poles of experience, for example of "can-do" and "no-can-do."

Here's an example of what fully experiencing the "underworld" aspects can look like. The dedicated wife and mother mentioned earlier crossed hemispheres from being overly other-focused for much of her life to what might appear to be overly self-focused. To honor the movement under way in herself, she might ask her children, who are at an age when they are capable of basic chores, and her husband to take more responsibility for their own lives. In areas where additional care is necessary, she might have to enlist the support of friends, family, or professional caregivers. If she resists the new imperative to tend to her own needs more of the time, she might get sick, leave her marriage, or find another unconscious way to take the necessary steps to include more parts of herself. By midlife, the psyche will not be denied its full expression without consequences.

However our shifts take place, we have to follow them, not frustrate them. Although it might appear that in doing so we are irrevocably up-ending our lives, we are, in fact, only dipping below the surface or turning a corner. For now, we must endure the loss of control and step away from the helm of our ship. Life will direct the process. Over time, we will notice ourselves inhabiting a wider range of possibilities for who we can be than we had before we capsized.

Self-Inquiry

Make a list of some hidden, disowned, or shadow aspects of self. To help you do that, answer the following questions:

* What are you afraid someone else might see about you?

* What are you most afraid of finding out about yourself?

* Who are the people you dislike, and why do you dislike them?

* Who are the people you admire, and what are their qualities?

The Uprising Moves Us Toward Freedom

By releasing all that has been confined, overlooked, or denied, we are opening up the boxes that hemmed us in at the outset of our midlife journeys. During the uprising phase of our journeys, we are laying the groundwork for a blessing that is currently still hidden to emerge later on; that blessing is an opening that allows us to expand without being constrained from moving in any particular direction. As we will see in later stages, we are developing the capacity to be located somewhere, everywhere, and nowhere. This is an entirely different reality matrix than the one we have been living in, as will become clear when this capacity strengthens later on in our journeys. Meanwhile, what lies between us and this freedom is a stretch of untrodden ground, the next three stages of midlife that we turn our attention to now.

Time Down Under

❧⁓⁓❧

Of all the stages we will experience during our midlife journeys, our time down under is often the most challenging. By now, the internal and external structures of our lives have broken down sufficiently that we can no longer renew the lease on our old selves or resuscitate them back to their former sovereign state. At the same time, nothing new is taking shape. In this place, we may feel dry, empty, lonely, helpless, or hopeless. We often don't have much energy to engage in our lives and, whenever we do participate, there is a haunting absence of pleasure, passion, or joy. Frankly, this stage feels more like an endurance test than a developmental passage.

Still, most of us will continue during this time to go to work, fold the laundry, pay bills, change the litter box, and take care of loved ones. Looking at us from the outside, the general public won't notice that we are barely holding it together. Feeling the situation from the inside, we will want to reach out for help – and sometimes we will – but we will also have to deal with our self-judgment and fears that we are weak, overly dramatic, or needy.

The best way to traverse this stage is to think in very small increments. Very much like terminal patients, we have to take it one day at a time, one action at a time, one breath at a time.

It will also help enormously if we remind ourselves that we are meant to lose some or many of our life structures during this time because those structures reinforce the ego identities that need to break down for a larger and deeper sense of self to emerge in us.

One of the reasons we create social structures in our lives – by doing things like having children, joining churches, getting involved in our communities, working, and affiliating with clubs and teams – is that each of these contexts gives us a sense of purpose, a direction, a place to be, and a way to be. In each of these settings, we know what we have to do, and we do it. Until midlife, most of these structures and contexts are expressions of the social contract. When we enter Stage 4, Time Down Under, these contexts are taken away from us – or they deliver less satisfaction – leaving us without a sense of purpose, direction, or knowing how to be. In the words of a client when he entered this stage, "It felt as though the Earth was shifting away from below my feet and then I went into a free fall. Since then, it's like there is no solid ground to stand on."

Solid ground is not the only thing that vanishes; we might feel that we ourselves disappear for a while as well. As our sense of who we are becomes less and less secured to our usual self-images, behaviors, feelings, and thoughts, our sense of identity gradually becomes less sharp and fixed. We might begin to feel blurred or faded. Less attached to our ego identities, we can no longer stand in any position with confidence. The result is confusion, disorientation, and alienation.

The ego is very resilient, however. Even this far into the midlife passage, it will try to create a new framework to help us hold ourselves together, to direct us, or to fill up the emptiness. As an antidote to our perceived decline, the ego will, once again, prompt us to initiate new projects, start new relationships, take on new hobbies, renew our new year's resolutions, go back to school, join new groups, attend new church services, and visit new places. However, most of these options will offer little more than a weak promise of new life. In most cases, the momentary updraft of hope is unsustainable.

The ego-driven strategies that worked for us during the first half of our lives get us nothing here. The ego's familiar emphasis on doing, producing, succeeding, being ambitious, achieving, visioning, leading, and goal-setting increasingly takes a back seat to the opposites: doing nothing, wandering, wondering, sitting still, daydreaming, resting, and all other forms of slowing down and stopping.

In contrast to Mark Twain's bold advice to "throw off the bowlines" and "sail away from the safe harbor," we find ourselves cast off, without mooring or sight of land, drifting at the whim of unknown winds and tides or becalmed in an endless and unfamiliar body of water. In this place we lack personal agency. We have no rudder, no motor, no sail, no map, no compass, and no known destination. We are not forced to merely give up command of our ship; it can feel as though our vessel is being taken apart beneath us, plank by plank.

In our first session together, Terri told me that for years she had pushed her unhappiness in her marriage under the rug for the children's sake. "You can fill yourself up on a lot of things," she told me. "I used food, entertainment, the children, and running the household to help me forget myself." In these years of her married life, she was a "go-getter, a good listener, and a cheerleader for others."

Around her 53rd birthday, the situation in her marriage worsened considerably. Her husband's addiction to pain medications led to an alcohol problem. He became increasingly unpredictable, erratic, and emotionally volatile. She never knew when she'd have to get the children out of the house at a moment's notice to protect them from his outbursts.

She felt herself coming apart under the stress of trying to normalize the environment for herself and the kids. "I felt engulfed by his neediness. My stomach felt as though it was permanently in spasm. Sometimes it felt difficult to breathe." Then, around her 50th birthday she began the descent into her time down under. She lost steam where once she had felt energized. She wondered if what she was going through was hormonal. She started taking anti-depressants, and they buoyed her, but only for a short while.

"I felt like I did when I was a child. Dad's moods ran our household; it's so engrained in me to detach and cope. I'm supposed to go away and entertain myself. I guess by now I've walked so far away I can't find my way back; I can't remember who I am or who I belong to." She fell into a state of chronic anxiety. Unable to make the monumental effort to try to manage her home situation any more, she felt overwhelmed and unable to move in any new direction. This anxious, drifting state persisted, on and off, for a couple of years.

The inner darkness can feel thick and impenetrable during this time. And when this inner darkness is partnered with the inability to move our lives forward, it can stimulate fears of dying or even a desire to die. As we will see shortly, we react to this darkness in one of two ways: we become either exceedingly lethargic or, like Terri, exceedingly anxious.

Do not lose heart; as the Turkish adage offers, "this too shall pass." But our time down under cannot be *bypassed*. This dark leg of the midlife journey melts us down to nothing, which is a necessary part of the alchemical process that will reveal our new form, as we will soon see.

The Tao says: "When you go into the dark and this becomes total, the darkness soon turns to light." Until the darkness lifts, however, what we need to do is be kind to ourselves.

What does it mean to be kind to ourselves? At the core of kindness lies authentic concern. The feeling is friendly, and the quality is compassionate and generous. Being concerned, friendly, compassionate, and generous toward ourselves when mired in these dark times, we open the door to light entering the darkness. Even though we cannot see or feel the light at the time, patience and gentleness will bring us through the dark wood.

Much later on in our journey we will no longer fear the dark, but, for now, it helps to remember what the mother dolphins taught us: love is always the highest response. If we can find ways to hold ourselves and our experience with love and kindness, at least for moments at a time, that will ease our way.

What this looks like is allowing ourselves to feel whatever we are feeling, patiently and without judgment. Also, and this might come as a surprise to many, we need to feel sorry for ourselves. This does not mean to become victims but to authentically feel pity toward ourselves for the difficult place where we are currently residing. Last, as I will repeat many times before our journey's end, being loving and kind toward ourselves means admitting we need help and seeking it out.

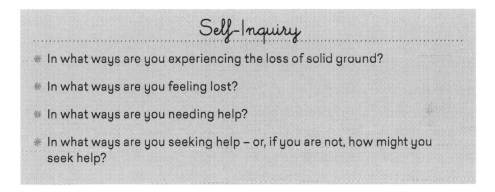

Self-Inquiry

* In what ways are you experiencing the loss of solid ground?

* In what ways are you feeling lost?

* In what ways are you needing help?

* In what ways are you seeking help – or, if you are not, how might you seek help?

Entering the Chrysalis Time

It is easier to be kind and loving to ourselves during our time down under when we understand what is going on. The concept of *metamorphosis* explains what is happening to us when we are in the darkness.

The process of metamorphosis is probably most familiar as the process by which some insects transform, through successive stages, from an immature form (a larva or caterpillar) to a mature form (for example, a butterfly). When a caterpillar is ready to undergo metamorphosis, it begins to wander in what appears to be an aimless pattern until it stops entirely. This is similar to the way we begin to behave after we have gone through a number of midlife entry shocks, started coming apart, and endured a host of unconscious uprisings from our underworlds.

The less identified we are with our ego selves, the less interest we have in the lives that have been fashioned by those selves. The less we act in habitual ways, the more lost we feel. The more lost we feel, the deeper into the shadows we travel. *The deeper we allow ourselves to go into the darkness – whether this darkness is experienced as lethargy or agitation – the more we are cooperating with the transformation that is under way.*

No longer sure what life is about or what we are looking for, we eventually, metaphorically, come to the end of the road just as the caterpillar about to build its chrysalis has reached the end of its time in caterpillar form. When the caterpillar stops its seemingly aimless movements, it begins to spin a small silk casing or chrysalis in preparation for changing form entirely. After spinning the chrysalis around itself, the caterpillar releases enzymes that digest its own tissue, converting itself into a rich culture fluid. The entire internal contents of the caterpillar – the muscles, digestive system, heart, and nervous system – dissolve. Later on, from this source of life energy, a new form is built, literally.

In the heart of the dark down-under stage of midlife, the human psyche enters a process similar to that of the caterpillar in its chrysalis. In Murray Stein's words, "...an old person is passing away. And, until the pit of death is entered, the process of internal transformation cannot move to its conclusion, for at midlife, too, a new person is being born."

In this stage of midlife, the parts of our egos that broke apart in the first three stages are being melted down like the organs and structure of the caterpillar. We sense ourselves reducing to nothing. Our identifications – both the "I-am's" and the "I-am-not's" – begin to disappear. We no longer have sufficient ego strength to resist, fight, or pull ourselves back together. As the ego releases its hold, we lose our physical, emotional, and mental boundaries. The resulting open space can feel like an endless stretch of uncertainty.

Warren is a film editor. He tumbled into midlife suddenly when, after 20 years with the same company, he was put on probation for poor work performance. "After the initial shock, all I could think about was trying to keep my job. I was suffering from a lack of sleep, and one day I froze during a presentation. I was overcome with anxiety and the bottom fell out." When the bottom fell out, Warren dropped into the time-down-under period of his midlife transformation.

In response to my asking him to tell me more about what the "bottom falling out" means to him, he told me about a movie where a dark crystal is used to suck the living essence out of people, reducing them to zombies. "I'm talking and moving but there is no essence in my veins. I'm just going through the motions." Pointing to his chest he tells me, "There is no *here* here. It's just one big empty cavity."

This slowing down or draining out of our life processes typically does not happen all at once. In most cases, we enter the chrysalis stage in increments. And, once inside, we do not hibernate, and our lives are not on hold. Instead, we enter a profound state of introversion in preparation for the dissolving process that will reduce us to our most elemental natures. All the experiences of our lives up to this point – everything we collected within our ego identities – will start to be absorbed and transformed. As the caterpillar metamorphoses into a butterfly, at the end of this process we too will emerge in an entirely new form.

We are metabolizing our history in this phase of the journey, and most of this process takes place in the dark. We are not able to consciously witness and participate. When we are in the dark and formless stage, we can feel hopeless. When we are in this state, it often helps to know that this process is creating the opportunity for our souls to make contact with us (to be discussed in Stage 5), after which we will have the opportunity to participate consciously in our transformation (to be discussed in Stage 6).

During this period of the journey, *we are meant to feel helpless as we repeatedly struggle and fail to compose, control, and get ahold of ourselves.* A friend likened his experience to that of a bug in a bathtub. "I can't get a grip. Neither struggle nor strategy affects the outcome." This state of struggle and repeated failure creates the perfect alchemy for the transformation that is under way. The outcome will be a flexible identity, as we will see later on in our midlife journeys, characterized by a dynamism and fluidity that an ego-fixed identity precludes. *Hopelessness and helplessness are the two catalyzing elements that foster our necessary dissolution from the fixed and predictable to the flexible and dynamic.* These catalysts must be powerful enough to set in motion a process that will not allow the ego to restore itself in the form it has taken during the first half of our lives. Instead, our hopelessness and helplessness take us down into a state of depression.

The Great Depression

The following discussion assumes no strong personal and family history of biologically based depression. If such a history exists, it is advisable to seek professional assistance from a trustworthy guide for support through this portion of the midlife passage. Relatively few of us have this kind of history. However, most of us have been thoroughly indoctrinated into the Western view of depression as a psychiatric disorder. This viewpoint presents a formidable challenge during our time down under because, for many, this leg of the journey can be dominated by depression.

To mine the riches of our time down under, we must consider setting aside the clinical mantle of the term "depression." Although psycho-pharmaceutical orientations do not accept depression as a healthy, natural response to loss, at this stage in our midlife journeys, *depression is a normal and inevitable result of the loss of our known worlds.* Even persistent depression is not, in and of itself, cause for alarm during our stay in the time down under.

Depression occurs naturally when we radically withdraw ourselves from our everyday, ordinary human concerns. It gives the necessary time and space to transition away from over-allocation of energy to activities and directions that no longer nourish, satisfy, and refresh us. We need time and space to redirect our energy toward discovering the larger agenda that is at work. Anything that prematurely lifts us from this darkness and restores us to normal functioning may compromise our chances of rebirth.

Hidden below the blanket of depression that deadens our feelings during the down-under period are highly transformative agents such as anger, fear, and grief. But we must not rush to try to uncover them. These feelings are incubating until they are strong enough to surface, or, more precisely, until our egos are dissolved enough to be transformed by these feelings. Depression detaches us from outer concerns while this inner process is under way.

Our experience of depression may take two forms:

1. Lethargic Depression

Lethargic depression shows up as paralyzing. We feel flat, indifferent, and apathetic. Our spirits are low. We feel unsympathetic toward others and unconcerned about the well-being of those close to us. We experience depletion, exhaustion, and a lack of energy. Connection feels like a burden or an obligation.

2. Anxious Depression

In the nervous form of depression, anxious depression, high levels of uneasiness and distress accompany the symptoms more commonly understood as depression.

We feel worried and apprehensive all the time; we experience irritability and feel as though we are living with a short fuse. We might also feel less in control of our actions.

Many midlife journeyers say that their sense of depression during the time down under feels connected to a deep sense of dissatisfaction with themselves and their lives. Rumination is common as are overreactions to minor stressors. Anxious preoccupations can lead to insomnia in some and excessive sleep patterns in others. Many experience an overall loss of pleasure in most if not all activities and fear that they might never feel happy again. It is common to hear people say they are afraid that they will no longer be able to function or provide for themselves if they give in to their depression.

Periodically piercing through the darkness of our flat or anxious depression, we might experience a very deep kind of emotional pain. This pain does not manifest in a tearful or volatile manner but as a piercing-to-the-core kind of sorrow. When I am in the presence of this depth of pain, I think of this line by the poet Emily Dickinson: "There is a pain so utter, it swallows being up. Then covers the abyss with trance, so memory can step around, across, upon it."

The following excerpt from a client's journal offers a sense of the onerous weight of lethargic depression:

> It's back: the depression. I can't think clearly in this thick fog. The endless longing and search for a reason why. I feel like I want to go to sleep – permanently. I thought I had turned a corner and then once again I plummeted down. Everything feels dark on the inside no matter how bright and sunny the weather or my circumstances. I'm not happy. Inside of me and outside of me, all I see are shades of dark gray.

In contrast, the following excerpt from another client's journal reflects the quality of anxious depression:

> When not experiencing a full-blown panic attack, I'm feeling the jitters. The body aches and pains – and the chronic headaches – feel

fatiguing. The dizziness and vague stomach pains come and go and seem related to nothing I am doing or not doing. I can't stop worrying about what may happen, what has happened, what hasn't happened, what should have happened. I'm irritable and I am walking around like a time bomb, ready to explode for no apparent reason.

From inside the torpor or emotional instability of our depression in the time down under, we repeatedly try to imagine a new life. But a new life is built on a new self, and our new self is not born yet. As a result, we might feel as though we are dying. Some consider suicide, either casually or seriously, during this period (if you are contemplating suicide, it is imperative that you seek professional assistance).

Whether we are anxiously scurrying around, lethargically crawling, or feeling broken from sorrow, there is little we can do that will make more than a passing difference other than to track and validate our suffering. Even though we might want to accept that there is something larger at work, the depression might feel too uncomfortable to allow that understanding to suffice. The thought that maybe we really do have a chemical imbalance requiring medical intervention will return again and again, and we might periodically wonder whether we should take medication.

It's very challenging to distinguish the purifying fire of a transformative depression from the degenerative disease of a psychological depression. This makes it hard to know when to turn to prayer and when to seek treatment. There may be long periods of time when we will be unable to discern the best way to respond.

All we can do is allow discernment to develop over time by giving ourselves permission to explore different options; this is part of the journey. I have seen people use anti-depressant and anti-anxiety medications in a conscious way during their time down under. Medications can take the edge off the seemingly endless experience of depression during this period. But there is no doubt in my mind and the minds of many others that anti-depressants and anti-anxiety drugs are prescribed more often than is merited. At the same time, some who could benefit from their use shrink back because they estimate that the benefits do not outweigh feared negative consequences.

Use of medication should be considered carefully and with the help of a holistic professional. A holistic practitioner looks at the whole person and analyzes not only physical but also nutritional, environmental, emotional, social, and stage-of-life issues. Although not averse to drugs or surgery, such a practitioner encourages and provides support to clients to seek meaning rather than focusing on a quick fix with potential long-term consequences.

The Hidden Blessing of Depression

Depression changes our relationship to the world; it rips us away from our lives, undermining meaning, hope, and identity. At the same time, although in our time down under we have the sense we've lost many of the qualities by which we had defined ourselves, we also notice that something essential remains at the core.

As we are melting down to nothing, some part of us might be able to sense the unfolding story of the phoenix within our dissolution, and we might begin to wonder what the essential thing is in us. When we are in the throes of depression, we can scarcely expect to experience the rich well of insight that will one day become the source of our inspiration, but afterward many report depression to have been a prerequisite to deep soul contact.

During my depression years I had a dream that my mother had breaded and baked an eagle for dinner. In the dream I was panicked to learn that the eagle was put in the oven while it was still alive. I appealed to everyone to stop the baking but couldn't get anyone to respond. I was horrified, heartbroken, and despairing. When my mother pulled the baked eagle out of the oven, I was shocked and overjoyed to see the eagle brush the bread crumbs from its wings and body and stand there in its full regal glory.

Contemplating the dream the following morning, I realized that my state in the dream before the eagle emerged reflected how on the edge I had been feeling and how much I had been suffering. The dream, which clearly has overtones of the phoenix story, also told me that even though I had been feeling anxious, heartbroken, and despairing, I would, like the eagle, emerge okay from the process of being cooked down under. I understood that it meant there would be light at the end of the tunnel even if I was still far from that light.

Sean, a client I worked with a number of years ago, was plunged into his time down under after a car accident nearly ended his life. During the year of rehab, he was very depressed. Nothing felt trustworthy to him anymore: not his body, not his friends, not his ideas.

While lying in his hospital bed, he felt he was watching the moments of his life dissolve in present time as he was listening to the ticking of the clock; he wondered who he would be – what it would feel like – when nothing was left. Much to his surprise, he felt a tremendous sense of relief. Then he felt what he describes as a vibration, or hum, in the core of his being. He held his breath and waited. The soft hum continued. "That felt like the turning point," Sean told me with a smile. "That is the moment I found myself, I think. I can remember it clearly. The humming continues to this day. I call it my heart murmur; it is a source of great reassurance and joy."

Sean's turning point came when he gave himself over to feeling the full experience of his dissolution. We experience a sense of power when we commit to feel what we are feeling. A fidelity and personal resolve to have, as fully as we can, the experience that is present for us is often mentioned as a turning point in the depression times. In contrast, reaching for premature relief can sometimes be a sign that we doubt our own resources or doubt life itself. If we can resolve to stay with our experience during our time down under, we develop a capacity to converse with ourselves at a deep level. We might not yet be conscious of this conversation, but it is under way. (We can support ourselves during this time; commitment to stay with our experience does not preclude simultaneously seeking nutritional, medicinal, and other forms of aid.)

Sooner or later, something will awaken within each of us as it did within Sean; a murmuring of a potential new life will begin to whisper to us, whether in fleeting incidents during waking hours or in our dreams. Until then, all we can do is feel what we are feeling and trust the process.

One alternative to the negative view of depression is to consider one of the dictionary definitions of it as "an area that is sunk below its surroundings." Depression is supposed to bring us down, to take us below the surface realities and routines of our lives. And during midlife it is meant to do this for an extended period of time to help dissolve our outer identities (although these identities are extraordinarily resilient and will reconstitute at any possibility they see for getting back into the swing of our old high-stimulation lives).

A helpful practice during this time is to reflect on what depression might be trying to bring into our awareness. Perhaps the depression is a sign that our soul is withdrawing its support and energy from what is no longer satisfying. Perhaps the depression is a deep hunger for something more than we are currently experiencing even as we are not clear what will satisfy that hunger. Perhaps the depression is a natural response to the necessary losses we are experiencing (losses always precede a rebirth).

Contemplating a range of perspectives like these brings light into the darkened spaces and might naturally lead to further more hopeful wonderings such as: what is useful about depression? In what ways might the experience of depression be a truer guide than other emotional states we have valued thus far in our lives?

Self-Inquiry

If you are experiencing depression currently:

* Is it the occasional moderate kind or more intense and prolonged?

* Does it feel like the depression is pointing out a quick course correction, or does it have more of the quality we are talking about in this section, that it is part of a longer, more intricate process?

* What might the depression be helping you feel or come into contact with?

Understanding Ego Dissolution

A tremendous dialogue is under way in the deepest, darkest reaches of our psyche during our time down under. A larger presence within us whose existence we have previously intuited and might have called by different names – our soul, our true nature, or our authentic or higher self – is rising up and overwhelming the survival-based urgencies and certainties of our ego-based self.

Our souls are showing us that all the heroic things our egos have been promising are nothing but a house of cards. The depression, ennui, anxiety, restlessness, and boredom we experience during the time down under are telling us that our egos have played their final hand. It's time to leave the gaming table. *It is not until we thoroughly exhaust the script of the ego – in addiction terms, until we "bottom out" – that we begin to shift our journeys from the ego's heroism to the soul's deeper understanding of reality.*

What we are learning in this very important stage is to welcome the great rhythms of life that exist quite outside the ego's agenda. Rather than trying to find a way to transcend life's natural ebb and flow, our task is to be willing to be pulled down, against our will, into the dark places that scare us. These times emotionally enlarge us, expand our consciousness, and prepare us for the next step in our journeys.

Remember, what is dying in this stage is not our actual self. It is our constructed self: our self *identity*. The truth is, there is no ego separate from the soul. The egos we have identified with are our souls, encased in mental structures. Nothing actually dies in our time down under; rather, the ego identity dissolves like the body of the caterpillar in the chrysalis. Although this loss is often initially experienced as a death, in later stages of the journey we see that the dissolution of the ego frees the soul, just as the caterpillar's dissolution gives rise to the butterfly. While we are in the time down under, however, many of us cannot perceive anything remaining in the darkness. It can feel like the death of experience itself.

This process happens in stages and in varying degrees. And, even as our ego resumes its relentless arising, most of us will, from time to time, have an experience or glimpse of our true selves in the depth of the immense stillness underlying the ego's efforts. The experience is similar to deep rejuvenation after deep sleep. What is most important to understand is that the soul is actively engaged in transcending its ego structure even though we might not be directly aware of this underlying process at this stage in our journeys.

What we learn in Stage 4, Time Down Under, is that what we have mistaken as our demise is, in reality, a change in form. Day flows into night and back into day; light flows into darkness and back into light; what's visible becomes invisible and then, once again, becomes visible. The more deeply we travel into the dark side of these cycles, the closer we get to the point where we will emerge back into the light (Stage 7). We are traveling an unbroken circle, a flow of life. We are learning that we are a part of the life cycle. With each successive experience of ego dissolving, the soul is further freed, and our consciousness grows.

We will return to this discussion in later stages, but, for now, the key thing we need to know is that what we may be experiencing as a death is really a change within life, a change from one condition of consciousness to another that is more suited to our further unfolding.

Sparks of Life

As the process of dissolving the ego continues, we begin to experience small but noticeable sparks promising new lives. A client calls these sparks "fireflies" for the way they ever so briefly break the monotony of the darkness. The sparks show up in the most unexpected places. They are magical and momentary.

A spark of life is a sudden experience of feeling alive, just for a moment or two. A flicker of life may arise when we hear a song, read a poem, find a penny on the sidewalk, or see a movie. A spark may come while spending time with a friend, reading a book, sitting in a therapy group, or attending a spiritual function. We may feel momentarily enthused while engaged in a physical activity or while sitting perfectly still.

Although, for the most part, these sparks are unexpected and short-lived, there is one human-fashioned version that I have observed so many times I feel compelled to mention it. I have noticed that, during the seemingly interminable time down under, many people decide to adopt a kitten, puppy, or pet of some other kind. They often explain that they need to remember that new life is possible, and bringing a new being into their lives – especially a young one – helps brighten the passage. In this vast emotional desert where each moment blends into the next without distinction, bringing in an animal seems to offer some relief.

Other than adopting a pet, the sparks usually show up on their own. They will be brief but enough to reveal that we are not cold stone dead. Like the hint of green breaking through the melting winter snow, they suggest that some part of us might one day make a comeback.

You might recall an earlier version of these vague energetic impulses from Stage 2 when we began to notice confounding compulsions that didn't make sense at the time. The sparks that appear during our time down under might or might not make sense, but, if one comes with a message, it is important to follow that message for a while.

These sparks are affiliated in some way with the new energetic field that we are starting to gestate, so it is important to notice them when we can and to respond to them in whatever way feels right to us. We might feel a spark of life in response to seeing a flock of birds, which may call on us simply to appreciate the flush of joy we experience as they sweep across the sky. We might feel a spark in response to hearing about a new play; if so, we must go to the play and see what message is there for us. We might experience a spark when we hear the title of a new book, so we buy it and explore why it has called to us. We need to respond to the sparks because they have to do, in some way that we might not yet recognize, with the next step we are to take in our journeys. They are breadcrumbs on the path through the darkened forest.

The moments of contact with each spark begin to matter *a lot*. An act of kindness, a feather on the side of the road, a reassuring dream – these little things offer small rays of possibility. They hold us for a moment here and a moment there.

A friend who is submerged in her time down under as I write this chapter reported on a wonderful spark of life in the form of a reassurance dream the other day. My friend is suffering terribly in her time down under. Her family structures are crumbling, and she is physically challenged to the max. She is struggling to get through one day at a time. Last night she dreamed that she was in an airport with a baby. She was trying to get an airline representative to make a change to her ticket when she realized the baby was missing. She began asking everyone she could, "Have you seen my baby?" She was frantically looking everywhere in the airport. Suddenly she saw the baby. It was climbing on a chair looking around in wonder, exploring and finding delight in the simplest acts. My friend told me that when she woke up, she knew that she was the baby and that everything was going to be okay, much as I had felt after my dream of the baked eagle. She was touched to tears recounting the relief and reassurance she experienced from this flicker of nighttime hope lighting an otherwise dreary daytime landscape.

As our time down under works on us, the ordinary and simple become more fulfilling. We begin to feel less need for big things to happen, and the commonplace becomes more precious. The fulfillment of our lives happens in these small moments, and it begins to matter less what we are doing or achieving in the world of daily action as old fantasies of who we are and what we must accomplish fade.

The flickers or sparks that visit us during this period might not always take a "positive" form. A spark is characterized not by the positive or negative valence of its energy but by the degree of passion that arises and the life force we feel in response to it. We might, for example, discover a spark in talking to someone we dislike. What is important is to notice the degree to which the person, event, or thing captures our attention in a deep way. The energy or fascination we experience is very important whether it feels positive or negative. We will learn more about this in the next stage when we discuss the opening of our spirit door.

In the beginning, the sparks only offer reassurance and a break from the darkness. Over time, the sparks will ignite the deeper forces that are waiting to flame up as we proceed through our midlife passages. For now, we might think of the sparks as wandering pilot lights in search of a furnace.

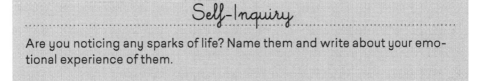

Self-Inquiry

Are you noticing any sparks of life? Name them and write about your emotional experience of them.

Each Stage Offers Blessings

Even if we cannot manage to befriend the nighttime part of the midlife journey while in the midst of the experience, we will certainly appreciate it in retrospect when we see how much we were changed by our extended time enveloped in an inner darkness. Carl Jung's most creative years – which speak volumes because his entire life was very productive – followed his many years of depression.

When not completely overwhelmed and overtaken, we must remember that every state brings blessings in the form of wisdom to impart; even the most wretched experiences have value. Although that value may be hidden from view while we are going through the experience, everything we are experiencing is precisely what we need if we are to continue to evolve into our most expansive and genuine selves. We will not directly or immediately experience the expansion after we emerge from Stage 4 and the two stages that follow, but our time down under is necessary preparation for the expansion that will eventually come.

If there is a goal for our time down under, it is this: as full a separation as we can manage from all that we have identified ourselves to be. To help us achieve this, life circumstances or a loss of will to overcome the obstacles in our way will again and again thwart our efforts to press forward. Sometimes we will not be able to fully absorb and digest the extent of the losses we are experiencing. All past attachments must be released. We are repeatedly exposed to the fact that we cannot transcend our fates, no matter what we do. Although scary, this inability to move forward is very supportive of the deeper, underlying process of our transformation. J. R. Tolkien has written: "Not all those who wander are lost." We are, in fact, on a path and it is, in fact, leading somewhere.

A part of us has to die to make this transformation, and the unlived possibility of us dies if we don't. Which part will prevail: what has been or what may be? When our desire to really show up for life – to be more alive, more present, more conscious, and more awake – overwhelms our desire to be safe, comfortable, and in control, the darkness shifts from tomb to womb, from a place of crucifixion to one of resurrection. At this point, although we might continue to feel like a still-life painting hung in a hallway between what has been and what will be, something changes. Like the figures in the paintings in the Harry Potter series, we begin to feel some personal agency – the ability to move within our frames and ultimately outside of them altogether. As we will see, the opening of our spirit doors in the next stage moves us beyond the sovereignty of the ego, a transformative event that often takes us completely by surprise.

Opening the Spirit Door

❧ ～～ ❧

In the background of our discussion of the spirit door in this stage, the overall midlife program of ego dissolution drags on. We continue to confront our ego's built-in expectation that life will turn out in our favor. We continue to suffer defeat when we operate based on our belief that if we act in accordance with the "rules" (each of us has a different set of rules depending on our conditioning), we will prevail. We continue to feel lost and disoriented. And we continue to need to remind ourselves that the experience we are having is necessary for us to transform into larger, wiser, kinder, and more genuine human beings.

In this stage we explore what happens when the process of our ego dissolution shifts from what has felt like a "stuck in the mud" quality to more of a "rising water table, bordering on flash flood" quality. This shift in depth and velocity occurs when our spirit door opens.

The term "spirit door" originates from Native American traditions in which basket, bead, and textile artisans put an inconspicuous "mistake" into their creations. They call this purposeful error the "spirit door." Native American artists believe that placing a "mistake" in the perfection of a piece of art allows an encounter with a larger reality, one they refer to as "spirit." Synonyms for spirit in the way we will be using the term in this stage are the mystery, our soul, the sacred, or whatever lies beyond – or outside of – our current, ego-directed comprehension. At this stage of our journeys, spirit is experienced as a force larger than us that threatens to overwhelm us.

Although our ego usually keeps us well defended against overwhelming contacts that disrupt its stability, there are some familiar ways that we come into contact with the hint of a world larger than ourselves. One way is when our "ego sphere" meets the biosphere: for example when the majesty of a star-studded nightscape draws us toward it in wonder, or the chaos of a tornado makes us shrink back in fear. When we are in the presence of something unexplainable, amazing, and otherworldly, we touch the larger reality of spirit: crop circles, the pyramids of Egypt, and Stonehenge are all examples of amazing phenomena that expose us to the mysteries of a larger life outside of the tiny confines of our ego.

In our dreams, too, we meet experiences that are outside the ego's familiar constructs. The marvelous and unpredictable array of characters and settings we encounter in the threshold (liminal) space of sleep offers a repertoire of possibilities for experiencing ourselves from perspectives outside our usual conceptual framework. If we take psychedelics or entheogens and meet the "plant teacher" within the "medicine," we expose our smaller consciousness to a larger consciousness that can feel overwhelming as well.

The spirit door is the imagined – or magical – passageway through which these encounters take place. The brief and occasional encounters we have with spirit in nature, awe-inspiring otherworldly sites, dreams, or meeting a "plant teacher" usually last only minutes or hours. By contrast, at some point in the heart of what feels like the darkest part of our midlife passage, we have a much longer encounter. Something wedges itself in the spirit doorway, forcing it to remain open for as much as one to three years. *This plummets us into our interior world – or an alternate experience of waking reality – with little reprieve.* During this time, we might feel as though we live our waking hours in a dream world.

This extended stay in altered space and time pulls us into deep, previously unknown realities. At first, the content of these realities will appear to be an intensification of our journey thus far, and they might be difficult or painful to experience. Then, as we move more deeply into the journey, the nature of the spirit door landscape changes. It can become both terrifying and electrifying; it may feel like everything we don't want and everything we do want at the same time. The experience of being wedged in the spirit door is the next hidden blessing we will discover in our midlife journey. Like the other blessings of midlife's early stages, this one might not feel well hidden and not like a blessing while we are experiencing it. However, as we will see later on in this chapter's stories of midlife journeyers' spirit door experiences, the blessings of this stage often reveal themselves in retrospect.

To give some context, let's look ahead at how our understanding of our spirit door encounters will evolve in the course of our journey. *Further along the path, we will recognize that our very own souls are the architects of the spirit door meeting.* Although we are not able to live in the soul's full inclusiveness and openness now, we might be able to engage with the experience in a way that supports our unfolding if we understand the spirit door event is often our first visible point of soul contact.

As sweet as "soul contact" might sound, and the touch might indeed include moments of exquisite sweetness, the initial contact, generally speaking, will feel challenging. This is because, as mentioned above, at this stage in our journeys, we are still not convinced that there is something beyond our egoic sense of ourselves, and meeting something much larger than our egos can manage or understand can be an overwhelming experience. Nonetheless, like the sparks of life we met in the previous stage – and the compulsions that took us over from time to time earlier in our journey – the spirit door and the contact with our souls that it initiates also can feel like a beacon of hope in our dreary or agitating times of depression.

Prior to midlife, encounters with dimensions of reality outside the norm are generally not sustainable in our everyday consciousness because of the ego's attachment to predictability and stability. At a deep level, we are closed to encounters with that which is larger than us – or beyond our comprehension – because we are afraid of being overwhelmed. Because we do not believe that we can handle the bigger reality of spirit, and we resist disrupting our familiar lives, we fear encountering spirit and create emotional and psychological defense structures against it.

Like most elements of the midlife journey, the spirit door experience is not a neatly defined event. Although the door can open at almost any time, in this chapter we will focus our attention on the initial experience of this midlife phenomenon so that we can recognize it when it happens and give it the importance it merits. If we can manage to acknowledge the opening of our spirit door, we will have at least a couple of oars in hand as we continue the journey, whether we encounter stagnant water or treacherous rapids.

In the same way that our midlife entry events can come in the form of "big shocks" (like cancer, divorce, or a deadening malaise), or "little shocks" (like a frozen shoulder, being laid off, or not finding a mate despite hours searching through online dating services), the spirit door phenomenon can come in large or small forms. I will focus our attention primarily on the "large" form of the spirit door opening – the opening that can feel like the door will never close again – because this form of the spirit door is the one that tends to be most difficult for midlife journeyers. However, interspersed throughout the discussion, I will address other less dramatic or "small" ways that we might experience this midlife event; these are typically of shorter duration but have the same characteristics as the "large" spirit door events. I do not mean any judgment about the value of the experiences by using the words "large" and "small," and those who cannot identify a large spirit door experience in their journeys should not feel as though their experiences have less merit. The terms "large" and "small" are meant to simply characterize the scale and duration of the types of experiences that are possible.

When our spirit door opens and puts us in contact with that which is larger than our ego-based frame of reference, this contact shifts us away from our habitual perception that we are the center of the universe. This habit is a result of the ego's belief that we are separate. When we inhabit this belief, all we can see is ourselves; ironically, this leads us to feeling alone as we think that whatever happens is entirely up to us. *Because of this fundamental orientation of the ego toward sep-arateness rather than connectedness, the universe beyond ego that we meet in the spirit door feels overwhelming and beyond our control.* The high price we pay in the spirit door meeting is our sense of security (or whatever remains of it in the wake of our other ego-dissolving midlife experiences thus far).

The spirit door opening and the ensuing contact "from beyond" can come in both desirable and undesirable forms that simultaneously astonish and threaten us into a deeper relationship with a larger universe, as we will see in the examples later in this chapter.

Spiritually speaking, we are still deeply asleep at this point in our midlife transition. When the spirit door opens during this period, the fact that the soul contact feels as if it comes from a realm below or beyond us rather than within us reveals how spiritually lost we are. We do not yet understand that what feels as if it is outside of us is, in fact, the soul that dwells within us. The spirit door is meant to draw our attention to an underlying reality that there is more to us – and life – than we know. This reality is shocking to our struggling ego identity, trying to hold onto the belief that it is the center of the universe. Much later on in our journeys, we will learn to search for and enter this door intentionally.

The Key to the Spirit Door

As we dive into this stage's material, the key guideline to bear in mind is to "go in the direction of the energy": when the spirit door opens, our task is not to inte-grate what we experience into our known world but rather to *allow the experience to catapult us out of our immediate context into a larger field that is unknown and uncertain.*

Going in the direction of the energy might look a little "crazy" from the ego's perspective. Because the spirit door experience might ask us to behave in uncon-ventional, unexpected, or even outrageous ways at times, let's turn to a "crazy wisdom" teaching story for guidance:

> *Nazrudin is crawling around on his hands and knees late at night under a streetlight near his house. A neighbor wanders by and asks*

him what he is doing. Nazrudin tells the neighbor that he is looking for his lost key. After joining the unsuccessful search for a while, his neighbor asks Nazrudin exactly where he lost his key. Nazrudin points down the street. The neighbor is speechless and wants to know why they have been searching in the street in front of the house all this time. Nazrudin replies, "Because this is where the light is."

Nazrudin was a legendary Middle Eastern Sufi character who is well known for his "wise fool" teaching stories. Although these tales can be told superficially as jokes, they have a deeper side that confounds the rational mind. When the mind is stopped – when we cannot relate to what is being taught through logic or intellect – we are forced to journey beyond familiar realities and step away from the coordinates of the known and comfortable.

The neighbor in the story above presents the logical view: we should look for the key where we lost it. That makes sense. Nazrudin, however, is teaching us something outside of the obvious or rational perspective. He is taking us where the ego cannot follow. The story suggests that there are times in our lives when we need to interrupt – at least temporarily – our normal way of seeing and responding to a situation. *If we respond in the same old way, we will see the same old things.*

Nazrudin's choice to look for a key under the streetlamp in front of his home when he knew he lost the key a block away doesn't make sense. More accurately, we (represented by the confounded neighbor) cannot make sense of Nazrudin's response.

There are times when the willingness to suspend ordinary consciousness and everyday assumptions is vital. Midlife in general is one such time. Perhaps a key that cannot be found – a "lost key" – will open a door that cannot be seen. Perhaps it is more important to look where the light directs us than where it seems logical to look or where we think we "should" look. As confounding as this "crazy wisdom" may sound, sometimes the *inability* to bring things to completion is more important than successfully bringing them to closure.

When life situations do not resolve for uncomfortably longer periods of time than we are accustomed to, we are stretched beyond our familiar perspectives. In everyday terms, it is possible that, when we lose a job, it might be better for us in the long run if we do not successfully land another one. Sometimes not being able to immediately resolve a painful issue with a loved one leads to a deeper result over time. Oftentimes, suffering, although not something we would consciously choose, teaches us the deepest lessons.

Maybe our spirit door experience comes in the form of an on-again-off-again relationship with a friend or a legal dispute with a neighbor. Perhaps it is the inability to change jobs or a physical symptom that no one can diagnose or that doesn't have a cure. A mentally ill son or daughter, the decline and death of a beloved pet, end-of-life hospice with a parent, divorce, or a child leaving home can all be spirit doors if they create an ongoing, irresolvable emotional, psychological, or physical condition.

If we allow our mind to relax in a way where "making sense" and "logic" are less important than hunches and intuitions, we may be able to sense that not being able to nail an issue down, resolve it, and move on may offer more personal growth for us than handling it and moving on with our life as planned. When we cannot achieve the outcome we think we want, we have the possibility of discovering something that is more vital to our lives' unfolding than what our egos would have envisioned. Although it is crazy-making for our ego-directed minds, this kind of thinking responds to a deeper set of realities that are not immediately visible in our everyday view of our lives. That is, this way of thinking recognizes that safety, comfort, and control don't develop us into more authentic, mature human beings.

To appreciate the role of the spirit door, we must suspend our conventional conceptual apparatus and approach the experience like Nazrudin would. A deep-seated shift is under way that will allow us to open to new and mysterious possibilities. But *we have to consent to a period of chaos and uncertainty before a new sense of order can be established.* This chaos and uncertainty are what we experience when we allow ourselves to live in — and ultimately in the space between — the two worlds that we meet when the spirit door opens.

Self-Inquiry

* Are you currently experiencing an irresolvable or disturbing life experience? What is this like for you?

* Can you relax the reflex of trying to "make sense" of this challenge and instead enter crazy-wisdom space by asking: How does not being able to resolve this situation and move on offer more personal growth than handling it and getting on with things as you had planned or would like to do?

The Attraction and Aversion Doors

While the look and feel of the spirit door will be different for each of us, the pull into the doorway will generally feel either intensely attractive or repellent.

If we enter through what I call the *attraction door,* we will be swept into an entirely new reality, one that feels powerfully alluring yet frightening. Becoming intensely attracted to someone, meeting a teacher and wanting to leave our lives and follow him or her, and being drawn into a new career path that promises riches or recognition are examples of the attraction door.

Alternatively, the spirit door might open in a way that makes us recoil. I call this the *aversion door.* Similar to the opening of the attraction door but without the allure, the aversion door sweeps us into another plane of reality, one with its own rules and laws that appear to operate in opposition to life itself. Classic examples of the aversion door are bereavement, illness, the loss of a career with no other options on the horizon, sudden debt, an extended lawsuit, the arrival of divorce papers, a prison sentence, or being swept back into the thorniest patterns of our family of origin (often via issues related to parental health care or inheritance).

Through the attraction door, we can experience ourselves in ways that we have deeply longed for but have not had access to or felt the permission to explore. These include feeling attractive, wanted, special, or powerful, especially if we haven't felt these things for a very long time. Often these feelings will evoke confusion and grief over how much of our lives have been lived without this very thing that the spirit door opens up in us.

Through the aversion door, we are forced to confront deep-seated fears and feel the destabilization that comes with the loss of our fantasy of safety, comfort, and control – an even greater loss than we have experienced so far during our midlife journeys. Most of us experience aversion to circumstances like illness, incapacity, loss, and feeling overpowered or abused. We can also feel aversion to a person, to a situation, or to restrictions on our control or personal freedom.

Bear in mind, I am talking here about the large or shocking form of the spirit door experience, the one that people find most challenging. I will talk a bit later about more subtle, "smaller" spirit door experiences.

Whether we enter the spirit door through attraction or aversion, we are forced to face, for an extended period of time, something that feels dangerous, indigestible, or unresolvable. This, in turn, obliges us to go to places inside ourselves that we prefer not to visit because they are generally experienced as an insult to or defeat for the ego.

The more ineffectual we feel while in the spirit door, the more permanent the transformation that we will experience on the other side of it. And, similar to all of the elements of the midlife journey we have discussed thus far, we might find the spirit door opening more than once in the course of our midlife journeys.

One client's spirit door opened when her daughter, whom she experienced as her best friend, left home to go to college. Although my client knew full well that her daughter needed to pursue her own life, the loss of her daughter's physical, daily presence resulted in inconsolable grief along with feelings of deep loneliness and abandonment. Her daughter's departure opened my client's spirit door and exposed her – for a protracted period of time – to parts of herself that she had lost (or lost consciousness of).

A neighbor's spirit door opened by way of a double mastectomy and the emotional turmoil she felt from the physical disfigurement and what she believed to be the loss of her femininity. The physical changes dislodged her from her primary identity as physically attractive, exposing an underlying sense of worthlessness and brokenness.

A high school friend's spirit door opened when he blacked out on tequila, fell down a flight of steps, and ended up in the emergency room at five in the morning with his wrist gushing blood as the result of landing on broken glass. "I feel like I fell through a spiritual door that evening when I fell down those stairs," he writes in an email. The next day he returned to the Alcoholics Anonymous program he had previously left and began a struggle through recovery that lasted for a number of years.

To open to the midlife phenomenon of the spirit door, it is enough for now to notice the emotional effect of small interruptions or ways that we cannot get something working, cannot move forward in the direction we have chosen, and cannot figure out something that feels scary to leave unresolved.

A Spirit Door or Midlife Entry Point?

Until we have experienced the difference, it can be hard to understand the ways in which a midlife entry point is different from the spirit door opening. Although we will experience many entry points throughout midlife, most of us will have only one or possibly two "larger" spirit door experiences.

Any of the examples of entry points mentioned throughout this book could also function as spirit doors. We can no more predict what will open our spirit doors than we can predict whom we'll marry; although we can imagine a list of non-negotiable traits in the perfect partner, the person we choose rarely has all, or in some cases, any of them. In the same way that we cannot know why one person has the power to reach down into the center of our being and another doesn't, we cannot know why one event has that same power and another does not. It's a mystery and might forever remain one. As mentioned earlier, the spirit door doesn't always appear as a dramatic event like a love interest or a diagnosis; sometimes the experience of feeling firmly pinned to a corkboard and unable to wiggle free – for example, by the demands of family or a work situation – can tilt us into the spirit doorway.

The major difference between a midlife entry event and a large spirit door event is the length of time we spend caught between two worlds or assaulted by a flash flood of uncontrollable experience as a result of the event. The spirit door is a long process of feeling caught between two realities whereas a midlife entry point initiates a sharp disruption or change in a trajectory of our experience. A "small" spirit door experience might not last as long as a large one but will still have the strong quality of placing us between two worlds in a way that we cannot resolve for an uncomfortable length of time.

At the same time, the length of time and degree of destabilization produced by a midlife struggle are not guarantees that it is a spirit door opening. Menopause, for example, has spirit door potential in its length of time and power to keep women out of balance, but it does not reliably open the door and plummet everyone who experiences it into the rising tide of magic or misery found in spirit door experiences. It opens the spirit door for some but not for everyone.

Who we are by the time we get to the spirit door is also a key factor: by Stage 5 we are less defined, less defended, and less capable of defense, which leaves us more susceptible to the spirit door encounter. Perhaps we are more willing to trust intuition and non-rational forms of knowing (note that "non-rational" is not equated with "irrational" here) than we might have been at the outset of our midlife journeys. At this point in our passage, we might be more willing than we would have been earlier to surrender a prudent choice in favor of other, largely neglected options or even extremes. Also, by this point in our midlife transition, growing parts of us want to break our containers open. We long for a change and thus might be more willing to make a mess, which is often what happens when the spirit door opens.

During a large spirit door episode, we cannot regain composure, and, after the experience, we can never be the same. The beginning of the experience rivets our attention for an extended period of time, which carves out a space within us – a receptor site. This receptor site is eventually filled with our new selves.

In a few moments, I will describe two characteristics that clarify the look and feel of large spirit door experiences in greater detail, but first I want to acknowledge that, if we open our apertures to the widest setting, the entire midlife transition is a spirit door process; that is, midlife is a large spirit door event that we all share. Midlife pulls us out of what's comfortable and familiar and catapults us into a journey of mythic proportion in which we are suspended between our old familiar ego-based lives and a new, unknown soul-based life for an extended period of time. I mention this so that no one feels concerned if he or she does not experience a discrete "event" that is recognizable as a spirit door event. Within the larger framework of midlife, however, most of us will have at least one experience that has sufficient teeth to it that it won't let us wiggle free and that puts us in contact with an underlying reality that affects us deeply.

I also want to mention that unless a person is tracking his or her midlife process closely and consciously, as we are doing here, many will have spirit door events that they will not remember clearly afterward. I have noticed, while working with clients, that a sort of amnesia sets in after the spirit door event. This might be part of our reflex to put painful or difficult periods in our lives out of our minds. Once we get to the other side of such experiences, we may have an aversion to thinking about the difficult process that got us there.

Regardless of what opens our spirit door, the opening brings us face to face with aspects of life that appear to be unresolvable. The result is great emotional turmoil. If we can remember to remain under the light as Nazrudin did – i.e., not focused on the resolution but instead using the issue to take us well beyond what we can currently be open to – we will find the lost key to our new home.

Two Defining Characteristics

If both of the following defining characteristics are present simultaneously, then our spirit door has opened in a pronounced way:

1. **We are presented with a situation or dilemma we cannot resolve for an extended period of time (at least one year for a "large" spirit door opening).**
2. **We experience ourselves living in two worlds at the same time or suspended between two worlds, unable to occupy either fully (true in both large and small forms).**

A Seemingly Irresolvable Dilemma

The first and most apparent distinguishing characteristic of an open spirit door is that we are presented with an impossible dilemma, *one that cannot be resolved*. For one reason or another, completion is not possible. If cancer opens the door, even if the tumor has been cut out or "cured," we will find ourselves confronting big life questions that we cannot resolve from where we stand at that time.

Whatever opens the door, it won't let us rest. We cannot find peace. We cannot understand it. It will not allow us to be passive around it, nor will it permit us to go back to the comfortable narcosis of an ego-encapsulated existence. As a result, our lives feel massively disrupted.

This condition of facing something irresolvable will persist for what will feel like an unbearable length of time. As I mentioned, in my experience a spirit door passage can last for as little as a year and as long as three years. In some cases, I have seen the door remain open for five years, as in the illustration that will be given shortly.

The situation might be continuous, with no break in its emotional intensity, or it might come and go and come back again. As mentioned earlier, a medical crisis might open the spirit door. So might an on-again-off-again relationship where we find ourselves unable to stay or leave. An extended legal dispute can open the door, as can a seemingly never-ending divorce, significant hearing or other physical loss, or taking on the full-time care of parents in the final years of their lives.

For better or for worse, from the ego's perspective there is no traditionally happy ending to a "large" spirit door experience because the experience's value – its hidden blessing – lies in its inability to be resolved (whereas the ego's worldview is that it can manage and resolve anything that befalls us). It is the very fact that we cannot resolve the situation in what we experience as our real or waking world that forces us to become different in relationship to it. And because the spirit door can remain open a year or longer, it can catalyze a transformation of profound depth.

A note about the nature of the smaller versions of the spirit door phenomenon might be helpful here. A smaller spirit door opening takes place whenever we experience an altered state of consciousness that places us in a liminal or threshold state between two worlds. For example, as I said earlier, dreams are small spirit door events in which we enter a world beyond waking reality and then return. Using entheogens (or psychedelic) substances opens our spirit doors for short periods of time by taking us to other dimensions of experience outside daily reality (although the fallout of such an experience can sometimes become a large spirit door event). When a precious animal companion passes away suddenly or tragically, we can live in two worlds at once as our grief pins us to our broken heart in our inner worlds while we still have to commute to and function at work in our outer worlds. Although "smaller" spirit door openings don't last as long as the larger and more shocking ones, they offer access to the key elements of the spirit door experience: we find ourselves between two worlds, unable to resolve the resulting dilemma, for a period of time that is long enough to noticeably disrupt the smooth functioning of our daily lives.

To the degree that we can stay in the spirit door experience of ambiguity and lack of closure – whether for a short time in a small spirit door opening or a really long time in a large spirit door opening – this experience holds a "lost key" to the larger reality we discover during midlife. In terms of the Nazrudin story mentioned earlier, it is the key to a larger psychological, emotional, and spiritual home than the ego-constructed one that we have been renting for much of our lives. When we are in the spirit door's in-between state, ungrounded in either world, we are invited to experience the groundless world of spirit and soul, as we will see further along in our journeys.

Self-Inquiry

* Can you identify a small or large spirit door opening in your life?

* Is it an attraction door or an aversion door, or both?

Two Worlds

In addition to being presented with an irresolvable dilemma, we experience a second distinguishing feature of the spirit door: a sense of living in two worlds at the same time. We are unable to fully occupy either but also unable to get free of either. We find ourselves not only suspended between two worlds but forced to *live in both simultaneously.*

This is called "metaxis," from the Greek word that Plato and Aristotle described as meaning *between and in* at the same time. As we know, when we are in midlife we feel as if we are between our "life before midlife" and our "life after midlife." And, within midlife, when we are in the difficult challenges of Stages 4-6, we are also in a metaxis, the time between an ego-centered existence and soul-centered existence.

We might feel "torn between two lovers," unable to choose one person over the other. We might feel as though we went to all this trouble and pain to divorce our husband only to find ourselves tethered to what we experience as his insanity as we try to co-parent our children after the divorce. We might be thrown from our horse and wake up to find our lives permanently changed, as actor Christopher Reeve reported when he described living after his accident with a whole and healthy body in his dreams but a faintly functioning body in the waking world. Or, a spiritual opening in the course of a long retreat might afterward leave us experiencing ourselves *in* this world but no longer *of* this world.

Self-Inquiry

Are you currently having the experience of living in two worlds at the same time or living between two worlds, unable to occupy either fully? Describe the ways this is showing up for you and what the experience is like emotionally.

Living with the spirit door open has a quality of indeterminacy; we feel stuck "between," without promise of closure or positive outcome. When we are forced to live in two worlds at once, we cannot find peace. *That the situation cannot be resolved is the spirit door's special gift: we cannot let go of it, and it will not let go of us.* Over time, we become more capable of living with our inability to categorize our context or ourselves in a finalized way. We learn to hang out with the lack of clarity. *When we are caught between worlds long enough, we take up residence in the in-between space itself.*

The capacity to tolerate ambiguity will become increasingly important as we move forward in our midlife passages. That capacity is, in part, developed through the experience of instability. Whether we are of two minds, two hearts, two physical locations, or two experiences of ourselves, the overall sense is that we cannot unify. We cannot stand in one place for any length of time, so we cannot experience stability, certainty, or predictability.

It bears repeating that the spirit door experience, in its large form, keeps us destabilized *for a long time*. That is its power and its value; we can't quite get ourselves organized in the face of it. Every time we try to land somewhere – by fabricating an explanation for what is happening, creating a rule about how to be in relationship to it, or forcibly trying to affect the situation – our state defies categorization or control, and we find ourselves back in flux.

In what I am calling the "smaller" versions of the spirit door opening, we might learn to become comfortable, over time, with leaving the fixed, controlled terrain of the familiar and entering the terrain of the unknowable. One example of this could be attending church or engaging in spiritual practice; if we allow ourselves to really step into the ritual space each time, ritual and practice can be small spirit door events in which we leave the literal world and enter a more numinous and ineffable world.

A client of mine spoke harshly to his daughter; seeing her crestfallen expression, her tear-filled eyes, and her hands going to her stomach as if he had punched her physically, he wanted to take it all back and enfold her in her arms. Instead, he stood frozen as she walked upstairs to her room and cried herself to sleep. His remorse and grief felt excruciating for him. Even after talking to her the next morning, apologizing again and again, he felt haunted by the event. It took him weeks to feel all the feelings that flooded his system and during that time, he experienced himself reliving that moment – or living that moment – over and over as he went about his day. For him, this was a small spirit door experience. In this moment he became aware of an unkind – even violent – part of himself that he was not aware of before. While he had directed his anger at others in his life, he had never felt the damaging effect of his anger like he had when he saw himself through the mirror of his daughter's eyes. For a long time afterward, he felt suspended between his self-concept as kind and the reality that he could be violent and cause harm.

All periods of ongoing destabilization loosen, soften, and open us. Over time, we grow a capacity to live with small and large overwhelming situations without losing ourselves, a developmental capacity that exceeds the abilities of the ego. Sexual attractions, opportunities that evoke jealousy or greed, the possible loss of loved ones, tragedies, illness, and threats of separation and divorce are large, overwhelming life experiences. Church, retreats, psychedelics, a new product introduction that fails in the market place, a new relationship that can't quite get off the ground, and minor injuries and medical procedures are smaller but nonetheless overwhelming life experiences. The midlife developmental task is to live through experiences like these by learning to occupy the empty space they open up, which our egos experience as destabilizing.

Living in two worlds at the same time forces us to grow large enough to hold both even when they appear to contradict one other. This can be a slow and arduous process from the ego's point of view, but, if we stay with the tension, we will expand our sense of ourselves, of others, and of the world we live in. On the other side of the process, having developed our capacity to live with contradiction and instability, we will emerge with a capacity to be dynamically present in situations of flux without requiring that certain conditions be met in order for us to survive those situations.

Close Encounters and Near Affairs

To illustrate the large form of the spirit door opening through attraction, we will focus our discussion on love interests although this is only one form in which attraction spirit doors open. Each of us will experience the opening in a way that is appropriate to our own lives. Many people will experience the attraction door in forms, large and small, that are other than a love interest.

Love can be beyond understanding and beyond control at any stage of life; its allure is one of the most powerful forces, and its shadow one of the darkest. Affairs of the heart turn our worlds upside down and turn us inside out. A great deal gets stirred up inside and around us.

When the evocative, compelling allure of love strikes in a way that cannot be grasped or realized objectively in our outer worlds, it becomes a doorway into our interior lives. At midlife, this is often a spirit door ushering us forcefully into other worlds and dimensions that are usually inaccessible to us.

Everyone knows the phrase "love is blind." This is not entirely true. *Love is blind only to the world we came from, not to the world it opens up in us.* Although love can make us look and feel giddy and unbalanced at any age, it also forces us to extend beyond what we thought we were humanly capable of enduring and experiencing. It unearths core material in our psyches and forces us to face what we spend parts of our lives avoiding.

Strong attractions are overwhelmingly real and at the same time seem unreal. We enter what can feel like a virtual or dreamlike reality. In this state we are neither here nor there, unable to exclusively inhabit any one reality. We often feel split in two; we show up for work each day and go through the motions of our jobs as always, but inside we are in a tumult.

The general experience of love is that someone appears in our lives – or we appear in theirs – and we begin to feel powerful emotions and overwhelming sensations. We think or fantasize about the object of our affections obsessively. We experience ourselves in ways that we haven't for so long that we have almost forgotten what it feels like, if we ever knew. We feel a depth and force of desire that threaten to destroy us as well as the world we have created. We feel desired by and desirous of another.

Even as one part of us might know that the experience is risky – and at midlife it can feel a great deal more risky than in youth – we find ourselves orienting toward something other than safety, security, and success, the goals of an ego-directed life. Even as the situation is scary and produces anxiety, it is also wildly exciting and enlivening. We are terrified that we won't be able to hold things together, but we cannot walk away. We experience extreme states, and the emotional chaos pushes beyond our attempts to normalize it.

Spirit door love interests catapult us out of the orbit we have been in and give us some distance to look back at ourselves, and our lives, to see what is missing and what is needed. They also invite us into shadow material that is beyond our capacity to evoke on our own.

Attraction Spirit Door Case Study

A client, whom I will call Kim, is married and a mother of three young children.

She tells me that she "fell in love" with a man she met on a family vacation. In her mind she made the relationship okay by telling herself that he was "just a friend," and it was "entirely harmless." Harmless until the night she found herself "opening to him sexually."

After she had had a six-month, long-distance affair, her husband confirmed his suspicions by accessing her email account and reading the ongoing intimate exchange. "The shit hit the fan," Kim said with her characteristic candor, "and I found myself in the middle of a big mess."

When this spirit door opened for Kim, she became able to see that, although her marriage had some wonderful aspects, it also had some serious flaws. Kim's husband expressed his anger in inappropriate ways; she felt abused by the outbursts of rage that he used to control her and the children when he didn't get his way.

Kim had not been looking for someone else, but falling in love with this "other man" helped Kim to see the places in her relationship where she was afraid and hiding. She realized she had created an unconscious agreement with her husband to remain dependent on him so that she did not have to face her fears of being incapable of supporting herself. Furthermore, she realized that she had shut down sexually in order not to feel the pain of her self-censorship in the marriage.

Given that Kim felt fearful much of the time, the fact that she risked an affair was a surprise to herself and everyone who knew her. Reflecting on this, Kim came to recognize her heretofore-unconscious coping strategy to emotionally collapse when upset or confused. She realized that, up to this point, she had had little personal authority regarding her life and had felt overtaken by self-doubt much of the time.

During the two years following the discovery of the affair, Kim felt as though she was living in two worlds simultaneously. There was her inner world where she felt "married" to the man with whom she had the affair and an outer life in which she was cohabiting and co-parenting with her husband.

Spirit door experiences bridge worlds, and we cannot fully occupy either one. This is massively frustrating. Despite our best efforts we cannot bring a new form into existence, one we can live with and live in. Nor can we fully disentangle ourselves from the life we've created.

In Kim's case, she could not leave her husband because she could not support herself. She was also concerned about the impact that a divorce might have on her young children, and she felt a responsibility to not leave her marriage until she explored whether or not the marriage could be re-visioned.

At the same time, she could not stop thinking about her lover and her desire to leave her life – and herself – as she had known them to be. She felt inexorably drawn to the experience she had of herself while with her lover, an experience she could not create up to that point without him.

She describes the experience of her lover this way:

"When I first met him, I felt so deeply moved. It was as spiritual an experience as it was physical. I felt like I was looking into an ocean of love and kindness. I felt his presence deep inside me, in my belly. It felt very physical and very real. Every time we had to say goodbye to one another, I'd experience gut-wrenching anguish and pain."

Kim continued. "I struggled with my feelings for a very long time, seeking the support of group therapy but also individual sessions with various guides over the years. Eventually, I began to notice I was feeling less of *him* in my belly and more of *me*. I cannot describe how this happened or why. Now, five years later, I feel full of me for the first time in my life. I feel here for the first time in my life. I feel whole for the first time in my life."

Even though Kim ended the affair in her waking reality, she was unable for a long time to end it in her mind, heart, and dreams. It took an additional couple of years for the energy constelled in that affair to transform itself so that she no longer felt anything (except a fullness of self and gratitude for him) when she thought of her lover.

As she was pursuing her inner work with the help of a therapist, Kim could not tolerate acting as though things were "back to normal" in her marriage. Although she continued to feel afraid of her husband's rage, she noticed herself less and less willing to "make nice" as she had in the past. In fact, as Kim felt more of herself inside herself, she felt more powerful, clear, and grounded. She realized that she had brought her lover in as a means of equalizing the tremendous imbalance of power she felt in her marriage. She was no longer willing to be in the child role in the marriage.

She felt so grateful for the shift in herself and her marriage that she made a promise to herself that no matter how much her husband bullied her, she would never pretend to be contrite about the affair. Her commitment to stand behind this deep truth within herself became the scaffolding for the new sense of self that was under construction.

By the time the entirety of Kim's process of having her spirit door experience and working with its aftermath was over, she was already well into the final stages of her midlife passage.

Kim's story follows a progression that is common in love-affair spirit door situations:

1. We "fall in love" – or find ourselves intensely attracted to someone.
2. We experience a powerful desire to leave our lives but lack the internal or external support to do so.
3. We spend much of our time thinking about our lover in our mind yet feeling tethered in various ways to our lives as we have known them to be.
4. We find ourselves bouncing between the two worlds, inner and outer, unable to reconcile them.
5. We begin to live in both worlds simultaneously.
6. Over time, we occupy the space between the two worlds consciously.

The more we live *between* the two worlds instead of bouncing back and forth from one to the other, the more we set the process of rebirth in motion. As we increasingly *inhabit the space between*, a new experience – of ourselves and of our worlds – begins to materialize. This process of inhabiting the gap will be the central theme of the next stage, Filling in the Gaps.

What Kim noticed as she began to live in the gap is that instead of focusing on the two men – and bouncing back and forth between them – she began to focus on *herself* more, separate from the two men. She also noticed that her need to have these two men direct her life lessened.

She shared the following from a couple's counseling session with her husband: "I told him that I felt deeply sorry for causing him so much pain. I also told him I would do it all over again in a heartbeat because the affair saved my life. I do not believe that I would have been able to pull out of the orbit I was in with my husband without being swept entirely into another world for a period of time. I am so grateful for the experience of the affair, which helped me see that what was missing in my life was me. I hope that one day he will be able to understand that."

The fact that she could say this to her husband without flinching was proof positive that she was no longer living in her old world and no longer orbiting around him as her reference point. "Nor do I intend to become a moon orbiting around any future lover's planet," she thoughtfully informed me during our final meeting together.

Although the paring down of Kim's story here to illustrate key elements of the spirit door experience might give her experience an appearance of simplicity and ease, her process took arduous inner work over a long period of time. The struggle matured Kim, and it was anything but simple and easy.

I must mention a caveat here: when the spirit door opens as an attraction door with a love interest, it is generally compelling enough to end or severely challenge marriages. What we are feeling seems to be as real as anything we have ever experienced. And, on one plane of reality it is. But that plane of reality is often a "temenos," a sacred container where something very deep is being worked out. Although I suggest that clients take what is unfolding as seriously as they can, I also urge them to slow the pace down as much as they are able. The aim is to help them occupy two worlds at the same time instead of destroying their old world and jumping into a new one.

The Wilderness of Illness

Illness is a common form in which the aversion door opens. Minor ailments may open the door for a short period of time, but serious conditions such as cancer or the nervous system disease multiple sclerosis can fling us "off the map of the knowable," as English doctor Oliver Sacks wrote after his own bout with illness. Illness is an unknowable terrain. Illness keeps us in suspense – or suspended

– because we cannot know with certainty what might happen next or how it will ultimately turn out.

Whereas attraction door experiences usually prompt us to rush out (at first) into the arms of the waiting world, aversion door experiences cause us to shrink back, withdraw, and pull deeply inward (between flurries of searching for a remedy).

When sick, we drop out of sight or into the background of life. During the course of an illness, we can experience ourselves as shut in or walled off, as if we cannot get to other people in the outside world. Life outside the confines of the illness fades into the background. When we "fall prey" to an illness, we feel as though we've been culled from the healthy flock and isolated, made into pariahs. Much is written by those in love. In comparison, scarcely a whisper is heard from those afflicted with health challenges.

Even if we have a curable illness, we feel the full weight of our aloneness and the fear of ending in oblivion. We feel poised on the brink. Sometimes we feel as though we will go out of our minds from all the internal chatter that erupts. Other times, the silence can be so deafening that we imagine ourselves to be in solitary confinement, the desert, or interstellar space.

Like the love door that we explored earlier, the aversion spirit door experience gives us an exceptional vantage point from which to challenge our self-perceptions after the initial flood of emotions and activity subside. But, unlike when we enter the love door, which can feel like a fairy tale, our initial step through the illness door will feel more like a nightmare.

Aversion Spirit Door Case Study

A client I have been working with for several years, Martin, experienced his spirit door open more slowly than most. He began to feel a loss of energy, first physically, and later on emotionally and mentally. Thinking back to the onset of the experience, he shared: "It felt as though someone had pulled a cork out of my chest, and I began to leak energy."

Highly sensitive people often report that before becoming ill – whether in minor or major ways – they are aware of losing energy and interest in their usual lives; they slow down or feel a bit lost. At first Martin tried to hold back the night with a host of energy-boosting supplements and sheer force of will, pushing his agenda forward despite signals that he was not feeling well. "Over time, the loss of energy just became another layer of too-muchness in my already too-much existence," he reported.

Whatever the severity of the condition, when we become ill, most of us feel strange – depressed, drained. The lack of psychic energy can be astounding. We often feel angry about being forced to attend to something not on our agendas.

Martin describes himself as "a tough nut and a remedial patient." He claims to have spent more time in the denial stage "than anyone else on the planet." He goes on to say: "After denial, I got stuck in 'guilt'; I felt as though I had done something wrong, and that's why I was sick. I believed I was being punished and that I deserved what I was getting."

Leaning back in his chair, he reflects, "Fear was present throughout. While it moved from the front burner to the back and then to the front again, it never went away, at least not for me."

The more energy Martin lost, the less he felt like himself. He underwent countless medical exams and tests with inconclusive results. He explored andropause (the male version of menopause), as well as various immune deficiency syndromes, all to no avail.

After working his way through the Western medical establishment's arsenal, he sought help from a full range of alternative health care practitioners. Still not finding a cure to the ongoing energy loss there, he began working with various psychotherapeutic modalities. He also worked with psychics, spirit channels, energy healers, and astrologers.

Over the course of his illness, Martin left his mid-level manager job in an engineering company, applied for state disability, and subsequently engaged in full-time self-study. To this day, Martin's illness remains undiagnosed, but, with his characteristic quirkiness, he has named it his "nutcracker" – drawing on the famous fairy tale by the same name – because he sees it as having cracked him open and allowed him to transform from a "thing" into a real, living human being.

Like all spirit door experiences, serious illness presents us with a situation we cannot resolve, often for a long time if ever. We are not only pulled off course from our lives, we fear being pulled out of our lives entirely. We hover between the world of the living and the world of the dying, each of which has its own needs, concerns, and occupations.

The parameters of our worlds shift dramatically when we are ill. Although these parameters appear to shrink by outer-world measures, the opposite is true by inner-world measures. Dreams become more real, and waking reality feels less real. If we have a meditation practice, the states we achieve while meditating become just as valid as "normal" consciousness states. My clients who are ill report that the distinction between states of consciousness blurs, and it becomes difficult to distinguish them.

In the course of living with an illness, we explore life and death in ways that most of us have not done before. And all of our struggling melts us down into our elemental state of utter humanness. A serious illness can divorce us from our egos so that we can achieve the enviable state that someone who has accepted death achieves at the moment of passing: acceptance, peace, joy, and gratitude.

Through the course of his illness, Martin began to wake up from his egoic dream and grew to appreciate the intricacies, complexities, and simplicities of life in ways that were not possible for him before he became ill. The more he felt included in the interweaving of all things, the more in love he felt with all of life. Nevertheless, as Martin often reminded me during the course of our work together, "the moment I have a 'good day,' I am back off to the races, rushing here and there, sometimes in mock self-importance. But if *recovery* would mean *covering over* the wise and gentle man I have become, I would not choose it."

⁓⁓⁓

Some of us might not be able to identify a condition or experience that opened our spirit doors, but we might identify an experience of metaxis, feeling ourselves completely, simultaneously in two different worlds. Any time we are present at a birth or death, we experience metaxis. Any time we spend time in a prison or a hospital, we experience metaxis. The same is true with nursing homes, halfway homes, hospices, rehab centers, and psychiatric wards. These are all places that house those living between the worlds and in multiple worlds.

For most of us, a hallmark of the spirit door is failure. Whether we enter though the attraction or the aversion door, the failure to make something work within one world requires a larger world. *We begin by failing in one world, discovering another, and oscillating between them until, one magical day, we find ourselves occupying both as well as the space between.* Unbeknownst to us now, we will eventually notice that we feel larger as a result of this experience. Like the f/stop on a camera, our aperture setting widens as a result of struggling with our spirit door experience, allowing in more light and a wider, panoramic view.

At some point we will emerge from the spirit doorway – excruciatingly slowly, or forcefully spat out – and we will be different. We will hear ourselves saying, "I'm changed" even if we cannot articulate the difference at first.

Stage 4, Time Down Under, drops us into the void. An open spirit door keeps us floating, destabilized, within that space. Working with the ways in which we have separated or abandoned ourselves – in Stage 6, next – begins the process of filling that space, often for the very first time.

STAGE 6

Filling in
the Gaps

෧ඁ෴ඁ෧

Before we can emerge fully from the emotional darkness and destabilization that characterize our time down under and our spirit door events, midlife requires us to reach downward and make contact with "the magnitude of the pain that has been entrusted to (us)," as a Sufi prayer says. This pain lies deep within the wounds we experienced in early life, in response to which our ego developed defenses, believing that they would protect us from further hurt. As midlife continues to dissolve our ego identities, our resistance to directly meeting these unclaimed parts of our personal pasts lessens. We are invited to dig through uncomfortable personal material of many kinds throughout our midlife journeys; during this stage, we focus specifically on encountering our past *traumas*.

Rumi writes, "The wound is the place where the Light enters you." As we investigate our past wounds and begin to fill in the gaps that these wounds created in our consciousness, we invite in the light. Bringing daylight into our dark inner landscape is a process I call *"filling in the gaps."* This light will help guide us in assembling the new self that will emerge from the ashes of our former ego-based lives. The work of filling in our gaps can be arduous, but, like our descent into darkness and encounters with the spirit door in the previous stages of mid-life, this work will reveal itself, often after the fact, as one of the many hidden blessings of our midlife journey.

The Power of the Past

To fill in our gaps, we must focus not on who we were as children but on what happened to us as children. Until we learn to distinguish between these two, what happened to us as children will continue to distort our perception of what is happening to us now as adults. Focusing on what happened to us when we were young takes us into the trauma layers in our psyches, which were created to manage the times when we had to leave or disassociate from ourselves because we could not handle certain experiences or encounters.

Before continuing, let me say a word of caution: almost all of us will inevitably become frustrated or impatient with the difficulty of healing our wound-structures, so we must muster as much kindness and patience with ourselves as we can during this process. Although not exactly encoded into our DNA, the reactions formed from our childhood experiences are deeply embedded in our nervous systems. These hard-wired survival reactions are linked to impressions left by our personal experiences in early childhood. *Because these patterns of response are – or feel as if they are – tied to our survival, examining and attempting to change them feels like a threat to our very existence.* For this reason, we may resist changing them even if we understand that healing these patterns is one of the key blessings that our midlife transformation brings.

In preparation for our exploration of what happened to us in the past, let's briefly review some basic psychological concepts that describe how we experienced the world when we were very young.

As infants, although we were able to differentiate among experiences, we didn't actually understand that experiences were separate from one another. Back then, the touch of a hand on our cheek, the milk we drank, and the crib we rested in were all parts of a unified field of experience for us.

This unity began to differentiate when we started experiencing pleasurable and painful sensations that were too much for our central nervous systems. As these two types of experiences repeated, the impressions were archived in our developing nervous systems, first in the form of body-felt memories. On the foundation of those memories, concepts and expectations were built. As we discussed briefly in Stage 2, The Unraveling, this is the process by which our ego identities were formed.

Because our first differentiations were between pleasure and pain, the distinction between these two responses becomes overarching and persistent for us. We could say that *every psycho-physical event that rises above the threshold of our consciousness is emotionally colored or charged by either pleasure or pain, and each event produces a sense of stability or instability within us that correlates with the degree of pleasure or pain experienced.*

We move toward pleasure and away from pain. This movement can be understood as the well-known push (pain) – pull (pleasure) dynamic so common in primary partnership and marriage, where we try to get our partners to do the things that provide us pleasure and to not do the things that cause us pain.

In addition to pleasure and pain, another type of early childhood experience adds an emotionally charged layer to our egos. When our caregivers are unable to attune and respond to our every infant need, we experience *survival anxiety.* When we are infants, if someone does not arrive to feed us as soon as we are hungry, we become afraid that we will not be fed and therefore will not survive. Our reaction to this anxiety is a contraction in one of two forms: withdrawal (shutdown) or rage (although rage might appear to be an explosion rather than a contraction, the physical experience we have when enraged is of reflexive contraction of the pupil of the eye and other bodily functions).

Whether we shut down or become enraged, the experience disconnects us from our infant state of unity with our environment or caregiver. Then, after the provoking distress passes, we return to our essential infant state of repose in non-differentiation. This natural cycle of contraction and relaxation repeats each time an experience elicits survival anxiety in us. However, in some cases, when the sensory stimulation is sufficiently extreme – for example, when we have to wait longer than our infant systems can tolerate before we are fed – this natural rhythmic oscillation between closing and opening is interrupted, and something that psychoanalyst Wilhelm Reich calls "armoring" occurs.

Armoring is a protective response of the body in which our muscles contract when we feel repeatedly threatened. To illustrate this concept, Reich used the analogy of the amoeba that, when undisturbed, expands and contracts in a fluid natural rhythm. When the amoeba is pricked by a pin, however, it instantly pulls away from the painful stimulus, and its fluid movements become restricted. After a period of time, the amoeba will return to its natural pulsation. But if the environment continues to subject the amoeba to pain, eventually the contracted state of restricted movement will remain permanent. This is what Reich refers to as armoring.

In human terms, when we armor or enter a state of permanent withdrawal and contraction, this forms a trauma site in our psyches where disproportionate amounts of emotionally charged energy are collected and stored. We will talk later in this chapter about the nature of these trauma sites and the work of softening and unwinding them. For now, we just need to keep in view the kinds of somatic responses that indicate armoring. These include stomach tightening, throat closing, brain fog, fatigue, forgetfulness, suddenly feeling very hot or very cold, having trouble breathing, experiencing a fast heartbeat, shutting down emotionally, developing sweaty palms, and feeling paralyzed.

Family environments where we experienced excessive criticism, aggression, shame, humiliation, volatility, neglect, competition, or coercion result in emotional armoring. But the emotional conditions do not have to be this dramatic; we all have created armoring to greater or lesser degrees, depending on the depth of trauma experienced.

Later in life, these armored trauma sites are the emotionally charged landmines that we spend so much time gingerly sidestepping in our relationships with others. This armoring may result in a sensitivity to being treated harshly or a pattern of acting out our own wounding by treating others harshly. Either way, we are not experiencing our own natural pulsation but are acting out a response to a past trauma. Each of us has sensitivities like these that developed as a result of our childhood experiences and our emotional armoring in response to those experiences.

Contacting the Child's Reality

The concepts above are helpful for *understanding* our childhood experiences, but it is important to also *contact* the emotionally moving reality of our childhood wounds. To bring our childhood state into our awareness, it is helpful to experientially recollect the full extent of our powerlessness as children. That powerlessness to meet our own needs is the reason we felt threatened when those needs were not met by our caregivers (and, by extension, when we are not getting our needs met in our adult lives).

Children's capacity for sensory impression – especially in response to what is communicated to them through body messages – is extraordinary by adult standards. Every intonation, subtle gesture, eye movement, or change in scent and body position is registered in minute detail in a child's consciousness. American botanist Luther Burbank captures the degree of a child's sensitivity to impression in the following, sobering passage:

> *Imagine if you can a diamond made of sensitized plates like those used in the finest camera, and then conceive of the infinite variety of pictures that are printed – every day – every hour! on the plastic and impressionable mind of the child! You think that he does not see that quick, angry gesture, or hear that sharp ugly word, or feel the impatience in that push you gave him, or understand that nasty allusion, or pick up that slovenly habit; but you are wrong. All the pictures are there. Every time the lens clicks there is a permanent record.*

Abstract models and words alone are not really enough to evoke the lived quality of our most vulnerable human states. Often it is only when a significant obstacle or event in our lives brings us to our knees that we are able to pierce our emotional armor and feel, viscerally, the vulnerability we felt in our early years.

Dick Wagner's song "Remember the Child" brings to the foreground the defenselessness of our early lives and the reason we close ourselves down in response to painful experiences that we do not understand. There are a few You-Tube versions of Wagner performing this song. The immediacy with which he sings the universally painful lyrics can help us remember the vulnerability of the child within us, which is easily forgotten when our egos are in charge. Some of the videos of him singing the song include moving photos of young children. It's well worth the time to watch and listen to one of these performances in preparation for our discussion below because doing so helps us recall the child within each of us, who had to go to great lengths to shut down to emotional pain that was unendurable at times. Listen to the haunting voice of the performer who wrote this from his own experience, and open to the images paired with the song. For those not able to access a YouTube file, below are a few lines of the lyrics.

NOTE: The suggestion to watch a YouTube performance is for those who could use some help connecting to the vulnerability of their child selves in preparation for our upcoming discussion. If you are already experiencing a highly sensitized state as you are reading this chapter, consider skipping the song and the excerpt of the lyrics (italicized below) for the moment because it will not serve you to feel re-traumatized.

Here are some excerpts of the lyrics:

…. I'm sorry, Daddy take my hand,
Tell me what I've done so bad.
… I wonder, why are you so mad?
Don't you love me Dad?

Cross my heart, I swear Ma, I won't cry no more.
I'll just lay in silence down here on the floor.
Cross my heart and hope to die if you don't want me anymore.

… for you Ma, I won't talk so loud.
I won't laugh so hard, I'll shut my mouth.
… for you Mom, I won't make a sound.

... Mean and angry words are all I hear
Through my bedroom walls Dad, loud and clear
... I lie awake and shake with fear
And wish I had no ears...

Self-Inquiry

If you have just listened to the song, pause here for a while and allow the feelings evoked by the song and video images to move in and through you. You might also want to take a moment or two to write about your feelings if that will help you deepen your experience of them.

The child in the song doesn't understand why his father is so mad. He cannot comprehend that his father's anger might be an overflow of frustration from the workday or an effect of too much alcohol. For that little boy, his father striking him is personal and shocking because the boy is still in a state of oneness with his surroundings; he is continuous with his father.

The child in the song who decides to shut her mouth to avoid upsetting her mother doesn't understand that her mother might be overwhelmed by the demands of three children in her care or anxiety over the bills stacking up on the dining room table. The child views her mother's incapacity to cope as a message about the child's own inadequacy.

Bear in mind that when they were young, these parents did not have parents who were empathically attuned to them – which is also true of most of our parents. The legacy of feeling unloved or of not experiencing attunement from parents is what we hand down when we communicate our frustration instead of our interest and love for our children and each other.

At the same time, each and every event like these creates moments of differentiation or separation in us that shape our personal development and evolution. If these moments are too extreme or too frequent – for *us*, not by any external measure – they result in wounding or trauma.

Dual Fears: Overwhelm and Abandonment

Thus far we have identified the universal pattern to move toward pleasure and away from pain. We also know that, when faced with pain, an infant experiences survival anxiety. When the survival anxiety becomes too extreme for the child's central nervous system to tolerate, the child experiences one or both of two fears that are common to everyone.

The first is the fear of feeling *overwhelmed*. This fear might occur when a stimulus is too strong for us, as in the example from the song above when an adult yells at us. The second is the fear of feeling *abandoned*. This might occur when we need emotional or physical contact but are left alone for longer than we can tolerate.

These two fundamental fears, and the outgrowth of our intricate weave of coping strategies and adaptations to manage them, form the root ball of our ego-bound existences. *Almost every reaction we have today as adults can be traced to a fear of being overwhelmed or abandoned.*

Self-Inquiry

* Do you tend to feel more overwhelmed (that experiences are too much for you) or more abandoned (left alone when you don't want to be by yourself) by life or others?

* Do others in your life experience you more as overwhelming or abandoning?

The utter helplessness of the infant during an experience of feeling overwhelmed or abandoned creates "cognitive shock," which is the inability to do anything to affect the outcome of the events. By this point in our midlife passages, we are more than familiar with the sensation of shock; our arrival in midlife itself is often felt as a shock, and the issues and experiences that arise once we are on the midlife path also often have a shocking quality. Our midlife confrontations with our own futility mirror the helplessness we felt in infancy, an earlier time in our lives when we similarly could not restore ourselves to a sense of safety and control when we felt overwhelmed or abandoned.

Coping Strategies that Result from Trauma

Trauma, a word with Greek roots meaning "wound" or "to pierce," refers to experiences that, within a short period of time, present us with stimulus that is too powerful for our central nervous systems to manage in a normal way. In response to childhood traumas of overwhelm (too much of something) and abandonment (too little of something), we developed three coping strategies that should be immediately recognizable as leitmotifs in all of our lives:

1. Moving *against* the other, resulting in patterns of control, overpowering others, and manipulation.
2. Moving *toward* the other, resulting in patterns of compliance, pleasing others, and accommodation.
3. Moving *away from* the other, resulting in patterns of avoidance, withdrawal, and shutdown.

In the following discussion, most of us will recognize that we employ all three coping strategies in varying measures at varying times. We employ these strategies, often unconsciously, to remedy our infant-imprinted experience of powerlessness, which continues unchecked and unconscious in our present-day experience.

The first coping pattern, *to move against the environment*, comes from the basic belief that the "other" (initially a parent or primary caregiver) is more powerful than we are, and the resulting decision that we want to be more powerful than the other is. In this strategy, we decide to use power to gain control; in other words, we decide that we want to be the parents, the ones in control in our worlds. We want to overpower others rather than feel overpowered ourselves.

Some employ anger, physical force, or even violent and coercive strategies to overpower others, but there are many less overt ways of gaining control. Some will seek to become know-it-alls, getting degree after degree in their effort to feel a sense of intellectual control over their worlds. Others will seek fame or financial dominance to gain a sense of power over their lives as well as the lives of others. Still others will employ manipulation or humor to get what they need and want.

The second coping pattern, *moving toward the other*, is also rooted in the basic belief that the other (initially a parent or other primary caregiver) is more powerful than we are. Rather than becoming controlling ourselves, however, in this strategy we *give our power away* to the powerful other. This is most popularly known as co-dependence, whereby we defer to the other – or align with the other – and submit ourselves to the other's direction, needs, or care. We accommodate the other and remain focused on the other's needs and wants rather than our own. A fundamental split in our psyche results, creating confusion about when to attend to someone else and when to attend to ourselves. Lacking strong internal structures to maintain a healthy balance between self and other, we collapse into incompetence and seek external structures to take care of us, or we throw the full weight of our competence behind someone else's agenda.

The third coping strategy, *moving away from the other*, is widely known as the pattern of avoidance or withdrawing from interaction with others. When total escape is impossible, we exhibit forms of avoidance that distance us from feared situations. Forgetting, procrastinating, withdrawing, withholding, shutting down, denying, minimizing, judging, confabulating, becoming passive or evasive, and engaging in substance abuse are all examples of avoidance patterns.

Self-Inquiry

* In what situations do you overpower, manipulate, or try to control others? What behaviors do you engage in to do this?

* In what situations, and with whom, are you compliant and accommodating, giving your power and control to others? What behaviors do you engage in to do this?

* In what situations, and with whom, do you shut down, withdraw, or move away? What behaviors do you engage in to do this?

All three coping styles are actually *avoidant* at their core. Because we cannot tolerate the internal emotional experience of discomfort, we employ these strategies to try to stop (overpower), prevent (accommodate), or get away from (escape) the perceived source of our discomfort.

All three coping styles are also *disassociative*. We will discuss disassociation in some detail next.

Disassociation

To explore the ways in which we disassociate, we must identify the places where we have, over time, become unconscious; denied our experience; fallen asleep to what was happening; or chosen an emotionally buffered, avoidant, automatic, or numbed-out existence. Once we identify the ways in which we leave the present moment, our task is to find a way to stay. *We must learn to show up here and now for experiences that we were not able to face in childhood, particularly at times when we feel overwhelmed or abandoned.*

Before we can fully understand what is required of us in healing disassociation, we must both clarify the meaning of the word "trauma," and de-pathologize the word "disassociation."

Earlier I offered a definition of *trauma* as an experience that, within a short period of time, presents us with stimulus that is too powerful for our central nervous systems to manage in a normal way. The resulting disturbances produce long-lived coping strategies and patterns. *Trauma, then, is the result of a stressful event or series of events that overpower our perceived or actual ability to cope.*

The circumstances that lead to trauma and become associated with a feeling of overwhelm or abandonment could be an abuse of power; a betrayal of trust; a feeling of entrapment; or an experience of powerlessness, pain, confusion, or deep loss. Trauma can be the result of a one-time incident, such as being molested by a babysitter, or persistent experiences, such as living with a parent, caretaker, or sibling who is chronically volatile, critical, emotionally vacant, withdrawn, or angry.

When faced with trauma, the human psyche distances itself from the situation in any one of a number of ways. We might go into shock, shut down, leave our bodies, throw a tantrum, or go numb. Afterward, many of us forget the event altogether or remember the trauma without feeling. When we distance ourselves from a situation, we *disassociate*: we absent ourselves from what is happening and what we are experiencing. *When we disassociate, our presence and our vitality are absent.*

Everyone disassociates; in its mild forms, disassociation is a normal and necessary function. Only in its most severe forms does it potentially require professional intervention.

Most of us are familiar with war-related, natural-disaster, and human-caused shocks (plane crashes, etc.) leading to disassociation. We might not as readily recognize, however, the personal ways in which we have all been traumatized unless we have sought therapy or have explored personal-growth modalities where traumatic material – and its daily effect on our lives – begins to become visible.

The personal traumas that cause disassociation can run the gamut from mild, such as a single event that felt upsetting to us as children, to more challenging situations such as growing up in an emotionally explosive, critical, neglectful, or addiction-driven family. Severe examples include childhood sexual abuse; the early loss of a parent, sibling, or guardian; grave childhood physical illness; early childhood surgeries; and experiences of public humiliation.

Whatever the form and duration of our suffering, *we all have experienced trauma*; no one is exempt. As a result, we all disassociate, to greater or lesser degrees. This coping mechanism is a part of the human condition.

We are disassociating whenever we are on automatic pilot, navigating through the day without fully paying attention to where we are, what we are doing, and how we feel in the moment. We are disassociating when we are in uncomfortable social situations and turn to alcohol, overeating, or cigarettes to feel more at ease. We are disassociating when we have a fight with a loved one and react explosively or when we communicate with others (such as our parents) but erect emotional and psychological walls so that we do not hear what they are saying or feel our pain about the lack of a meaningful connection with them.

At this stage in our journeys, the work is to become aware of just how chronic our condition of disassociation is. Becoming acutely aware of how often we separate from our experience will give us the opportunity to do the reverse: to re-associate and reconnect with ourselves. We have the opportunity to come out of shock and experience ourselves being present for circumstances that felt overwhelming or abandoning in the past. This is what I am referring to in the title of this stage, Filling in the Gaps; when we are able to wake up in places where we habitually absent ourselves, we are filling in the gaps that traumatic experiences created in our ability to be present.

Revisiting Trauma Points

To illustrate this process a bit further, a few chapters from my own life might help.

In my late teens, I was assaulted by two men. That assault resulted in long-term physical damage and initiated a 30-year journey. Many years of therapy – psychological as well as physical – were focused to a large extent on the assault. In that process, I made many connections and progressed through many stages of healing and recovery from this traumatic event in my life.

During Stage 6, Filling in the Gaps, of my own midlife passage, I returned to therapy for what I thought was a separate issue: I wanted to address my fear of public speaking. The therapist asked me about the trauma points in my life, and I mentioned the assault, quickly assuring him in the next breath that, after 30 years of therapeutic work, I felt I had run that particular well dry; there must be another point of origin to seek out and work with. He wanted to pursue the assault, but I was resolute: I had worked that experience through.

However, all of a sudden, in the middle of the first session with that therapist, I found myself in Washington, D.C., once again, with the headlights of the men's turquoise car shining on me much like the camera lights during a television interview. But this time, for the first time, I felt awake for each and every blow of the assault. I felt the fear, the searing pain, my back pressed up against the parked car where I struggled to hold on to the door handle so as not to be forced inside. I felt the coolness of the November evening, the silence, save for the occasional sound of rustling leaves being swept up the street by small gusts of wind, and the insistent voice of the second man urging the first man to hurry up.

During that therapy session, for the first time in 30 years, I experienced myself coming out of shock and fully feeling the experience of the assault. To my surprise, my brain had recorded and stored every minute detail. In my re-experience of the event, I found myself looking into the eyes of the bigger man who did most of the beating, and I saw that he did not want to be there any more than I did. It was a profound moment. I felt sorry for him, I felt sorry for myself, and I felt sorry for what we were both going through. I was overwhelmed with compassion for both of us.

I felt awake, as though parts of myself that had not been able to remain conscious during the assault were recovered. Those parts of my psyche that had disassociated or split off to survive that overwhelming experience were now being invited back in, and the loss of self that had resulted from that disassociation was being healed. Afterward, I felt more whole and integrated.

When I recount this story, I am often asked if my fear of public speaking was changed as well. It wasn't. But the rest of my life was. A deeply held inner grievance about being unfairly accosted was lifted. Along with that, I felt less afraid walking on the street alone than I had been for much of my life. But, most importantly, I felt as though the part of me that had disconnected from humanity the moment I disconnected from my assailants was brought back in a way that expanded my ability to love – myself and the men who had attacked me. This allowed me to experience myself as a part of the whole of humanity, giving me back the sense of belonging that I had lost as a result of that and other traumas like it. I count this restoration of connection and compassion as one of the great blessings of my midlife journey.

Life brings us things that we cannot digest, integrate, and resolve; these experiences force us to grow. In the filling-in-the-gaps stage of midlife, we are stripped bare enough to see more clearly than we ever could before the ways in which we leave the present moment. As a result, we are given the opportunity to revisit the major places and times in our lives at which we experienced trauma. In response to these traumas, we disassociated over and over until we were reduced to a defensive shell instead of the full living reality of who we were born to be. One profound blessing of our midlife journey is the opportunity to retrieve and re-enliven the parts of us that absented themselves, leaving us in this lonely shell.

In the course of 30 years of therapy, I had periodically worked on the experience of the assault, and that work contributed to the completion I experienced during the profound therapy session when I finally relived the full experience. But those who have never worked a day on their past adult traumas have the same opportunity to revisit those experiences and be present for themselves in the way I did during that session.

In my private practice, I am often asked when is the right time to let go of a trauma story. Clients believe they should stop telling their stories and want them to be finished. But if the story continues to have an emotional charge, I wonder whether, instead of us stopping the telling of these stories, *perhaps we should get better at telling our stories*. How might we feel the wound more deeply (but not in a way that reinforces a victim identity)? I believe a story that persists is inviting us into a conversation about something important for our personal evolution. Those trauma stories – and their deep places of emotional wounding – that remain with us for a long time offer opportunities for soul contact.

To use our traumas to make contact with our deeper selves, we must enter the instinctual part of our beings, our bodies, because we left our bodies when we couldn't handle what life presented. Returning to our bodies is returning home. The more we are willing to be present in the vulnerable flesh and blood of our physical beings, the more open we become to receive life in all of its dimension and depth. Paradoxically, the more vulnerable we become, the stronger we are. It's counterintuitive, I know, especially if we have felt traumatized, but this kind of resolution is necessary because of the nature of trauma and the way it takes up residence in our bodies.

Becoming Personally Present to Our Personal Absence

The work of re-association is the work of becoming personally present to the places and circumstances where we have been absent in our pasts. Re-association work will unfold in most if not all areas of our lives during the midlife passage. As mentioned earlier, in order to re-associate, we need to know the ways in which we disassociate, i.e., leave our present-time experience mentally, psychologically, emotionally, and/or physically.

We can begin by inquiring into the places and times we emotionally leave present-time experiences that feel uncomfortable. Think of a few current experiences that feel challenging. Public speaking is one such experience for many people. Social situations, holidays, job interviews, performance reviews, competitive situations, dating, and conversations where there is conflict are some others.

Contact with members of our family of origin and primary partnership is where most of us hit the mother lode of opportunities for disassociation.

Next we want to understand the ways in which we disassociate. Below is a list of some common ways in which we separate from our direct experience in a given moment. This list is not complete; it is offered to stimulate your own ideas and could serve as a checklist if some of these ways of not being present feel familiar.

* Shut down emotionally
* Act out or dramatize
* Explode in anger
* Emotionally detach
* Forget
* Get mental (become rational and logical)
* Lose body awareness
* Engage in food, substance, behavioral, and emotional abuses
* Excessively talk, use the Internet, watch television, sleep, etc.
* Compartmentalize
* Go blank mentally
* Get confused
* Constantly engage in internal monologues
* Become delusional
* Feel chronically overwhelmed or anxious
* Rigidly impose our opinion on others
* Make light of: "it's not that big a deal"

Self-Inquiry

* How do you disassociate? Make a list of the ways.

* Make a list of situations where you are likely to disassociate.

* Make a list of people in your life with whom you are likely to disassociate.

If we experience difficulty in identifying the ways in which we disassociate (and we might disassociate differently with different people and in different situations), we can look for clues by focusing on our relationship with our parents if they are still alive, our relationships with our children if we have them, and our relationships with current or former primary partners. The question is: under what conditions when in the presence of these people do we not feel alive, emotionally open, fully present, awake, and responsive? Disassociation happens when we are only half tuned in, half listening, or carrying on an internal conversation while making it look as though we are paying attention.

Five contexts that reliably produce disassociation in most of us are:

1. **Serious health issues**
2. **Serious relationship issues**
3. **Serious money issues**
4. **Serious sexual issues**
5. **Serious parent-child issues (whether we are the parent or the child)**

These five areas offer dependable – and, when confronted, formidable – doorways to emotional and psychological material that triggers overwhelm or abandonment. As a result, we often disassociate in these areas.

When we cannot show up for a given moment with our hearts wide open, our minds clear, our compassion and power readily available, and able to accept each moment as it is without wanting it to be different, we are disassociated to some degree. By emotionally and psychologically reopening memories of the trauma conditions that initiated our habit to absent ourselves in the first place, we invite ourselves to recover what was lost and to be more fully present for what is happening in our lives today.

Waking Up Inside of the Reaction

The process of *re-association* will begin to occur organically as we start to notice when we disassociate and struggle to fill in those blanks with open-hearted interest, curiosity, compassion, and presence. The first step is to recognize when we are disassociating. Once we become able to catch ourselves checking out while relating to our partners, for example, there is an approach we can take right in the moment as we are on the brink of feeling overwhelmed, abandoned, or reactive in some other way.

Begin by thinking of a recent conflict with your partner or someone else with whom you have felt emotionally reactive. It should be recent enough so that you can still sense some emotional charge in response to whatever you experienced at the time, for example feeling unseen, not appreciated, dismissed, blamed, judged, controlled, or undervalued.

Next, acknowledge the feelings you had in response to the experience. Anger, fear, and grief are possible. You might also experience disappointment, frustration, sadness, hurt, hatred, or regret. If you have difficulty identifying feelings per se, try to acknowledge the sensations you experience in your body. For example, you might experience tightness in your chest, heat in your face, or cold in your extremities. You could look for tension, ringing in the ears, vertigo, or brain fog as well. Whatever the experience – identified in the form of feelings or sensations – acknowledge it as fully as you can. Exaggerate a bit if you need to, in order to fully contact the experience.

Next, while inside the experience, ask yourself: how do you view the other person with whom you have touched into this distress? Does that person appear to be shut down, critical, negative, hostile, controlling, dismissive, attacking, rejecting, indifferent?

Now, ask yourself in what ways this experience of the other person is familiar to you. Go all the way back to your childhood. Does this person in your current experience remind you of your father, mother, other caregiver, sibling? It is important to connect the experience you are having today to an impression you have carried with you from your past.

This final part of this practice is the most difficult. Deliberately peel off the projected image of the "bad other" that you have brought with you from your past and attached to this person. One way to do this is to pretend that you have never before met the person to whom you are attributing your current distress. Imagine you don't know anything about him or her and are encountering him or her for the first time. What would you notice, be curious about, or drawn to? Pretending this way helps us see the person in a different light and lift off the projection.

Another way to lift off a projection is to consciously articulate to yourself who the person in your current experience is, and who is being projected onto that person but is not, in fact, that person. For example: "I see you; you are my friend Jeanette. You are not my mother, Lorraine. Here are some ways I can list that I know you, Jeanette, as a three-dimensional person who is different from the memory of my 'bad mother' projection (list the reasons). Here are some reasons I know I care about and respect you, Jeanette, and you care about and respect me and do not mean to repeat or re-enact any bad experiences from my childhood (list the reasons)."

As you lift the "bad other" picture off the present-day person, are you able to see the person you are relating to in present time more clearly and completely? What is it like to see the present-time person without the negative impression from the past? Do you feel less emotionally charged? Does your brain fog, confusion, or other mental state clarify? Is there more space for you and for the other?

When they give this practice enough time and attention, most report feeling less emotionally charged and better able to think and communicate after they lift off of the present-time exchange the "bad other" projection from the past. Sometimes we even experience an insight about what the other person in the present-day exchange might have actually been thinking or feeling, producing understanding or compassion for that person or for both of you.

The midlife transformation requires that we re-engage with all the places in our lives where we have disconnected in some way from ourselves and, by extension, from others. Wherever in our past we had a life experience that we could not handle emotionally, we must re-engage with it in our present. Such experiences include molestations, rapes, illnesses, accidents, disloyalty, betrayal, humiliation, feelings of being judged and criticized, and loss of a parent (to name a few). Any experience in which we felt hurt, shamed, disappointed, shocked, attacked, abandoned, rejected, overwhelmed, or damaged can also feel emotionally intolerable and cause us to disconnect. During midlife, it's as if life puts these events in our way again in one form or another so we can relate to them freshly and fully at last. This work must be taken on in earnest before we can emerge into a new life and a new experience of ourselves.

Our knee-jerk reaction to experiences we don't believe we can handle is to make them "bad"; we believe that the traumas we endured as children and beyond "shouldn't have happened." We do this because we couldn't handle the experiences back then, and we don't believe we can handle them now. As a result, we try to distance ourselves from the emotional material that is evoked in response to these experiences.

Instead of distancing ourselves, our task now is to wake up and be present to the full experience, including the effects of the trauma. Then, the parts of us that believe we cannot tolerate the experience will begin to relax and unwind; our defenses will soften, and our hearts will open, as my re-encounter with my past assailants illustrates. Paradoxically, we will also feel stronger. The mother dolphins are our example here; the highest response in these places is to love, in this case love for our own young selves who are caught in the spell of a past overwhelming experience.

I used a very large example, my work with my teenage assault, of what it can be like to re-associate. However, this same work can be done on a smaller scale as well. We take steps to re-associate when we speak what is true for us even though we fear there may be consequences; when we feel the craving for porn and stop to wonder why; when someone yells at us and we feel scared but consciously stand our ground; and when we say what we want even though we fear rejection. The work of re-association is available in both large *and* small places.

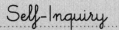

Self-Inquiry

If you regarded all challenges, problems, or difficulties (including difficult people) as things that life has put in your way to help you awaken a more authentic version of yourself, how would you experience your life differently?

It is not possible to re-associate and stay the same. When we re-enter experiences of trauma in an awake way, significant changes will result. Our lifestyles, our ways of being, what we choose to do for a living, and who we relate to might shift in new and unexpected directions. A very large part of the work of filling in the gaps is to allow the impact of our re-associations to fundamentally change our ways of being. This facilitates the discovery or recovery of a way of being that is more congruent with our deeper selves.

In Stages 4 and 5, we felt forced at times to be still, stripped of what we have known ourselves to be, and pushed into unknown fields and dimensions of existence. This kept us off balance for an extended period of time and brought us into contact with triggers that stimulate us to disassociate, to leave the present moment. The process of filling in the gaps in Stage 6 asks us to notice when we've left a moment and invites us to show up for that moment instead.

Just as the DNA of the butterfly is encoded in the caterpillar, we have our own blueprint for the future encoded deep inside of us. Reaching down, through our gaps – the places where we absented ourselves – and contacting this blueprint for our future life is a devotional practice. Over time, the process feels less traumatic and more like a homecoming.

A hidden blessing of liminal times like midlife is that they deeply destabilize our present state of consciousness. They come when, to harken back to Ken Wilber's concept of horizontal and vertical development, our horizontal growth has exceeded our vertical growth. We can think of this in terms of a tree whose branches continue to expand horizontally even though the roots are insufficiently deep. That tree will topple. Or, if we have up until now overemphasized a solitary, inner-directed life, we might have established very deep roots but have an inadequate amount of foliage – engagement in the world – to capture the light, photosynthesize, and nurture us.

Liminal times restructure the balance between vertical and horizontal by sending us in search of a deeper and more present experience of ourselves. To contact this deeper current within us, we must strive to be awake, present, and involved in all the places that we have avoided, checked-out from, or denied; that is, we must strive to re-associate. We will know we have filled in the gaps when *the spaces between places become spaces that unify rather than separate*. This awareness brings us to the next step of our midlife journeys, Stage 7, The Birth of a Unified Field.

STAGE 7

The Birth of a
Unified Field

⁓

When we arrive at Stage 7 of the midlife journey, gratitude and a sigh of relief are in order as we begin to emerge from the darkness. During the previous three stages of midlife, many of us doubted our chances of surviving the losses and emotional pain that we uncovered when we were stopped, depressed, suspended between worlds, and grasping the degree to which we have been disassociated from our experiences. During our sojourn in the depths, we might have occasionally feared that we would be forced to spend the rest of our lives replaying roles from the wounded scripts of our pasts.

But now we stand at the threshold of new life, emerging in two different ways. First, there is a sense of emergence that arises from stepping out of the darkness into the light or rising out of the depths back to the surface. Then, over time, the sense of emergence shifts, and we become aware that, like pupae en route to becoming butterflies, *we have wiggled out of the hard casing of our egos and have become more fluid and flexible beings as a result of our time in the dark.* Though we are not yet ready to take flight and inhabit the realm of air in addition to the realm of Earth (metaphorically speaking), we now begin to directly experience ourselves as belonging to a world larger than the one we inhabited when we were entirely ego-fixated. This is the stage when most of us first begin to sense in a more conscious and full way than earlier the blessings that our midlife journey is bringing to us – and that more are in store as we continue on the path.

When we notice a shift out of depression and hopelessness, it is not immediately clear what state we have shifted into; most of us can only report feeling that something is different, with a vague sense of relief. We begin, tentatively, to wonder whether we have made it to the other side of the darkness. However, after having been so thoroughly disassembled by the breakdown of our egos, we are cautious; we have learned not to get our hopes up and not to jump to grand visions of imminent rebirth. Our egos have been too humbled to spring back to their former levels of inflation.

If midlife is a marathon – and it is – at this point we've been running for 13 of 26 miles, and we are feeling the strain. We are not through the passage yet. There are more miles ahead. What will help us persevere for the remainder of the journey is the desire for our own fresh unfolding – as well as a lack of other options because some part of us knows that we can't go back to our old ego-based selves and find lasting satisfaction there.

The Emergence of New Life

Earlier in the book, I mentioned the parallel between the metamorphosis that transforms a caterpillar into a butterfly and the transformation we are undergoing in midlife. The darkness we emerge from now is the darkness of the chrysalis. Let's consider some new information about metamorphosis that sheds light on who we have been since the beginning of our lives, what happened to us in the chrysalis, and where we are headed as we emerge from it.

Although metamorphosis appears to have three distinct stages – caterpillar, chrysalis, and butterfly – it turns out that, in actuality, *these stages are not separate.* Those studying butterflies have learned that *the process of metamorphosis actually goes on continuously from the beginning of the caterpillar's existence.*

The seeds of metamorphosis are structures within the caterpillar that contain chromosomes carrying the butterfly's genes. These structures, called "imaginal buds," *are there from the beginning* – dormant, scattered in different locations within the caterpillar's body. When it is time to form the chrysalis, the imaginal buds become active, gravitate toward one another, and form clusters.

It is believed that the caterpillar's immune system responds to these activated imaginal buds as foreign to the organism and tries to fend them off (similar to the attitude of the ego when it first experiences soul contact and feels threatened). Only when the imaginal bud clusters gain sufficient strength can the caterpillar's immune system no longer suppress their aggregation. This triggers the dissolving of the caterpillar's body within the chrysalis. This is what happened to our egos during our time in Stages 4–6.

What this understanding of metamorphosis shows us is that *the caterpillar and butterfly are, in fact, one single organism that has the capacity to show up in two forms.* This is very important. Although some say that the caterpillar carries the blueprint for the butterfly, which reinforces the view of the two as separate organisms, the presence of the imaginal buds makes it clear that *the butterfly exists within the caterpillar all along.* So we could more accurately refer to this creature as a "catfly" or a "butterpillar."

When I was introduced to this information, it felt revolutionary to realize that the butterfly was in the caterpillar the entire time. But equally astonishing was the realization that the caterpillar remained present in the butterfly after the transformation. There it is in plain sight: the magnificence of the butterfly's wings had drawn my attention away from the caterpillar-shaped body to which the wings are attached.

The idea of the catfly or butterpillar is a stunningly helpful working metaphor for the relationship between our ego and our soul. *We are a single organism that can show up as ego or soul.* We exhibit more of the traits of the caterpillar when centered in ego consciousness and more of the traits of the butterfly when centered in soul consciousness. But regardless of where our consciousness is centered, *we are both!*

The relationship of the caterpillar to its own imaginal buds also helps us see why our ego and soul can feel as though they are enemies instead of successive stages of development. When the imaginal buds of our soul begin to cluster together in our midlife chrysalis (Stages 4–6), they are, like the buds in the caterpillar, beginning to build a new form that will supersede the ego and move us from being ego-centered to being soul-centered. Like the caterpillar's immune system, the ego tries its best to protect itself from and suppress what it sees as its own destruction. But, eventually, the ego cannot stave off its own dissolution and subsequent transformation.

A short journal entry written by a midlife retreat participant captures the hint of a new form coming into place:

> *I feel like I am in a very fine, subtle, and delicate process; I imagine this to be the weaving of a new psychological structure. I wonder what this new being taking shape out of the remains of me will look and feel like. I wait, hovering somewhere between what was once me and who I am becoming. When I do not worry if I'll get somewhere, I experience pleasure, peace, and even some excitement.*

Self-Inquiry

Are you noticing hints of a new self or new way of being? If so, how would you describe this new sense of self or new way of being?

As we move forward, we must allow ourselves to remain in this newly emerged and indefinable state. Our compass is in the process of re-setting itself, and we mostly experience a sense of space at first. Although the new terrain no longer feels dark and terrifying, we still cannot see recognizable landmarks by which to steady or orient ourselves or set a new course. Like caterpillars who know only the surface of the leaves over which they have crawled but not what it is like to flutter from flower to flower or to migrate long distances, it will take some time to learn how to orient and navigate as winged beings now.

Remember, the caterpillar (later to be transformed into the butterfly, capable of flight) is this creature's primary form during the first half of its life. Similarly, our ego is our main form during the first half of our lives. And, similar to what happens to the caterpillar, our ego will transform into a vehicle for the flight of our souls. As the rigidity of our ego melts away, it will be re-patterned and reconditioned into a vehicle through which our souls can open up fresh, new, authentic possibilities. Stage 7 and the two stages to follow are about the emergence of these new forms, a process that began with the dissolution of our old form.

When we first emerge from the darkness, the new subtle contours of our emerging inner and outer landscape might be hard to detect. Imagine how a being would feel that entered its cocoon as a crawling caterpillar and emerges as an entirely different form that has the capability to fly lightly above the surface of the Earth. Like the newly emerged butterfly, its wings damp and not yet unfolded, we do not know yet, as we emerge from the darkness, that we can fly. However, as we move further into this next leg of midlife, we will know with certainty that we have begun new lives.

Circumnavigating Ourselves

The state we emerge into now feels more whole and unified. To explore how this wholeness has come to be, we return to the diagram of a circle divided into two halves that was introduced in Stage 3, The Uprising.

As we discussed previously, the entire circle represents the sum total of who we are (psychologically, not spiritually, speaking). But, before midlife, we were unconscious of many aspects of our beings. As you recall, to illustrate the separation between the conscious and unconscious parts of ourselves, we divided the circle into two parts: the upper world represents the person we knew ourselves to be before midlife, and the underworld represents aspects of ourselves that we denied, did not recognize as part of who we are, or that were less developed.

The Upper World

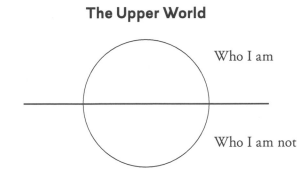

Who I am

Who I am not

The Underworld

During the uprising portion of our journeys, we experienced our primary identifications (the "I ams") begin to break down, allowing disowned or shadow parts of ourselves (the "I am nots") from the underworld to force their way into our consciousness. As an example of how the circle diagram applies, we talked about someone who had identified for much of his life as super-competent and a "can-doer." At midlife, when his dis-identified underworld aspects emerged, he began to experience himself as less competent or as a "no-can-doer."

You might remember that the suggestion for working with the material that arose from the underworld during the uprising stage was to allow our familiar identities to "capsize" and to inhabit the aspects of ourselves that emerged from our underworld rather than trying to reassert and reinforce our primary upper-world identifications. Doing this – allowing ourselves to be "no-can-doers" rather than trying to reassert our "can-do" identities, for example – took a great deal of courage. Thankfully, life kept the pressure on, forcing us to confront our underworld aspects rather than scurry back to our familiar identities.

After living for an extended time in our underworld identifications (the no-can-do place in our example above), we emerge in Stage 7 and cross back over to our upper world qualities (can-do, in the example above). At this point we have *circumnavigated* or traveled the full circumference of the two hemispheres of ourselves.

A Unified Field

In the example above, we moved from a primary identity of "I can" to a primary identity of "I can't" and then back to a primary identity of "I can." However, when we arrive back at our primary identity of "I can" in Stage 7, there is one monumental difference compared to our states leading up to this point: *when we return to the original position, we have erased the dividing line between the two hemispheres* as depicted in the diagram below:

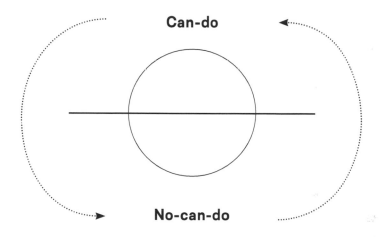

We have integrated all of ourselves and become a unified field.

Before I explain what this means and why this is such an important blessing of the midlife process of awakening, let me remind us that, as mentioned in Stage 3, the reverse of the can-do/no-can-do example is also true. If, for much of our lives, we experienced ourselves as "no-can-doers," chances are that during the shock, breakdown, dismantling, depression, disorientation, and disassociation of Stages 1–6, we began to feel more capable, or we made it more of a priority to be capable. The amusing aspect of this is that, because lacking capability was our original upper world identity, we felt more capable while in a dark place, which is where most people would feel less capable. Feeling capable while in the underworld builds a sort of back-door confidence so that, even as we return to what might initially appear to be a place of less capability on the surface (our starting point identity), at a deeper level we have experienced ourselves as capable, and we bring that awareness back into the upper world with us through the miracle of circumnavigation.

Whatever our starting point, we will know that we have circumnavigated ourselves when we no longer feel as inflexibly identified with one way of being or the other – that is, to use our example of competence and incompetence, when we don't feel exclusively like either "can-doers" or "no-can-doers." This is vitally important to recognize and consciously validate. *Once we have known ourselves both as someone who can and someone who cannot, we are no longer attached to being seen as – or seeing ourselves as – one or the other.* Our identification is less rigid, our reactions are less severe, and our ability to experience and enjoy life *as it is* increases significantly. *Our once-separate upper and underworlds have unified into a single field.*

Looking at circumnavigation through another lens, if we identify as thinking types and deny our feelings, once we have circumnavigated ourselves, we will likely experience more permission to feel and to express our feelings than we once did, but our thinking functions will remain fully available to us.

The following anecdote from a client is an example of what can happen after we have circumnavigated ourselves:

> *I was at a meeting in D.C., when the group I was consulting with asked me to facilitate an off-site training. I just said, "sure." Talk about out of character! For years they have asked me to do this, and for years I have explained that facilitating off-sites is not something I do. I have been referring someone else to them to handle this every year. But yesterday I agreed to do it without thinking much about it. I'm not attached to whether I can or can't, or if the way I do it will be as good as the way someone else would or not. I feel unattached and at peace with the decision. A decision that in the past would have kept me awake at night is not stirring a blade of grass in my universe.*

After the birth of the unified field of us, we have the possibility of being less attached to one identity or another and can feel more free to experience ourselves as able to do some things and unable to do other things without feeling either inflated or deficient.

This is quite an amazing turn of events – and it gets even better. Over time we will notice that we have *less preference* for one state over the other. Although on the one hand this can appear to be a process of letting go – and it is – on the other hand it reflects a reduced tendency to hold on; *we are becoming less inclined to rigidly identify with any state or role.*

Because we are less attached, we are able to respond to situations in an objectively appropriate manner. We are more skillful, attuned, focused, and capable of responding in whatever ways are most helpful and meaningful. This fluidity and flexibility are the most important blessings of this stage of our midlife transformation.

Self-Inquiry

* In what ways have you circumnavigated or are you circumnavigating yourself?

* Can you identify underworld aspects of yourself that you have experienced during your midlife journey, and their upper world counterparts?

* Can you identify an example in which you no longer have a strong preference for a particular role or state that was once important to you to maintain?

An Inclusive Identity Center

Coming full circle, through the hemisphere of our denied aspects, means that we are made *whole*. We are no longer subdivided into two worlds. Inhabiting this unified field means that we are less likely to identify ourselves as broken, inadequate, and not enough (or too much). From this point on, we increasingly experience *inclusive identity centers* that embrace *all* aspects of ourselves – allowing us to respond in a fitting way to any experience.

"In the human spirit, as in the universe, nothing is higher or lower; everything has equal rights to a common center which manifests its hidden existence precisely through this harmonic relationship between every part and itself." What the writer Goethe is saying here is that all of the parts of us – our "part selves" – are of equal value; no one is higher than the others or deserves greater privilege. I see this as each part self sitting together at the same banquet table: the inner controller, child, optimist, caretaker, sullen one, protector, etc. sitting at a round table where every part self is equal and served equal portions at the same time. We no longer care for some part selves and reject others.

There are still some challenges, of course. The more we stop identifying with any one "preferred" state, the more we clearly see that there are many voices inside of us. At times, our inner group of identities can feel a bit overwhelming. We might think to ourselves, "There isn't a table big enough to seat them all!" When we had fixed identifications with one way of being at a time, the rest of the group was more in the background. Now, as they all come into the foreground, many perspectives can present themselves in the course of a moment or an hour. These multiple voices or identifications can be present simultaneously or can come and go very quickly. "I hate this and want to kill myself" can exist simultaneously with "I love this experience and want more of it!" This can get a little confusing, to say the least.

At first glance, it can appear similar to the active imagination of children, but it is not the same. In midlife, developing the capacity to notice ourselves successively identifying and dis-identifying is a part of the transformative process that is under way and leads to larger and larger integrations, even though in the early stages it might feel as though we are trying to listen to a 50-piece orchestra with each part playing a different song. Over time, as our part selves coordinate, synchronize, and harmonize to the soul's key – this is the "harmonic relationship" of our part selves that Goethe mentions – we experience less dissonance and more harmony. We'll talk more about that in later stages.

Do not be confused by thinking that our newly birthed, unified fields have static boundaries and fluid interiors; the entire system now becomes fluid. Japanese farmer and philosopher Masanobu Fukuoka says it this way: "In nature, a whole encloses the parts, and yet a larger whole encloses the whole enclosing the parts. By enlarging our fields of view, what is thought of as a whole becomes, in fact, nothing more than one part of a larger whole. Yet another whole encloses this whole in a concentric series that continues on to infinity." The ever-widening aperture that Fukuoka describes will become more and more available to us as we move on in our journeys and will become an embodied realization in Stage 12.

Inhabiting Our Fluid, Inclusive Identities

Inhabiting our fluid identities does not mean trying to be a certain way; the more we detach from any single identity or role, the more connected we feel to the full range of human possibilities, and the more clearly we know that any particular state or identity is a fluid, transient experience of a deeper, permeable core self, which, as we will come to understand in subsequent stages, is our soul.

An inclusive identity center allows all elevations and amplitudes of our human experience to be present. It welcomes the entire spectrum so that we include and inhabit all that we once excluded, and we do not attach to any particular state. *Whether we are undone, bored, at the peak of a creative endeavor, or in the valley of an emotional crisis, we realize that all of those states are moving through us; they are not the same as us.* Our various identities or states are the *content* of our experience, and we are starting to realize that we are larger than that content; we are the *context* within which the content unfolds.

That last sentence bears repeating: Our various identities or states are the *content* of our experience, and we are starting to realize that we are the *context* within which that content is unfolding. That context is our core self, our soul, the being that lies beneath all of our various identities and through which they flow. Who we are now, the experiences we have collected over our lifetimes, and the seeds of what is to come are being joined together in a kaleidoscope of self-images and potentialities. The resulting totality will go well beyond the parts.

Oscillating Between Our Old and Emerging Selves

We do not shift over to new ways of being all at once. Our new selves have not yet fully emerged, so they have not yet formulated a vision of what our new lives will look like. However, a space has been created from which those new selves will emerge. As they come forward, and as we get to know ourselves better in the freshness of their emergence, new choices and new lives will follow.

To help deepen the realization of our increasingly inclusive identity centers, we can learn to distinguish between our "old selves" and our "emerging selves." What this means is that we notice and name those aspects of who we are that are subsiding, declining, and losing energy, and those that are getting larger, brighter, and more apparent.

Here are a few examples: A colleague explains that she feels less dependent on her partner when it comes to making decisions about their finances now; at the same time, she is noticing that her emerging self is more socially aware and looking for opportunities to respond to the needs of marginalized groups. My tax preparer reports that he feels more relaxed in relationship to accomplishing tasks than he used to be and is noticing that his decades-old habit of living according to the dictates of his to-do list is retiring.

The emergence of our new selves will take time. But the question has shifted from "*What is to become of me?*" (the query that arose during the dire experiences in Stages 1–6), to the more hopeful wondering, "*Who am I becoming?*" We will not become another static identity; our becoming will be more like a river, as John O'Donohue suggests in this short prayer: "I would love to live like a river flows, carried by the surprise of its own unfolding."

To live our lives as they are presently unfolding, we must continue to leave our old lives and prior levels of consciousness behind. Noticing our changes helps us trust in the unfolding process and supports our new growth. It also relaxes our natural impatience regarding how slowly organic processes proceed. A good friend of mine likens the pace of organic processes to watching rocks grow. Sometimes it can feel just like that. But indestructible foundations are made of that very stone.

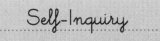

Self-Inquiry

Are you noticing yourself oscillating between old and emerging selves? Explore this question by answering the following sentence several times:

I am more _____ (for example, willing to make mistakes)
and less _____ (for example, needing to be right).

Wavering between the old and the new, we can feel as wobbly as a newborn foal. We long for a more solid sense of our new birth and fear a return to the constrictive ways of our old life and form. Until we trust what's emerging, our insecurities can overtake our curiosity, especially during lulls when our changes feel less apparent.

Our task is not to try to catapult ourselves into the new reality but to mindfully attend to the shifts and changes. The feel of this is captured in actor Errol Flynn's response when asked how to hold a sword correctly: He said, "In the same way you would hold a bird, not too tight and not too loose. If you hold it too tightly the bird dies, but if you hold too loosely it will fly away and you're left with nothing."

In Stage 9, we will learn how to cultivate our new growth in ways that are neither too tight nor too loose. Until then, and until our emerging selves are fully formed, our job is to allow ourselves to live in both worlds – in our old selves and our emerging selves simultaneously. We already had plenty of experience living in two worlds during Stage 5 when our spirit doors opened. Our emerging selves are just that: emerging. They have come out of their chrysalis but don't know how to fly yet.

The Assemblage Point

Socrates taught that soul is closer to movement than to fixity. This is why we experience the absence of soul as feeling stuck. When our self-images were constituted of boundaries – physical, emotional, and conceptual limits on who we thought we were and what we thought we could or should do – our range of experience, perception, and possible actions was limited. However, as our beings begin to open into a more inclusive and vast area of actuality and possibility that encompasses the territory we have circumnavigated – all the parts of ourselves that were previously disowned or suppressed – we experience ourselves as more flexible and spontaneous. In other words, *we become less defined and less definable.* This does not mean we feel ambiguous and vague, as was true of our experience in Stage 4, but rather that our identity centers are becoming more fluid and able to respond flexibly, as needed in each moment.

To help understand this shift, I borrow a term from Carlos Castaneda's teachings. Castaneda writes about what he calls an "assemblage point." This is the point where a person's awareness converges. When our assemblage point is fixed, we perceive our world and ourselves narrowly: varying dimensions of reality and wide-angle perceptions are excluded.

Castaneda taught his students to consciously move their assemblage points and thus widen their perceptions. When working with clients, I modify Castaneda's approach and employ this concept in two different ways. The first has to do with cultivating a "fluid perspective."

Fluid Perspective

To consciously loosen places when we feel emotionally fixated, I use a practice I call "emotional switching." In workshops I ask a volunteer couple to choose a sore topic that produces strong feelings between them. Let's say the couple is a man and a woman, and the topic is his habit of prioritizing work over their relationship. In this example, the man might start out feeling unappreciated, and the woman might start out angry. I then ask the couple to discuss the same issue but to switch from their starting positions to focus instead on the sadness they feel in relationship to the topic and not to allow any other feelings to come forward. Then I might ask them to feel happy and continue talking about the issue. Because happiness is the opposite feeling from their starting points, it is more challenging. The task is to connect with their internal state of joy and then bring in the issue, not the other way around. Then I might ask them to switch to anger. For some couples anger is very uncomfortable – especially if both are expressing it at the same time – while for others it is familiar territory. Then I might suggest that they continue the argument or discussion from a place of deep disappointment.

At some point in the process, the couple notices that the emotional charge on the issue softens or disappears altogether. In that moment, as everything drops away from the drama they were in, they realize that the fight was more about feeling forced to occupy one side of the issue or of themselves, or to fixate in one feeling state, rather than the real need to have something between them be a certain way. In that moment, it feels like a spell has been broken. Although the issue may still exist, they are no longer stuck in any one position and can discuss the issue from a more emotionally open and inclusive place (inclusive of all parts of themselves as well as inclusive of all parts of each other).

From this point on, the conversation usually includes more insight, compassion, and depth. The man might talk about the internal, emotional pressure he feels to perform and provide, and how difficult it is for him to step away from that area of his conditioning. He might share his feelings of inadequacy over not having developed himself as a more complete human being, something he fears might be noticed if he spent more time relating to his wife. She, in turn, might talk about her struggle to manage her anxiety when she feels lonely without him there to distract her. She might also talk about her realization that her fear about his lack of interest in her is really a reflection of her internal struggle to feel interested and invested in life now that their children have left the house.

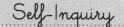

Self-Inquiry

If you have recently had an argument or disagreement with a friend or partner, try speaking about the emotional content of that argument, switching from feelings of sadness, to anger, to remorse, to disappointment, to happiness. If talking to the "other" feels too risky, use a journal to write out each emotional vantage point instead.

By switching our emotional positions, we become less fixed and more capable of being larger than who we can be when we are contracted or emotionally triggered. This moveable point of view that invites us into an open emotional field makes us more fluid and more resourceful when responding to situations that confront us. We become less of a noun (an identity) and more of a verb (an unfolding self), allowing something to come through us and express itself that is greater than our fixed ideas about how things should be. Over time, we develop the capacity to consciously shift our focus, and with it our sense of identity, as we will see in the next section.

Ad Hoc Assemblage

The second way I modify Castaneda's concept of the assemblage point is to investigate a phenomenon first noticeable for many in this stage of midlife: that we increasingly experience ourselves as "assembling" a self for an activity or a point of contact and then disassembling into a more fluid state after the purpose for assembling is over. It's a bit like a wave arising out of the ocean and then blending back into its watery home base.

For example, during Stage 7, I would find myself assembling to meet with a client; it would feel as though I was born freshly into my role in relationship to the client and into my responses in the interaction. After the session, I would dissolve into a state of openness. Then I'd get a phone call from my father and spontaneously gather my daughter-self together. After the call I would return to just *being*, in a state of readiness – but not waiting – to constellate again into the appropriate self at the next point of contact.

Although on the surface it might appear that I am moving in and out of identifications, the actual experience lacks the rigidity or investment that are characteristic of a fixed self-concept. Instead, the experience is spontaneous, fluid, and renewing. There is less agenda or attachment to the identity itself or to the outcome of the interaction than is the case when one inhabits a fixed identity, and little effort is used or needed. Assembling and disassembling is more like putting on a coat to go out in the snow and taking it off when returning indoors to sit in front of the woodstove.

A client, who had been an attorney during his 30s and 40s, decided to leave his law practice after entering midlife. At some point in the early stages, he decided to pursue a career as a social worker. Several years into his new profession, he was asked to lead a task force to study and subsequently challenge current state laws that his group did not feel sufficiently protected the rights of his target population, senior citizens. Before each task force meeting he would, in his words, consciously "dial up his lawyer self" in order to access a database and way of thinking that were no longer current for him but were still accessible.

Self-Inquiry:

Are you noticing yourself assembling and disassembling? When and with whom, or in response to what situations?

As we've seen, when we hold on to self-images – and the ideas of right and wrong and should and shouldn't that are attached to those self-images – we become stuck. We also polarize: I am this, and I am not that. I can do this, but I cannot do that. I can say this, not that. When we have circumnavigated ourselves, we are less attached to any one self-concept, so it is possible to behave in any way and be anyone that is fully authentic and genuine. We are freer to be responsive to what each moment requires.

The result is that we don't have to hold on so tightly to who we think we are; we don't have to defend or prop up an identity or fixed sense of self. We also don't have to worry about losing ourselves to who we think we are not. We don't have to be afraid of the ways of being that we denied before they forcibly entered our conscious lives during the uprising stage of our midlife journeys. *Now, we notice that every time we feel "assembled" into a particular way of being, it is an ad hoc state: we become some way for a given moment and for a given purpose.*

Those struggling with letting go might notice more acutely the times when their identity is disassembled than the points when their identity assembles, and the experience of having a more fluid identity center might feel alarming or uncomfortable at first. We can project onto the experience of being disassembled that it is forgetfulness or even dementia as, for example, we leave behind our "therapist" selves once a client leaves the office and perhaps do not remember the specific details of the interaction when we are no longer assembled in the form of a therapist. What is really happening is that we have shifted away from a familiar state to one that is larger, less defined, and less recognizable. We are now able to do this because we are newly grounded in an indivisible wholeness that results from having circumnavigated ourselves and brought our disowned underworld selves into the fold. As we become more used to and accepting of this mutable quality, we begin to function more efficiently and with less fear. We see what is needed more clearly and have a wider range of responses available to us. We begin to trust the flow of our lives and even look for more varied contexts that bring out other parts of ourselves than the identities and roles we are used to inhabiting.

In fact, the capacity to completely shatter our held notions and worldviews at any moment opens us up to the infinite perspectives and options available in any given situation. Ultimately, it will free us in a very deep way. It will mean that we can do anything we truly feel called toward because the value of our existence depends less on trying to have an experience that makes us feel good or important and more on what arises spontaneously within us. As we become less fixated on our survival, we experience the blessing of new possibility: the possibility of living larger lives than we have previously inhabited or imagined.

I am completely different.
Though I am wearing the same tie as yesterday,
am as poor as yesterday,
as good for nothing as yesterday,
today
I am completely different....
I patiently close my eyes...
and glimpse then, inside me,
one beautiful white butterfly
fluttering towards tomorrow.
—Kuroda Saburo

Now we flutter forward to Stage 8 where the lamp of our newly unified fields is ignited by our soul's flame.

STAGE 8

Lighting the Lamp

 ❧〜〜❧

During the first six stages of midlife, our ego was exposed to its own lack of integration and forced to dissolve in its own ineffectiveness; meanwhile, our soul, which has been present all along below the surface and is the motivating force for our midlife evolution, began to emerge. We saw flickers of our soul's wakening presence very early in our journey in the form of compulsions, again a bit later in the form of sparks of life, and stronger still in the attraction and aversion experiences when our spirit doors opened. Our first felt-sense of the soul's emergence, in Stage 7, was our experience of a more inclusive and fluid identity within our newly unified field. This unified field of self now, in Stage 8, becomes the womb for our ego's higher form, the soul, to develop into its fullness.

The Lay of Soul Land

To get our bearings in the land that the soul will gradually illuminate as it develops a brighter and brighter flame, let's look at an overview of the process of ego and soul evolution using a simple, sequential illustration of the larger and larger realms into which our consciousness will expand:

Reading from the bottom of the schema to the top, we see that the unintegrated ego develops into an integrated ego. The integrated ego, in turn, develops into the first stage of soul recognition where we make contact with what we can call the *personal soul.* This is the stage we are currently exploring and will continue to explore in Stage 9. (Further along, in Stage 12, we will delve into the "group soul" that lies above the personal soul.) As our soul develops from its more primitive forms into its more evolved forms, all aspects of our earlier uncoordinated or fragmented ego are transformed and absorbed.

For most of us, crises (large and small) continue to be the main catalysts of our progress from unintegrated to integrated ego and then to an increasingly soul-centered life. Although at this point in our midlife process the demands of our daily lives can, in large part, be met by an integrated ego, our crises cannot.

Crises tug on the spiritual thread of our newly expansive lives. Each crisis offers an opportunity to take another step in our ego-soul progression – not only in our progression from unintegrated to integrated ego but from there to a deepening felt-sense of the personal soul, which we will discuss in this chapter. When the full resources of our soul are called on to respond to a crisis, the soul turns up its flame, lighting the way for our ego to shift toward the next, higher state of evolution. As we have been discovering in earlier stages, midlife is a repeating cycle of crisis or stress that stimulates our evolution into more and more soul-centered beings. Each crisis reveals the hidden blessings that mark our individual journeys. In this stage, we will look at how the challenging experiences that continue to arrive at our door strengthen our soul's flame.

The Personal Soul: A Boundless Singularity

Thus far we have been referring to the soul loosely as a metaphor for our innermost selves, the core or harmonizing force of our unified fields, or who we are below all the layers of identity and the roles we play. In this stage, as I mentioned, we are focused on the *personal soul*, which is the form of the soul that we contact first in our midlife journeys. The personal soul is who we are at our most authentic and elemental level – the truest version of ourselves as unique beings.

> *Four thousand volumes of metaphysics will not*
> *teach us what the soul is.*
> —Voltaire

The feeling we get when we touch into our personal soul is an intuited sense of our unbroken self, whole and at the same time very personal and unique. It is our highest evolutionary prospect at the individual level. Because the personal soul is individual to each of us, it's difficult to give a simple definition of it, but there are many ways to glimpse its qualities.

Poetry is one medium that can express the personal soul's qualities in a way that touches us but doesn't lock us into a single definition. David Whyte is particularly adept at this. His poetry captures the personal soul's characteristics in a light, deft manner, as we can see illustrated in the following phrases harvested from his poems:

* "the one line already written inside you"
* "that small, bright and indescribable wedge of freedom in your own heart"
* "The one life you can call your own"
* "the largest conversation we are individually capable of having with the world"

❋ "The shape [that] waits in the seed of you to grow and spread its branches against a future sky"

❋ "Your own truth at the center of the image you were born with"

❋ "A simpler, more elemental identity, truer to the template of our own natures"

Some of us might at first experience the soul as the form of consciousness that some spiritual traditions refer to as the "witness," the presence that lies beneath our reactions and thinking and can observe those phenomena. This is a useful perspective; the concept of a witness reminds us that we are more than the compilation of reactions and roles that we believe ourselves to be when we're running on automatic pilot or when we are swept into an emotionally charged exchange. Over time, the idea of the witness gives way to a direct experience of the soul's depth, genuineness, and living and evolving presence.

Self-Inquiry

What do you intuitively know about your personal soul?

"Deep," "profound," and "meaningful" are words that often come up in attempts to describe soul: deep feelings, profound insights, meaningful contact. Similarly, "old" might be another word paired with soul. We feel soul in the presence of a very old tree. We feel soul in a handmade piece of furniture that has been passed from generation to generation and very likely has a memory of its own. Soul can be experienced reading an old, milestone document like the Declaration of Independence. We feel the presence of soul while walking through a very old graveyard, like the Highgate Cemetery in London.

We might feel a quality of soulfulness listening to jazz or recognize a soulful depth in the eyes of a wild animal. Soulfulness can be experienced in the presence of something or someone we experience as complex, in a photo of a beloved grandparent, and in the presence of the sacred.

Self-Inquiry

Where do you feel your own soulfulness – for example, in the presence of a person, a place, a thing?

Soul is not static. It develops and deepens over time. An acorn has within it the possibility of becoming an oak tree, but it takes much for the acorn to realize this full potential. In the same way, the soul is as much about potential – who we can possibly become – as it is about who we actually are.

The more we inquire into what the soul is, the more mysterious it becomes. The soul can't really be defined because it is the evolving quality – the animating principle – within each of us, so it is infinite and ever-changing in its variation, expression, and expansion.

In this stage of our midlife journeys, we are coming into contact with our alive, multi-layered, multi-dimensional soul. This is our first conscious taste of the ultimate blessing that midlife offers. Like the stages of midlife we have been exploring thus far, the soul's phases of development will not unfold in a straight line.

As mentioned, we will explore group soul in Stage 12. For now, the important bit of that future discussion to contemplate is that our souls are both deeply individual and personal on the one hand and expansive and connected to something much larger than ourselves on the other hand. To distill this combination, I use the phrase "boundless singularity," which came to me in a dream. This phrase captures the soul's infinite nature as well as its personal, one-of-a-kind uniqueness; it speaks to the soul's connection to the vast web of life that is larger than our individual selves and at the same time reflects the soul's unique mission in our individual lifetimes, a mission that can be manifested by no one else, as this excerpt from dancer and choreographer Martha Graham's famous quote states:

> *...because there is only one of you in all time, this expression is unique.*
> *And if you block it, it will never exist through any other medium....*

Self-Inquiry

Recall an experience in your life that felt soulful. Allow yourself to remember what the experience felt like in your body and in your heart. Invite yourself to reopen to that moment – in its full authenticity and depth. If you feel drawn to, write about it in a way that deepens that experience in this present moment.

The Lamp and the Spark

In Hindu traditions, the activation of the felt sense of the soul is called "the lighting of the lamp," which is the title I have given to Stage 8 of the midlife passage. The lighting of the lamp signifies the movement from an inner darkness into the light of greater consciousness. In the metaphor of metamorphosis, it is the moment that the butterfly pierces the chrysalis, and the light enters its darkened womb.

The light and the lamp go together, but the lamp precedes the light. This means that we had to first create a vessel that could be lit. This is what happened when the imaginal buds of our soul aggregated sufficiently to bring us into a unified field that could be "ignited," metaphorically speaking. As the light of the soul infuses the lamp of our transforming beings, we further shift our center of gravity and identity toward the soul.

Bear in mind that evolution is a very gradual process. At this point in the journey, we are still more or less ego centered, slipping in and out of contact with the soul's light; that is, we continue to be in a state of transition between ego-centered and soul-centered states of awareness. But many of us become increasingly aware, by Stage 8, that there is a new, more meaningful world coming into view, and we find ourselves intentionally searching for ways to grow and deepen our experience of this new soul-centered world.

In the presence of more light, the unwilling parts of the ego that remain will resurface with a vengeance, pulling us back into unresolved and darkened corners of our childhoods. Most of us experience this upwelling of yet more difficult material from the past as a surprise and disheartening challenge given how much grappling we have already done with past traumas as well as the hopeful sense we have in this stage that we are emerging into the light. However, if we realize that this upwelling of old patterns heralds the blessing of an unparalleled leap in our consciousness, we are better prepared to greet this challenge as the opportunity it is. As the soul pours into these darkened areas of our psyche and illumines these patterns, we have to make a conscious commitment to come out of hiding, grow up, step into our largeness, and become spiritually mature adults.

First we will discuss the lighting of the lamp and what that means in terms of our midlife journeys. Later in this chapter, we will look at the steps we need to take to address our old patterns of fear and smallness when the light of the soul illumines them, offering us the opportunity for a new, more wholehearted level of interaction with life.

Over time, we become soul vessels filled with light, life, and, later on, love. But before we travel much further – and in the spirit of understanding the richness of the metaphor of the lamp of consciousness – we turn our attention to the nature of the spark that will dynamize and enliven our evolving substance.

The Spark

The spark that lights our soul's flame is a fragment of "source" energy that is banked deep within our soul. "Source" here refers to spirit, the life force, the divine, the sacred, the mystery, or god. Just as a spark is a small fiery particle thrown off from a fire, the spark that sets alight our awakening consciousness is a fragment thrown off from the fire of the divine, which enlivens the sacred in the realm of the physical. In other words, *the spark is a symbol for the animating and vitalizing fragment of divine illumination and inspiration that burns at the core of each of our personal souls.* This spark ignites our soul flame, which, in turn, sets alight the lamp of our newly unified consciousness. The soul's light will ultimately grow so bright that it illumines the entire distance between our human center and our divine essence.

We fan our divine fire and emit light every time we shift our center of gravity toward the soul. In practical terms, this happens every time we bring a larger scale of meaning to our everyday existence, every time we experience the inner friction of taking a moral stand within a quaking body, every time we inquire deeply into who we really are. We burn brighter when we disturb fixed patterns of thought and interrupt habitual, learned behaviors and open instead to inner guidance, wisdom, and intuition. We glow when we are vulnerable and undefended. And we throw off sparks when we inspire those around us with our inner strength, authenticity, kindness, and compassion.

Self-Inquiry

* What sparks the deeper, more meaningful, and profound currents of your being?

* What brings you alive?

For a while, the light we are bringing forth from within us will be flickering at best; it will appear to ignite and go out, ignite and go out. Over time, this source fire will free us from the gravitational pull of former conditioning and dependency. When that happens, "a mighty flame follows," as Dante Alighieri writes.

But even now, before the mighty flame, we begin to glimpse the truth of the well-known biblical phrase, "You are the light of the world." With each step, we long to walk more of the time in that soulful light. To accomplish that, we have, as mentioned earlier, a critical piece of psychological work to do now. This work is rigorous but necessary, and, after we do it, our midlife journey becomes more about the evolution of the soul than the evolution of the ego (although, as we know by now, the process does not proceed in the neat, orderly, and linear fashion presented here).

Time to Grow Up

As we noted at the beginning of this chapter, just as we begin to get a palpable sense of the presence of our soul, we will likely get thrown backward into the tangled patterns of our family of origin. When the soul's flame touches these patterns at this stage, it sets them alight; the resulting fire seeks to burn through the conditioning that is blocking us from becoming the flame itself.

Although the return of old psychological patterns can feel very disconcerting at this stage, it is not purely regression; it is a necessary fluctuation that can be a source of guidance. Maurice Nicoll writes: "As one's level of being increases, receptivity to higher meaning increases. As one's being decreases, the old meanings return." Moving forward, we will become more aware of this expansion and contraction of consciousness that Nicoll describes. This pulsation becomes exaggerated in Stage 8 when the lighting of the lamp illumines our "childishness," which has been hiding in the shadows.

At this stage we feel, more keenly than ever, the tightening bindings of our old emotional defenses, which make it difficult for us to show up or grow up to this day. In fact, we are not becoming more childish but are more clearly seeing things as they are and always have been. In the light of the soul, we see our constant fear of being controlled, overpowered, rejected, or ignored. We realize the extent to which we are afraid of making a mistake, getting punished, being criticized, being ridiculed, being made wrong, or being humiliated.

By this stage of our midlife journeys, we are getting pretty tired of living in child-based fears of getting into trouble, making someone mad at us, or being hurt by others — even as we continue to regularly feel overtaken by these and other seemingly regressive feeling states. This is our opportunity to work with these states so that they have less influence on our behavior and sense of self going forward.

Becoming Spiritually Mature Adults

In the Gospel of Luke, Jesus tells his followers that they cannot be disciples without turning their backs on their families; otherwise, they would not be free to accept the new consciousness that Jesus was offering. Jesus' statement might seem surprising. Why would he require his followers to choose between their families and their spiritual path? As I reflect on my own and others' midlife processes, I understand this teaching of Jesus as saying that we must at some point stop feeling and acting like children, caught in patterns of fear and smallness that originate in our family upbringing. We must appropriate the inner permission to finally grow up and become spiritually mature adults.

To do this we must continue the process we began earlier in our journey of uncovering the intricate weave of values, beliefs, and emotional imprinting that we received from parents or primary caretakers. This weave has been unconsciously incorporated into our psyches along with our cultural and social conditioning. Bringing this imprinting into conscious awareness includes recognizing and interrupting our reliance on religious doctrines, political figures, spouses, employers, and other authorities who tell us that they know what is best for us. In midlife our job is to attune our ears to the guidance of our own souls.

We noted earlier that ongoing compliance with some elements of the social contract – such as paying for services, keeping our agreements, and restraining ourselves from harming others – is important because it sustains the civil fabric of community. However, we shift now from across-the-board compliance with the social contract to conscious choices. We move away from obligations imposed by social and other external structures that are not aligned with our deeper natures.

When we do this, we come face to face with our fears of being cut off from the safety of the herd. For example, several of my clients who have become grandparents know that the socially acceptable role of grandparents is to help care for their grandchildren. When my clients don't want to participate as caretakers in this way, they feel criticized by their children, family, and friends and pressured to conform to an image of what it means to be a grandparent even if they do not feel personally called to engage in that way. "I raised my children," one client told me; "I don't want to raise my grandchildren." She goes on to say, "I love them and want to see them, but I don't want them to be the focus of my life going forward. There are other, truer directions calling to me."

Other clients are at the age and have the economic means to choose retirement. They have friends who are "living the good life," migrating to Florida or Mexico, playing golf, frequenting casinos, and wondering why my clients are not choosing to similarly "relax" and "be free." But not everyone is inspired by or drawn to these choices. My clients don't want to play. They have more they want to contribute; they have a desire to help, to serve, to participate in ways that were difficult to do when they were working or raising their own families full time. However, they fear losing their friends as their interests take them in divergent directions.

"It's hard to create new, lasting friendships at this age," one client said when sharing his fears about pulling away from his group. "But I'd rather die than spend what time I have left eating, drinking, and playing the slots." This is not to say that eating, drinking, and playing the slots is a wrong or lesser choice; for some, perhaps those who did not play when they were younger, those choices are the direction of greater authenticity. The issue I am addressing here is not the validity of a particular choice but rather what happens in us and to us when we move in a direction that differs from that taken by the rest of our particular herd.

The price of consciousness is high. As psychologist Carl Jung has written, during the second half of our adult lives, our task is to be neither well-adjusted nor normal; our task is to be ourselves. Aligning ourselves ever more completely with the deeper, inner demand for authenticity and originality is our main assignment whether that demand takes us to the golf course, an art studio, an ashram, a goat farm, or to serving those less fortunate in a soup kitchen. This is the path that our souls are beginning to illuminate for us as they kindle the lamp of our awakened consciousness.

The journey is no longer about adapting and adjusting to the needs of others or society at large but rather about being our unique selves and taking stands in alignment with our inner guidance. We begin to care less about what others think and feel about us and more about what we think and feel is right for us. We become drawn to the subjective experience of each moment and each encounter, to an endless, active participation in and involvement with the unfolding of our lives and of life itself. And when we participate in this way, we feel less self-consciousness, fear, and shame than in the past.

Self-Inquiry

* What don't you have time for any more? (For example, false pride, gossip, lying, relationships that don't serve you.)

* In what ways are you currently taking a stand against conventional obligations?

* In what ways are you beginning to live a different life situated in different values than in the past or than those held by your social circle?

In a very real sense, when we begin to seize the right to feel what we feel, express what is true, do what is right for us, and live our lives free from obligations that we no longer endorse, we are expressing a fidelity to a spiritual imperative. It is not easy for most of us to make choices that cause us to risk losing friends or the approval of family, but, in so doing, we are following the path illuminated by the soul's flame and stepping toward our true homeland: the life that is authentic and genuine for us.

How Far Did the Fruit Fall?

Next, we explore a framework that is designed to help us engage with, rather than resist, the powerful, internal pull that is urging us to move away from the dependencies of our youth and to focus instead on the inner light of our soul. This exploration is not meant to push us beyond where we are but rather to help us see more clearly where we are.

If we have any doubt whatsoever as to the lifelong effects of our family of origin, the four questions below will generally expose the degree to which we continue to be under the sway of our childhood conditioning. We answer the questions about parents (or other primary caretakers in childhood) for the period of time when we lived with them, which, for most of us, was from birth to approximately age 18. It's important that we resist answering the questions the way our parents (or whoever parented us) might wish we would answer; rather, we should respond according to the way we observed *they actually lived their lives from our childhood perspective.*

To benefit from this exploration, we need to take our time, and travel back in time, feeling the experience of being with each parent or primary caretaker when we were children, allowing ourselves to remember what it was really like. What did we see, hear, and sense? The more time we spend with each question, the more profound the realizations that will arise.

We answer the questions posed about ourselves in present time but with the awareness that most of our answers might have been similar for approximately the past two decades.

It is best to not answer these questions in our mind alone. Writing down the answers and reviewing them more than once will produce more profound and transformational results.

1. **What was the dominating preoccupation/worry/concern/anxiety in life…**

    ※ for your mother (or first primary caretaker)?

    (Example: Safety – How to be safe physically, emotionally, and financially)

    ※ for your father (or second primary caretaker)?

    (Example: Self-Esteem – How to get others to like and respect him and how to avoid criticism)

    ※ for you, now, in the present?

    (Example: Emotional and Financial Security – How to support myself and my family financially and do things the right way so I don't get into trouble)

    Reviewing your answers to question #1, what is the connection between your answers and those of your parents or primary caretakers?

2. **What were the dominating worldview and coping strategies…**

    ※ for your mother (or first primary caretaker)?

    (Example: The world is unsafe, unfair, untrustworthy, so she stayed separate, retreated from others, was very frugal, and didn't take risks.)

    ※ for your father (or second primary caretaker)?

    (Example: He saw himself as underprivileged and an underdog, so he worked hard as a small business owner to make what money he could to get the respect he wanted.)

    ※ for you, now, in the present?

    (Example: No one is going to help me/I have to do it myself, so I worked hard and became self-sufficient and independent.)

    Reviewing your answers to question #2, what is the connection between your answers and those of your parents or primary caretakers?

3. **What was the dominating source of satisfaction…**
    * for your mother (or first primary caretaker)?
        (Example: Her morning walks and the amount of money she had in savings)
    * for your father (or second primary caretaker)?
        (Example: Giving employment to others so they could provide for their families, and providing financially for his own family)
    * for you, now, in the present?
        (Example: Productivity, respect from others for my achievements, and providing financial security for myself and my family)

    Reviewing your answers to question #3, what is the connection between your answers and those of your parents or primary caretakers?

4. **How are you carrying the unlived lives of one or both of your parents?**
    (Example: I have lived out my mother's preoccupation with money as a means to be safe in the world and my father's need to feel good about himself via his accomplishments in his profession.)

As the saying goes, the fruit doesn't fall far from the tree. Despite best efforts, we end up:

> ▸ Identifying with our parents' patterns (e.g., I've become my mother or father)
>
> ▸ Living in reaction to our parents' patterns (e.g., rejecting making money because our fathers made that too important)
>
> ▸ Spending our lives trying to fix our parents' patterns in some way (e.g., if our parents were alcoholics, becoming a therapist or nurse to fix or heal this pattern)

While answering this series of questions might, at first, feel like a crushing reality check for some of us, the awareness and insight we find through this process will help us continue to deepen our awareness of our inherited patterns. The more we shed light on these patterns, the more clearly and steadily we can see the path illuminated by our souls, enabling us to step further and further away from the unconscious agendas that have bound us to the dynamics of our families of origin and ruled our lives.

The Need to Humanize Our Parents

After the disheartening discovery that we have unconsciously based who we are on the model of our parents, the good news is that we can now finally allow them to become human-sized, historical figures – and, in so doing, liberate ourselves from the influence of their patterns.

Below are several series of questions designed to put us in contact with sparks of gratitude that will burn through the larger-than-life quality we unconsciously ascribe to our parents or childhood primary caretakers.

1a. **Name 3 positive attributes of your mother** (or first primary caretaker):
  * _____ *(She loved animals.)*
  * _____ *(She was innocent and kind.)*
  * _____ *(She was self-sacrificing.)*

1b. **Name 3 things you are grateful to your mother** (or 1st caretaker) **for:**
  * _____ *(She gave birth to me.)*
  * _____ *(She sacrificed her life for mine.)*
  * _____ *(She believed in me.)*

2a. **List 3 positive attributes of your father** (or second primary caretaker):
  * _____ *(He loved to play.)*
  * _____ *(He was congenial.)*
  * _____ *(He knew how things worked.)*

2b. **Name 3 things you are grateful to your father** (or 2nd caretaker) **for:**
  * _____ *(He worked hard to provide for his family.)*
  * _____ *(He spent what time he could with me.)*
  * _____ *(He taught me how to fish, ride a bike, drive.)*

3a. **List 5 positive attributes you inherited from your parents** (or caretakers):
  * _____ *(Kindness from Mom)*
  * _____ *(Childlikeness from Mom)*

❋ _____ *(Hardworking from both Mom and Dad)*

❋ _____ *(Love of animals from Mom)*

❋ _____ *(Easygoing nature from Dad)*

These questions prepare us to contemplate the ways that we might more deeply value all that we received or inherited from our parents or primary caretakers. Doing so can join our basic humanity with theirs, healing any feelings of separation from them. As we fully feel the appreciation that arises, we come to know that the more deeply we humanize these people in our life, and feel gratitude for the role they played in our lives, the more *we restore ourselves to ourselves.* We can align with the light of our own souls when it is no longer overshadowed by larger-than-life images of parent figures and their expectations and rules. As we do this, we more fully understand the requirement of Jesus mentioned earlier in this chapter that his disciples leave their families behind. What he means is that *we leave the inflated and idealized projections onto our families, allow them to become human figures, and walk into a larger field of consciousness ourselves.*

⁌⤳⤳⁊

After Stage 8, we still have work to do to recognize patterns from our youth that stop the unfolding of our souls' aims and of the blessing of a fresh, genuine experience of our soul-directed selves. But the process is under way. Our old ego self is finishing up of its own accord, and something else is coming alive in us. Luckily, an evolving system can never return entirely to its past. New realizations and energy will continue to press us to take small steps and larger leaps to a higher order. We will be given more and more opportunities to deepen our commitment to and engagement with our souls. Through our loops back into the past and attending to our own conditioning, including the work of previous stages, we are becoming vulnerable to our own true natures now, to the fragility of the flesh and the durability of the spirit.

As John O'Donohue writes, "Once the soul awakens, the search begins and you can never go back. From then on, you are inflamed with a special longing that will never again let you linger in the lowlands of complacency and partial fulfillment. The eternal makes you urgent. You are loath to let compromise or the threat of danger hold you back from striving toward the summit of fulfillment."

One way in which this work unfolds next is through learning how to cultivate the new energetic pulses, currents, vibrations, and threads of possibility that are presenting themselves within our integrated fields in response to our soul's emerging light and presence. Cultivating those new signs of soul force is the topic of the next stage.

STAGE 9

Cultivating
Soul-fullness

❧⁓⁓❧

O ur attention in Stage 9 shifts from the illumination of our consciousness –
the lighting of the lamp that took place in Stage 8 – to the task of *cultivating soul-fullness*. This is a subtle, delicate process because the glimmer of soul-light is often barely perceptible at first, and its movements cannot be understood with the rational mind. And as if that isn't difficult enough, the earliest experience of the personal soul – when we are first learning to attune to it – is so varied and in most cases nonverbal that putting it into words can sometimes feel impossible.

So, with the understanding that we are trying to perceive the imperceptible and describe the indescribable, here are some of the ways our emerging soul might be experienced: as internal energy currents, vibrations, waves, subtle internal movements, body temperature fluctuations, inner quickenings, flashes of imagery or feeling, impulses, sound, color, and light. On perhaps a more familiar side of the spectrum of possibility, our personal soul might reveal its awakening presence in the form of inner knowings, intuitions, sensations, emotions, and longings. For simplicity, in the rest of this chapter, we refer to the soul's subtle movements as energetic impulses.

Sometimes these impulses will arise seemingly out of nowhere and at other times we will be deliberately listening, watching, and waiting for them as we wonder how to confront a life challenge or decision. Each of us will experience these impulses differently at different times, but often we will have a felt experience, however subtle and vague, generally in the core of our bodies, most commonly in the stomach and heart areas.

Self-Inquiry

Before continuing to read, take a moment to sense, to tune into, your stomach. Place a hand there and breathe into your stomach and breathe out with a relaxing sigh; do this a couple of times.

Can you sense anything there? A vibration or some heat; a faint sensation of anticipation or excitement? What do you sense?

Can you soften in the area of your stomach a little bit? A little more? Another relaxing sigh perhaps?

There is no need to rush. You don't need to get to the end of the chapter or even this page today. Immerse yourself in the sensations in this very moment. Extend the moment; allow it to flow effortlessly into the next moment; no need to hold on. What are you sensing now? The soul's stirring is often experienced as subtle sensations in the stomach.

Repeat the steps above, focusing on the area of your heart.

Another relaxing sigh. As you continue to read, notice the difference in how your stomach and heart areas feel.

In James Hillman's words: "Even in the sciences, you only begin to see the phenomenon in the sky or under the microscope if someone first describes what you are looking for; we need *instruction in the art of seeing.* Then the invisible becomes suddenly visible, right in your squinting eye." In the early stages of attuning to the subtleties of our soul's movements, we are simply learning to detect them. For this, we need to cultivate sensory and intuitive receptivity: watching for fine inner cues, listening for the arising of faint inner vibrations, sensing waves of energy or delicate inner shifts. Most signs will be on the borderlands of our perception at first and come in forms that we don't have much experience recognizing.

What is happening at this stage of our journey is that the imaginal buds of the soul have coalesced sufficiently to become active. At the same time as this is happening, our sense of our identities, the place where we locate the "I" when we talk about ourselves, is shifting from a fixed position to a fluid one as we discussed in Stage 7. The combination of these two phenomena moves us toward being more soul-centered. As this move happens, we fine-tune our perceptual capabilities to detect and follow the life pulse of our souls.

What we are undertaking here is like learning to watch birds. At first, as novices, we might not even see the bird that the experienced birders stop short on the trail to observe. Soon, with practice, we too become alert to the subtle movements in the trees or brush that signal that a bird is present. With time, our eyes become able to see the small form that is generating the movement, and, with more practice, we start to pick out attributes of that form: markings and colors, the length of the tail, the relative size. Eventually, we learn to recognize the characteristic plumpness and speckled chest of a sparrow or the crest of a waxwing or the long tail of a flycatcher. We begin to have a sense of what we are looking for and how to identify what we are seeing.

The amorphous process of trying to recognize what we don't yet know how to sense might feel daunting, but I can assure you from experience that the ability to perceive the delicate stirrings of our expanding soul will grow – in a non-linear way – with time, just as the novice birdwatcher, with repeated practice, begins to see what was not visible or recognizable before. Sometimes birdwatchers sit a long time in blinds in the cold predawn to catch a glimpse of a rare species. This is the kind of alert patience we need to cultivate in Stage 9.

Here is one example: a friend of mine was diagnosed with cancer during Stage 9 of her midlife passage. When her circle of friends did not see her take any action in response, we became concerned and asked her what she was doing.

She told us she was "tuning in" – sitting with the question of what felt right for her. As the days turned into weeks, we became quite upset with her. We were afraid for her life. She, however, was resolute that she was not going to take any action based in fear (fear is the ego's home base). She went on retreat, prayed, did research, continued to meet her daily obligations to work and family, and only proceeded when she felt a "certainty in her belly" letting her know that she had found a direction that resonated as true in her innermost being.

Like my friend, we will all experience times when we have just the barest threads of something that is being woven inside us, and we will have to wait, spinning yarn and tending our loom over time until a fabric of certainty emerges. We ask ourselves repeatedly: "Is this an authentic soul movement or just another trick of the ego?" "What is the guidance or message?" For deep, true answers, we have to wait and see. The movements of soul and consciousness proceed at a different pace than the quickness exhibited by the intellectual mind.

Next, we will look at two practices that will help us cultivate soul-fullness, along with a sizable pitfall that we must skillfully sidestep to ensure that we stay on the path to rebirth. At the end of the chapter, we will turn our attention to the psychological need that often arises at this stage of the journey: a surprising level of attunement that we need *from others* to raise our sacred self to its full measure of brightness and power.

The Practice of Silence

We can support ourselves in attuning to our soulful stirrings in many ways, for example by praying, chanting, participating in authentic movement, reading sacred poems, meditating, engaging in self-inquiry, journaling, fasting, reciting mantras, doing rhythmic and mindful manual labor, practicing yoga, and engaging in a host of other spiritual practices. Out of all the possibilities, one practice that is essential for radical transformation is *silence*. The practice of silence means consciously withdrawing our energy and attention from outer distractions in order to deepen our internal connection with our soul.

Virtually every sacred tradition maintains that silence is a prerequisite to spiritual evolution or transformation. I rarely take a firm stand on how the midlife journey should unfold because I deeply appreciate that we are all on unique, personal paths. However, I believe that making space in our life for silence is an essential element in maturing into soul-directed beings.

Self-Inquiry

Stop for a moment. Can you sense a subtle or strong longing for silence? Feel that longing for a moment. Breathe out with a relaxing sigh. Soften. Open.

Allow the longing to be there and notice with the longing comes just a little bit of what you long for. Give the longing and the silence that slips in alongside it more space inside of you.

Stop everything for 30 seconds and notice what you are sensing inside of you. You have all the time in the world. Take your time.

Reread this practice once or twice, without rushing through it, to see if your experience deepens.

Although those of us seeking an authentic, deep, meaningful, intimate life outside convent and monastery walls usually cannot take a vow of complete silence, we can purposefully vow to keep silence for an hour here, a day there, and periodically for longer stretches, perhaps in a natural or retreat setting. The more time we spend in silence, the more clear it will become that silence is indispensible to unveiling the mystery that is our soul. Silence brings us into our inner cloister where we can do the central work of Stage 9 – communing with our soul and cultivating its subtle energies.

Before we go further, let's distinguish between quiet in our outer worlds and silence in our internal worlds. They are related, but they are not the same.

Quiet is a condition we create on the outer plane, which opens up the possibility for silence on the inner plane. We must intentionally create quiet because the modern world is so deafeningly noisy. Creating quiet means turning off the television and the radio, removing newspapers and magazines, closing down access to all connective devices like computers and phones, and choosing solitude over social engagement. All natural sounds – like the ocean, the wind, and calls and movements of birds and animals – are a part of the stillness we want to create because these sounds foster connection with our inner plane and deepen the silence within.

If we do any reading during periods of silence, it is only of short passages of inspirational material by sages, poets, and others deeply anchored in the realm of the soul. The same holds true for listening to sacred music, which can help tune us to the soul's key. Self-inquiry, meditation, prayer, and contemplation can be among the activities we do in quiet to cultivate our "soul-sensing" capabilities.

When we quiet our outer environment, we shift our attention away from the distractions and seductions of worldly life and pursuits. The first thing most of us will notice when we do this is how noisy our inner environment is. We will become aware of the mind's busyness and seemingly unceasing need to be thinking, evaluating, planning, and strategizing.

To create an ongoing practice of silence requires some reordering of our lives. It means slowing down the pace and opening up space and time away from outer-directed activities. We must carefully examine our daily life and determine which elements enhance an inward-directed focus and which do not. For many of us, this will mean learning to say "no" to non-essential activities, meaningless entertainment, social engagements, and trivial conversations that disturb rather than nourish our experience of inner silence.

I cannot emphasize enough that a regular practice of silence is essential from this point forward if we are to create an ongoing relationship with our soul that will enable us to feel its mystery, be guided by its wisdom, and anchor a soul center amidst the worries, trials, and tribulations of ordinary life. In silence, we lance our residual ego-self-centeredness, impatience, and anxiety and fall into our soul's deep living light.

Self-Inquiry

You can create your own inner sacred space for communing with your soul by practicing silence every day. Here's how:

Schedule 10 minutes of silence every day in your calendar; commit to this time as non-negotiable (later, after a few weeks, increase it to 20 minutes, 30 minutes, and so on, building up to whatever amount of time feels right for you).

Make sure you will be undisturbed, that there is no access to connective devices, reading material other than spiritual texts such as are mentioned above, or outer engagement of any kind (including food). Sacred music can be an aid in this process, as described below.

Light a candle to symbolize the lighting of the lamp of your awakened consciousness.

Play some sacred music for a few minutes before shifting to complete silence. There are many kinds of sacred music from many different traditions; take some time to listen to pieces of music and select a few that feel soulful, slow you down, and bring you into your depths.

Breathe in the silence. Breathe out any thoughts that might pop up in your mind, any feelings that might come, and any sensations that feel uncomfortable.

At some point as you are breathing mindfully, you will notice that silence is not the absence of something but the presence of something. The something that is present is natural, spontaneous, and active. It is a radiating field of energy and life force. It feels peaceful, joyful, and alive. At first, this will not happen every time. With time, the more you experience this field that is always there, the more open and receptive you will become to your soul's voice and movements.

When the time in silence draws to an end, leaving this state takes some care. Being in silence is like being deeply under water. After being in the depths, returning and adjusting to life on the surface takes a few minutes. A helpful gesture when emerging is to place one hand on your heart and silently acknowledge what you love or feel grateful for in that moment. This will help ease you back into the world you cherish.

To complete the practice, blow out your candle before going about your day.

In this next section we will discuss a second practice, immersion, that helps us become more soul-full, as well as a significant pitfall – our unconscious reflex to mentally suffocate our soul's emerging presence.

The Practice of Immersion, and a Pitfall

Let's start by discussing the pitfall, which is a reflex that can snuff out nascent expressions of soul before they have a chance to manifest. This reflex is that, when we detect a flicker of soul movement deep within us, most of us have a tendency to move quickly toward turning it into something to manifest or obtain in the outer world. Instead of engaging with the energy of the impulse itself, circulating it inside of us and allowing it space and time to grow, we instead focus on an image of what we would like to get or achieve based on that impulse, and we circulate thoughts of action or completion: How would I do that? Can I do that? Where would I do that? Am I supposed to do that? Can I get that? How much would it cost? Would it be worth it? What would my friends say? What would I have to give up? How much fun would it be? What will the experience be like? When this happens, how will it affect the rest of my life? Can I make money at it?

These thoughts are thieves. When we ask these questions, we abandon the energy of the initial impulse and go into our minds and into the future, away from the here and now. We imagine better work situations, new lovers, other places to live, fresh ideas, more lucrative ways to earn a living, more or different sexual experiences, and new pursuits and ways of being. Some of us have been trained to call this "visioning." The visioning process can be useful during other life stages but is generally detrimental during most of our midlife transition and perhaps beyond.

Our reincarnation – or rebirth – depends, in part, on our ability to cultivate, in the present moment, the energy that the soul presents to us, and to allow it to develop in its own way and in its own time into the blessings that are uniquely ours to harvest from midlife. We need to guard against the tendency to go immediately into our minds, jumping imaginatively ahead in time to flesh out and quickly satisfy an impulse.

We had some experience noticing vague energetic impulses in our work with "sparks of life" in Stage 4. Now, the work of becoming soul-full requires not only that we notice an impulse, energy, or inner movement, but that we circulate, cultivate, relate to, and deepen our capacity to experience it without rushing to turn it into a goal or an image to pursue. Soul-fullness develops slowly over time. Like a hen sitting on her eggs until they hatch, we must allow the energy to gestate in its own time – not our time, but the energy's time.

Our work now is to pay attention to the energy itself – the actual state or feeling of the desire, impulse, or vibration – without allowing our thoughts to move out into ideas or images that might fix or satisfy the desire or manifest some other form of outer-world completion. That is, *we immerse ourselves in the direct experience of the energy, not knowing where it will lead.* If we cultivate the energy in this way, the rest will take care of itself. And whatever arises from this process will be 100 percent authentic and "true to life."

Here's an analogy to help clarify the process. Imagine that you feel fine overall but have a small pain in your neck. The practice I describe above means paying attention to the pain in your neck without becoming interested in any ideas, stories, fantasies, or images that might emerge in relationship to that pain. Don't let your mind wonder what caused the pain, what healing modality might resolve the pain, how long the pain might last, what if the pain never ends, whether the pain is due to a genetic predisposition or is a sign of a degenerative process or disease, whether the pain will interrupt your plans for the evening, etc. Don't even become interested in the pain as a message at this stage.

Instead, place your focus and attention on the energy – the pain in this example – itself. Perhaps it is best to not even label it as pain; just focus on the sensation, without any associations. As you do this, don't allow your mind to wonder or wander.

In this practice, by not allowing ourselves to create closure to the impulse or sensation, we are leaving some part of our world in suspension or even chaos, incomplete and unknown. This avoids the pitfall of suffocating the energy by jumping into how to manifest something. By remaining with the energy, we are opened up to the soul's aims for realization and expression. We simply remain receptive, experiencing the energetic impulse and not trying to control or manage it in any way; this allows the energy to develop on its own.

In the above example, what we label as pain is simply energy, and that energy is a communication from our souls (we will look more at somatic symptoms as soul communications in the next stage). In other words, pain is simply the "housing" for the energy. The example of pain is familiar to most if not all of us, but the same type of openness and engagement with the energy itself, rather than the "housing" in which it appears, applies to the other more subtle soul impulses that we are discussing in this chapter.

Desire is another form in which energy arises in us. Perhaps we have a vision of something we want, or perhaps we feel a longing but don't know what we desire. In either case, our first task is not to dwell on what might satisfy the desire but instead to stay with the actual feeling of yearning itself. I'll say more a little later about ways to engage with exploring the energy. For now, it's enough to think of our jobs as simply experiencing and observing what the yearning is like – what sensations do we feel?

Visions, some very compelling, about what might fulfill the desire, will appear and disappear. We can notice these, but our work is to *cultivate the energy itself until it ripens*. When it is ripe, something will manifest (which might or might not have anything to do with what we thought we were desiring at the outset). If we stay with the energy itself – allowing our focus, interest, and attention to cultivate it – the energy will move organically and often in surprising ways. It will seek to fulfill itself. The ideas and images that our minds put in the way are only distractions that interrupt the process. *The energy represents something unknown, a seed.* When we create an image around it, we suffocate the seed. And if the energy peters out on its own as we experience and contain it within ourselves, then we let it go; not all seeds are meant to grow.

Allowing energy to ripen is not easy. We are conditioned to respond to a feeling by immediately trying to figure out what it is and how to satisfy, complete, or fix it. Our inner addict (whether we identify as an addict or not) wants satisfaction. Addicts impulsively seek to gratify cravings. We can addictively fill our inner "holes" with images and ideas or with substances and behaviors; either way, addicts don't allow the energy of craving to grow inside of them.

Self-Inquiry

* Are you aware of a vague energetic impulse, current, or desire circulating in your consciousness? What does this feel like (simply describe the energy itself)?

* Can you stay with this subtle inner movement – the emerging soul force – and allow it to circulate in you without jumping to a way to satisfy or manifest it? That is, can you allow it to find its own way until it is ready to emerge into the true shape and form it is destined to take? If you cannot, what prevents you?

We can liken an energetic impulse inside of us to a young child, full of possibilities. Indulging in the mind's tendency to envision the completion of an energetic impulse is like taking that child, dressing him up in a three-piece suit, dropping him off at an office on Wall Street, and hoping he will bring home a paycheck later in the day. Children can't do that; they are too young. And, until they grow up, we won't know whether their work will take them to an office, a nightclub, a home, a construction site, or a university. Similarly, our cravings or energetic impulses need to gestate and mature into what they are meant to manifest, and we have to give them the space, time, and attention to do that.

Many people I work with say they want to find something new to do. Some want to write a book, for example. But they often need their new venture to support them financially. A creative spark or subtle energetic impulse is not powerful or sustained enough to support us. It must be cultivated into a flame and then a bonfire before it has sufficient strength to offer something back. At the start, we cannot know whether it has the fuel it needs to grow big enough to carry us somewhere; only time and ripening of the impulse itself will tell.

This doesn't mean that we don't do anything at all in relationship to a subtle energetic impulse or yearning. To help ourselves pay attention to the impulse, we might write in our journals, dance, draw, meditate, pray, or contemplate the experience of the energy. The key is to *not* make up stories about what it is and what is needed around it. *We drop all images and imaginings and stay closely connected to the energy itself so that it will ripen into itself.* In so doing, we shift our center toward our innermost core.

We might also take outer-world steps to explore the energy. We might go visit farms, talk to writers, or take surfing lessons in order to engage with and experience the energy of an impulse. When the juice is present to propel us in a direction without our manufacturing an image of what the impulse might become in the future, we go and see what's there for us. That is, we *explore* the energy; we don't *exploit* it by building an image of future gratification on top of it.

Returning to the metaphor of metamorphosis, we can see that cultivating energetic impulses is like activating our imaginal buds – our own seed impulses – and encouraging them to cluster. There are original cells or soul seeds inside of us that want to develop and mature. Some might develop into an awareness, others an ability or a capacity. There might also be seeds that grow into a creative project like a book, business, path, or relationship. The longer these seeds have to ripen, the more alive the outcome.

The inner stirrings I am referring to as impulses or energies alert us that something deep and genuine is trying to come through us. Whatever it is needs to be planted in cultivated soil, encouraged to grow in its own time – not ours – and tended with loving consideration. Our egoic habit is to reach for what we think we want rather than allowing the space for the energy of a desire to ripen. Here, we are breaking that habit and instead cultivating a relationship with our internal impulses. This cultivation creates deep alignment with our unfolding selves. We learn to stay with the ache, the longing, or the subtle energetic movement even when we fear our hearts will explode or when the feeling seems unbearable, and even in those places where we are not yet sensitive enough to follow the energy. *The process of cultivating is a process of immersion without action, much like the practice of silence discussed earlier.* Practicing immersion helps us develop the ability to perceive – to "sense" or "see" – the soul energy that, like a refreshing stream, spontaneously arises within us and offers us guidance.

Holding Our Vulnerabilities

As we increasingly immerse ourselves in the flow of the soul's subtle energies, many of us will experience yet another bewildering turn of events. At the same time that we are metaphorically in the process of giving birth to our emerging souls *within* us, we find ourselves in need of a womb *outside us*. As in Stage 8, where we felt dumbfounded to be thrust back into seemingly regressive psychological patterns from childhood just as we were first making contact with our souls, we are dumbfounded again in Stage 9 by the *need for help from others* as we move toward a soul-centered life.

Most of us tend to feel that we should be psychologically self-sufficient by this point in the journey. But the opposite is true. As we will see, developing our capacity to cultivate the soul's vague energetic impulses within the holding environment of our internally unified field is intertwined with learning to create and surrender ourselves to an external holding environment as well.

A Necessary External Holding Environment

It is important not to fall into the trap of self-condemnation when our deep vulnerability and need for a holding environment show up at this point in our journeys. A brief look at some of the psychological dimensions of what is happening for us at this stage will help us understand both the reasons for our particular vulnerability at this time and the nature of the environment that we need to support us in deepening our midlife transformation.

An infant needs attention, attunement, and support, all grounded in relationship to another, to grow. This is what psychologists call a "holding environment." Attention, attunement, and support, grounded in relatedness to another being, are not a wish list; they are non-negotiable *needs* when we are infants.

Similarly, even after we have started the work (in Stage 8) of *humanizing* our biological parents or childhood primary caretakers, our personal growth and development cannot unfold in a vacuum. At this stage in our journeys, as we surrender to the deep, mysterious domain of the soul, we contact a kind of vulnerability that has been paved over by the ego for decades. As our tender, vulnerable soul self begins to emerge, we are not meant, nor are we able, to fully satisfy our own need for attention, attunement, and support; we need others with whom we can engage in a dynamic and related manner. That is to say, we need actual attention, attunement, and support *from others* – an external holding environment that

is open and friendly toward our needs. Moreover, we need to consciously participate in this process by acknowledging our needs, accepting them ourselves, and
opening up to the support around us.

As author Harville Hendrix writes: "We are born in relationship. We are
wounded in relationship. We are healed in relationship." The drive to relate is a
core human drive, possibly *the* core human drive. Although we must continue
to meet our own emotional needs in many ways – such as through mindfulness
(moment-to-moment nonjudgmental awareness), self-empathy, and self-care – we
also need something from others. *We need someone to meet us in the areas of our
deepest vulnerabilities; we need someone to hold a space for us as we experience expansions in consciousness; and we need someone ahead of us on this journey to bear witness
to and affirm our unfolding process.*

In psychological terms, we could say that everyone is narcissistically wounded:
no one's primary narcissistic needs for attention and empathically attuned mirror-
ing are fully met in childhood. Well-adjusted adults learn to handle these needs
in one way or another, so we are generally taken by surprise when confronted in
the latter part of midlife by the urgent return of what can, at first, appear to be
a purely infantile need for holding in the form of attention and accurate mirror-
ing. On a spiritual level, however, this urgent need for a holding environment is
part of the shift in our center of gravity toward our soul. Vulnerability is directly
linked to the soul's strong but tender connection to the weave of all of life, as we
will see in Stages 11 and 12. The defenses that our egos built to protect us from
these needs only function, at this point, as walls that prevent us from being present, aware, and authentic. What is important at this stage is our willingness and
capacity to acknowledge, at least for ourselves, the depth of these needs.

For most of us, it is extremely vulnerable to truly acknowledge and honor our
need for a holding environment in a way that invites a partner, intimate friend,
professional guide, or others to see and respond to us. This acknowledgment is
risky in two ways: our need might be seen and responded to, which is frightening; or our need might *not* be seen and responded to, which is equally terrifying.
Why are we afraid of both outcomes?

Because, when we relax our defenses, the first thing we feel is defenseless. This usually feels like a trembling vulnerability. I am not referring to our egoic view of vulnerability as a state of weakness. I am referring to a deeper vulnerability that is more basic and central to our nature as human beings. This kind of vulnerability is a reflection of our basic openness. It reveals our exquisite human beauty. It is receptive and permeable. Inhabiting this vulnerability is a key element of living centered in the soul. When we touch into it we feel tender or raw, but we also sense the power and aliveness that is there.

In a very real sense, we now become aware of being vulnerable to direct contact with others – feeling held, hurt, rejected, met with sweetness – as well as being vulnerable to our soul's awareness, consciousness, and sacred essence. Vulnerability may not always feel desirable, but it is what we long for: connection to ourselves and others. The bottom line is that our midlife process is opening us to the great blessing of being permeable to all of life, and we might feel very sensitive and more than a little cautious about dropping our firewalls and allowing life to rush in.

The response from outside us – that is, whether we receive the help we are asking for or not – is particularly important at this stage, as is the depth of empathic attunement we feel toward ourselves while we experience our need and reach out for help. Once again, this statement might sound confusing in light of our corresponding urgency (discussed in the previous stage) to leave behind the emotional and psychological structures created in our families of origin. Here we are, striving with all our might to transform ourselves into mature, soul-centric adults, yet we are asked again and again to return to what appear to be earlier developmental stages.

To put it ever so bluntly, along with opening and aligning with the soul's impulses, we should expect to experience what can feel like a childish need to experience someone's undivided attention. We do, in fact, authentically need to have someone adjust and accommodate to us to the point that we experience that person as joining with us, in alignment with us, or in tune with us. We actually need to experience someone actively providing the precise response we need to help us withstand whatever we are going through in order to evolve into our larger presence.

For most of us, our histories and conditioning make it difficult to acknowledge and express our need for a holding environment. Those same factors can make it hard for others to extend the kind of holding and attunement that we require. If our friends and partners are in the midst of their own midlife passages, their capacity to provide this kind of support might be enhanced if they are engaged in their own deep, inner work or severely compromised if they are not. I'll talk later on about ways we can consciously create a holding environment for ourselves. Here, I'll just mention one of the most common ways that we elicit the attention and holding environment we authentically need to experience as part of our midlife unfolding: by developing a medical crisis. This is an entirely effective and powerful – albeit perhaps least desirable – way to get a holding environment.

When a serious medical diagnosis comes our way, friends and family typically pour out of the woodwork to support us. We move from one conversation to the next about us and our condition. On and offline communities gather to support us. We are wheeled to the operating room, wheeled back out, and lifted in and out of our hospital beds. Our meals are brought to us, and our vital signs are attended to. Beautiful flowers and cards expressing how deeply we are loved surround us. Our hearts feel open, and we feel vulnerable, permeable, raw, tender, heightened, exhilarated, and frightened, all at the same time.

Although no one consciously wants a serious medical diagnosis, those who have gone through a medical crisis report experiencing – among many other feelings – relief and pleasure at being so completely held and taken care of.

Those of us who do not have a medical emergency to help us obtain support will have to find the strength to self-validate our need. Although it's harder to dial 911 for ourselves, that is just what we have to do. The first step in being attended to in the way that we require is to connect to the deep, profound truth about what we are needing when we experience letdowns or meltdowns that cause us to feel out of control, sad, in pain, or hopeless. The unvarnished truth is that, at this stage of our journeys, we sometimes need the same attunement and support that we imagine only infants require.

Self-Inquiry

* What is your deepest truth about what you are needing and not getting in your life?

* What hungers and needs feel emotionally crippling to you and in what ways?

Asking for Help

When we reach points of incapacity, grief, and defeat – in the tiniest of ways or to the extent of experiencing an entire lifetime as a failure – we ask for help. In the 12-step process, this is called "turning it over." It is the moment when we have done all that we can, and we can do no more. These are the times we drop to our knees and pray. We don't have to be at death's door. We just have to feel exhausted, with nothing left inside of us that can respond. This complete sense of our own powerlessness to help ourselves makes the asking *authentic*. Authentic asking is most likely to get us an authentic response.

The core emotional experience of desperation or helplessness is very hard for the remaining parts of our unintegrated ego to tolerate. So as we notice our needs at their most primal level, we experience our powerlessness as much as our egos will allow us to do. When the ego has reached the end of its resources and is forced to call on a greater power – something outside itself – to come to its aid, this opens us to guidance from our souls. However, at the moment of need, the ego, with its knee-jerk response to control outcomes, interprets our distress negatively; it finds fault with us and accuses us of being weak or deficient. A stream of critical inner voices can overwhelm us in moments of crisis or deep need. We have to learn to ignore these voices and create a new reflex: to open up to being helped, guided, and held.

An interesting thing about the authentic experience of being in need, feeling vulnerable, and asking for help is that these states can, paradoxically, make us aware that we are not alone. When the need and asking for help come from an authentic place, a place where we have no more resources within ourselves, we discover a force in us that is actively guiding and powerfully engaged with our unfolding process; we feel our soul's commanding presence in the form of "a thousand unseen helping hands," as Joseph Campbell writes. Over time we come to learn that a larger field is deeply invested in our succeeding in our soul's earthly quests for self-realization and creative self-expression.

Self-Inquiry

* When in your life have you had to "turn it over" because you felt a help-lessness or desperation that was too large for you to handle?

* What was it like for you to feel this low, powerless, or terrified?

* What does it sound/look like when you really need help and you ask from a deeply authentic place?

I am not suggesting reverting exclusively to a state of dependency or requiring that others do for us what we can do for ourselves. I am encouraging us to seek out, ask for, and open to receiving help *in the places we feel the most exposed, fragile, and vulnerable,* the places where we cannot help ourselves.

For example, a client who found himself feeling raw and fragile in the face of multiple deaths among family and friends while he was in Stage 9 acknowledged his deep grief to his church's men's circle, a group to which he had belonged for several years. When he broke down with chest-heaving sobs, the group remained silent but expressed their support by holding each other's hands and offering him their undivided attention. No one tried to make him feel better. No one tried to cast his experience in a positive light. No one tried to rush him to pull it together in any way. When he looked up, he saw all that he needed to see in their eyes: they were one with him in his sorrow and holding him with their concern.

In recounting his story to me, this client said he felt like they formed a lap that he just crawled into and fell apart within – they were his refuge in those moments. He said he never felt so much kindness, compassion, and love before and now refers to these men as his brothers. Parenthetically he added that the circle's members shared later that he formed them into a true family that night when his need inspired them to respond in a way that was more loving than they realized they could be toward one another. For this client, the experience of becoming vulnerable in this way was one of the great blessings of his midlife passage – and his fellow group members felt blessed too, in their experience of spontaneously coming together in loving response to his pain.

When we acknowledge an authentic need and ask for help from that place, we will be able to receive more deeply than we might have in the past because, at this stage of our journeys, there is more of us consciously present to feel the impact of the gift. As we genuinely receive support, we feel the tender vulnerability of relinquishing control and surrendering to the full experience of being helped. And, when our request for help is met at these times, the result is always a deep sense of gratitude and blessing that arises of its own accord in both the one needing help and the one responding to that need.

Practically speaking, it might not always be possible to get the need for a safe holding environment met by our friends and family. They might not be available or capable. Sometimes professional help is necessary. I strongly encourage those who have the means to consider working privately with a guide – someone wise, caring, and capable of holding space for deep process. The quality to look for is *empathic attunement* rather than someone who offers advice or opinions or sees his or her role as trying to fix us or improve our situation (tempting though that can be).

It is also helpful to attend workshops, go on retreat, or join a therapeutic or spiritual support group. Twelve-step programs as well as hospital, church-hosted, and peer and co-counseling groups are free or lower-cost alternatives to private work with a personal guide. Spiritual communities dedicated to centering prayer and meditation are also valuable forums for the support we need.

Regardless of the modality, path, or person we choose to create and facilitate holding, *it must feel right for us*. We must trust our intuition and allow ourselves to try various people and approaches. This is the time to invest in ourselves; our future during the remainder of our life hangs in the balance.

Self-Inquiry

* Who in your life relates directly to you, offering you attention, attunement, and support?

* What help are you needing in your life? Can you acknowledge that?

* Can you create a holding environment for those needs and express those needs from an authentic/vulnerable place in front of others?

The development of a mature capacity to need and to be taken care of is one of the more challenging tasks during our midlife transition years, whether we have lived a more dependent or more autonomous life up to this point. This capacity is essential for us to deeply attune to our soul's vibration and then open enough to be directed by its guiding radiance into the full expression of our most authentic selves.

As I have mentioned numerous times, although the transition from ego-centrism to soul-centrism can be broken down into steps, these steps do not progress sequentially or in a straight line. A better metaphor now is that of a spiral, in which we move forward and circle back, revisiting different degrees of depth, breadth, and height. "It is not so much that we go anywhere, but that we fill out," in the words of Carol Pearson. "Filling out" is the quality of the experiences in Stages 7, 8, and 9.

In the next stage, we move beyond detecting the soul's vague and subtle movements and consciously enter into direct dialogue with more developed aspects of our soul. Our engagement will be kicked up a notch, and the messages from the soul will be more directly felt so that they cannot be overlooked or denied. With fear, faith, and a fidelity to expressing our vulnerability, we will learn how to work with dreams and physical symptoms to actively engage with our souls in ongoing conversation about the direction of our unfolding.

Through the Sacred Gate

༄༅~~~

Now we arrive at the place in our midlife transformation where "intuitive possibility is on the threshold of tangible manifestation," in the words of Jungian analyst and author Jean Shinoda Bolen. Whereas in Stage 9 we worked on developing finer senses of perception that could discern the subtle stirrings of our soul's awakening presence, in Stage 10 *our soul comes to us in a more developed form,* inviting us through the *sacred gate,* the hidden doorway to the invisible inner world where the soul abides.

The sacred gate is another name for the spirit door that opened for us in an overwhelming way during Stage 5. By Stage 10, this doorway between the visible and invisible worlds — between the worlds of matter and spirit — is more familiar, inviting, and compelling. We feel drawn toward this gate, on the other side of which resides another of the blessings of midlife that have been largely hidden from our view until now: a new, deeper, more genuine, and meaningful life. As we move again and again through the gate, into the soul's invisible world and back out into visible reality, we weave a thread between the two worlds, bringing them closer and closer together until there is an unbroken flow between what once might have been perceived as worlds apart.

In Stage 9, we learned to detect our soul's stirrings in the form of energetic impulses. In Stage 10, we deepen our ability to discern the soul's direction by learning to recognize its guidance. Our soul is always speaking to us – *always*. It has many ways of communicating – through feelings, thoughts, hunches, intuitions, gut instincts, dreams, synchronicities, somatic symptoms, subtle energetic movements, projections, epiphanies, and our relationships, just to name a few. However, we must learn the language of the soul to decipher its guidance.

Many teachers suggest that we simply personify the soul and begin a conversation, but I have found that, at least in the early stages of this work, the soul we personify is often an inflated image of the ego. The same can be said for thoughts, feelings, and other means that might, later on, be strong avenues for a lively dialogue; in the beginning, these are often taken over by the ego's aims rather than being a true expression from our deeper self. I prefer avenues that remain slightly beyond the grasp of our minds – just outside the capacity to fully understand the guidance we are receiving – so that we maintain a humble relationship with that which will always remain larger than us. This ensures that our conversations with our soul remain dynamic and alive.

Opening to the Unknown

We know that the physical world is composed of forms such as molecules, atoms, and subatomic particles that are invisible to the naked eye. In these later stages of our midlife journey, we are learning about an *invisible* dimension of the world that is even harder to grasp – the flow of life itself. Our soul is part of this life flow.

Knowledge of the invisible world is called *gnosis*.

The invisible world has two dimensions: the parts of ourselves that are hidden from us and can be understood from the perspective of psychology (our unconscious patterns, for example) and the larger, vital, energetic forces that are choreographing our individual unfoldings, which we are coming to know as the soul, and which can be understood through the perspective of spirituality.

In this stage we will learn to use two "louder" and more familiar phenomena by which the soul communicates to us – dreams and bodily symptoms – to cultivate gnosis, a personal and direct experience of that which generally lies beyond ordinary states of consciousness.

Martin Luther King, Jr., spoke of the ineffable forces below our conscious awareness that shape and direct our energies when he said, "Everything that we see is a shadow cast by that which we do not see." Earlier in our journeys, we caught glimpses of the forces from the invisible world of which Dr. King speaks when our disowned aspects were released, when our spirit doors opened, and when we became naturalists, learning to notice the subtle stirrings of our emerging souls. Now, in Stage 10, we move forward as mystics, extending our vision to converse with the flow of life that lies beyond normal human perception and that casts the shadows that make up our visible experience.

As mentioned earlier, before midlife, we rarely caught a glimpse of the hidden matrix upon which the visible world rests. At the outset of midlife, when confrontations, disillusionments, and failures of expectation cracked open our logical, ego-based stories of self-sufficiency and heroic accomplishment, the unseen world began to seep through these fissures and into our consciousness. Now, at this stage in our midlife transformation, the invisible becomes much more perceptible and accessible, bringing into our field of perception more of midlife's previously hidden blessings.

Enter the Greek Chorus

In ancient Greek theatrical productions, the chorus was a group of actors whose role was to comment on and explain the play that was under way. Often, the chorus's job was to express to the audience what the main characters could not say – their hopes, fears, motivations, and secrets. The chorus also offered insights directly to the characters themselves, to assist them in moving forward in their roles. The Greek chorus was the voice in the play that told it like it is, without sugar coating, rationalization, or excuse. And, because Greek theatres were so large, the chorus's message often had to be exaggerated to get across to the assembled audience.

Similarly, our soul communicates to us in numerous pronounced ways that offer an ongoing, truthful, in-depth evaluation of how life is going for us and instructions for expanding consciousness from our soul's perspective rather than our ego's more contracted and fear-based vantage point. In Stage 10, we learn to notice and decipher the unique style of communication that the soul's "Greek chorus" uses to speak to us through two avenues that are the least co-optable by the ego. These avenues are dreams and somatic symptoms. By engaging in the ongoing discourse that takes place in these borderlands where our psyches meet both their disowned parts and the world of the divine, we will discover a constant source of guidance that comes from and nurtures our souls and, by extension, reveals more of the deep narratives of our lives than is visible on the surface.

Dreamwork

Dreams are encounters with a simultaneous but seemingly separate world or dimension within our soul. These encounters offer healing, insight, and an opportunity for unleashing energies that allow the dreamer to know his or her deeper self.

It is well beyond the scope of this book to offer a complete primer on dreamwork. Our focus here is to learn a distinction between dreamwork that is more psychological in nature (ego-soul integrative dreamwork) and dreamwork that is more spiritual in nature (soul-centering dreamwork). A mix of the two is important for inviting meetings with our soul's mystery through the sacred gate.

We'll begin our conversation about dreams with a brief description of the ego-soul integrative approach and then discuss, at greater length, soul-centering dreamwork and how it helps us move through the sacred gate that opens up in our dreams.

Ego-Soul Integrative Dreamwork

The basic starting point when working with a dream from an *ego-soul integrative* perspective is to ask ourselves how we feel about the dream. When doing this, we contemplate both the feelings during the dream and the feelings resulting from the dream. Because dreams remove censorship filters, we tend to experience our feelings in a more amplified way while in a dream as well as in response to the dream when we awaken. Dreams reveal unconscious judgments or alert us to places where we are seeking release from constrictive energies and beliefs. In our dreams, we are also more likely to act out aspects of ourselves that are repressed, overlooked, neglected, and disowned.

Next, we place the dream in context. We try to connect the dream material to what has been going on in our waking lives. Often a dream will be addressing something relevant in our current lives. To let us know this, the psyche might use images that we have seen recently, whether from waking life experience or movies we've watched.

The dream will often point out a situation or aspect of a situation that is currently unconscious or hidden from view. In ego-soul integrative work, we can regard the dream from a 360-degree view, looking at it from all sides as if we were turning it around in our hands to examine the different angles. As part of this examination, one helpful perspective is to explore the dream as being populated with different parts of ourselves. For example, if our father shows up in our dreams, we can contemplate the parts of us that are like our father and explore the dream from that perspective. If there is someone stealing something from us in a dream, we might inquire into the ways we are thieves ourselves, as well as the ways we are feeling stolen from in our waking reality.

Dreams that repeat, or a series of dreams containing a similar theme, are particularly important messengers. When a dream repeats, the psyche either is expressing a sense of urgency that we get a message, or it is letting us know that we are overlooking a very important dialogue that needs more conscious involvement on our parts. No matter how bizarre the dream imagery may appear, every dream image is an expression of something worthy of conversation. The more familiar we become with the language of our own psyche, the more skillfully we will be able to decipher these nocturnal messages in a way that is outside our ego's ability to censor.

Soul-Centering Dreamwork

Ego-soul integrative dreamwork can give us important psychological insights that help us make sense of messages that our dreams bring us. But this method is basically about attempting to interpret and make sense of our dreams by bringing them into our waking reality's consciousness. In contrast, *soul-centering dream-work invites us to step back through the sacred gate into the dream itself.* In this style of dreamwork, we see dreams as offering opportunities to cultivate a deeper relationship with our soul, and, by extension, with all that lies below or outside of ordinary consciousness.

Soul-centering dreamwork harvests an emotionally or spiritually charged image or passage from a dream and then engages with that image or passage over a period of time. We re-enter the dreamscape each time so that the image or passage can work on us, transform us, and plant seeds in us.

Let's take a look at how this works.

When we are dreaming, we experience the dream as an embodied event occurring in space and time; we are convinced that we are experiencing a real event in a real environment. (A similar state arises when using entheogens – plant-derived, psychoactive substances used in shamanic or spiritual practice – or synthetic psychoactive substances.) The dream is a total world unto itself, and we feel awake within this world.

We experience this ever so slightly when we get swept into a movie and lose track for a moment here or there (especially during the most frightening or seductive parts) of the fact that we are watching a movie. From the perspective of the dreamer, the dream is a real environment, not a movie, and the dreamer is having actual experiences. Thus, as we step back into a dream, we enter a state of consciousness that lies beyond ordinary, waking consciousness.

Soul-centering dreamwork seeks to re-enter the landscape of the dream and to explore the dream's feelings, images, and experiences in a way that deepens and prolongs the experience. *The main distinction between ego-soul integrative dream-work and soul-centering dreamwork is that, in the former, we seek to digest the message of the dream, and, in the latter, we invite our soul to digest and transform us.* In other words, soul-centering work is the process whereby our smaller sense of self is dissolved and absorbed into our larger sense of self.

A soul-centering approach is best used when the dream contains an emotionally, psychologically, or spiritually charged image that feels edgy. If there isn't one, then we begin working with the dream in an ego-soul integrative manner, exploring associations with the dream as described earlier. This helps stir the pot of our intuitive awareness. We might find that the dream becomes edgier the more we engage with its material in this way; if so, then we might shift over to immersing ourselves in the dream using the soul-centering approach.

To briefly illustrate how one might work with a dream from a soul-centering perspective, here is a dream fragment of my own:

> *I was in a small Christian chapel or shrine room and a priestess was going to lead a ceremony. She had a Chihuahua-looking dog that had been shaved and was lying on her lap. I knew the dog was going to be sacrificed. The priestess was rhythmically stroking the dog's back to calm it. I moved forward to calm the dog as well when it bit me two times: once on my left index finger and once on my right index finger. I felt cautious about approaching the little dog again and felt ambivalent about being a part of a ceremony where a dog would be sacrificed. There was a small door that I used to leave but then felt that I didn't want to abandon the dog; I wanted to bear witness to its sacrifice.*

This dream was so disturbing that it woke me up. The theme and images were so troubling that my initial response was to try to forget the dream. I tried to shake it off. In the days that followed, the image "dogged" me until enough of the emotional charge drained off for me to be willing to re-enter the dreamscape through journaling and contemplative exercises.

Being bitten on the index fingers stood out as the edgiest, most powerful image: the bites, the physical experience of shock and pain, the blood being drawn.

During my meditation, I repeatedly stepped back into the dream at the point of being bitten and began to sense that something I was not entirely signed up for was under way, that I was involved in something that would require a sacrifice. I sensed that a contract had been struck, and those bites and the blood that was drawn sealed the deal.

As I immersed myself in this dream event, I remembered another dream I had had the previous month of the Last Supper (which was when Jesus predicted his death). An awareness arose of the powerful symbolism of sacrificial blood in the Christian tradition. In the dream of the dog, a sacrifice was under way despite my ambivalence. Entering the experience of the dogbite again and again became a practice of surrendering to a powerful energetic current that was gaining momentum in the deeper waters of my soul. This current attracted my curiosity about what new path was being opened for me as a result of the two related dreams and the compact made in the second one.

Through repeated immersion in the feelings and sensations attached to the image, I eventually experientially contacted a part of me that had unconsciously harbored ambivalence and even revulsion in relationship to the Christian path of my youth. In this process, I recognized an invitation to positively appreciate and open wide to the mystical side of Christianity in the same way I had, over the years, welcomed the perennial wisdom that other spiritual traditions offer.

Soul-centering dreamwork is difficult to describe because the impact of dream images is so personal. The foundation of the work rests on simply experiencing the image – and the feelings and sensations it evokes – over and over *without analyzing or explaining*. This is similar to the practice of immersing ourselves in the energy of impulses that we discussed in Stage 9. In soul-centering dreamwork, we let the dream images and feelings work on us, like an alchemical fire works on the substances that are subjected to it. As we immerse ourselves in the immediate, raw experience of a dream image, our cells shift in response, and insight and awareness arise without our engaging our minds in deliberate analysis. The awareness that coalesced for me was that the bites ratified my re-opening to mystical Christianity as a done deal, leaving me to accept and sort out what to do next to integrate this soul-centered, in-dwelling realization.

Self-Inquiry

Pick a strong dream image and then draw the image, or find a similar image on the Internet. Make this image your screen saver or desktop background on your computer, or print it and paste it near a location where you sit or work daily. Each time you see the image, pause and let it affect you however it does, just for a moment here and there. Write down any insights that come.

The goal of soul-centered dreamwork is not to reinforce an identity or self-concept, derive understanding, or "improve" ourselves with lessons drawn from a dream. Although the dream terrain we enter is real, the compass is always broken, and long periods in suspended states or wandering are required (we learned to do this in our waking reality during Stage 4 of our midlife journeys). Unlike ego-soul integrative dreamwork, soul-centering dreamwork doesn't tend to offer a nice, cozy feeling that we are getting ahead or learning something specific. It can, however, offer reassurance and guidance.

Like the spirit door, a dream that brings a soul message gets our attention with a high-voltage contact that can, at first, be disturbing. This kind of contact is rich with potential revelations and invites us to cross again and again through the sacred gate to allow the dream's images and feelings to work on us. This is a more experiential than mind-based approach of opening up a deep dimension that often lies beyond words. It offers something difficult to articulate that emerges over time as we continue to re-encounter the dream elements that were powerful for us.

Contemplation is not the only one way to do soul-centering work with charged dream images and feelings. We can engage with the material in other creative or kinesthetic ways as well: we could dance with the dream passage, paint a series of images in which we allow the dream to go in its own direction, write about it, or re-enact it with a group of others who are interested in exploring dreams in this way. Finding images and creating a collage that starts from a dream image and builds over time, with one image leading to the next, is another approach. Meditating on a charged dream image can also open up and extend the soul dialogue that is embedded in the dream. Or we might employ active imagination techniques such as selecting a particularly charged image from the dream and, in waking consciousness, letting the film roll: imagine what wants to happen with that image and where it wants to go. What all these techniques have in common is that they withdraw attention from the solidity of the fact-based world and take us through the sacred gate into the imaginal realm where we are more receptive to other orders of reality and the soul messages waiting there for us.

Symptom Work

Along with dreams, physical symptoms and illnesses are readily accessible avenues into the soul's invisible world. When our soul's Greek chorus speaks through symptoms, it often helps us become aware of the places where we are out of life's flow, where our life energy has become static and needs to return to its fluid state. Symptoms invite us into ongoing dialogue with our soul, a sort of revolving sacred gate, spiraling us across successive thresholds into deeper and deeper self-revelation and, ultimately, authentic self-expression.

As with dreamwork, it's beyond this book's scope to present a thorough discussion of the vast topic of somatic symptoms as avenues into the invisible world. However, we will look at several soul-centering approaches that engage with the energy within a symptom to consciously converse with evolving aspects of our being in a way that lies outside of our ego's ability to direct.

Although it might, at first, be difficult to accept that it is healthy for a body to produce symptoms, we can be sure that our soul is seeking conversation with us when a symptom arises. If we jump to trying to cure the symptom, we might end up curtailing the dialogue, cutting off one of the most important avenues we have for connecting to that which lies outside our ego consciousness.

We can hide from messages contained in dreams by refusing to remember the dreams or declining to converse with them, but we usually cannot hide from illness. There is no greater wisdom than the wisdom exhibited by the way things are! A somatic symptom is a message. The more dramatic the symptom, the more important the message. A symptom is not a sign that we have been bad; a symptom means that we are being invited into a *conversation*.

A Two-Faced Messenger

Symptoms always have two faces.

The more visible face is that *a symptom creates freedom,* a way of being that we are not able to inhabit without the symptom. An example of this could be feeling a deep need to rest or focus on our own development but not feeling the inner permission to be "selfish" in that way. So we develop an illness with symptoms that prevent us from being active – perhaps deep fatigue or a limitation on our mobility. The nature of the illness and its symptoms give us the freedom we were not able to give ourselves, to take time for ourselves and rest or engage with personal development.

A symptom also has a less visible face: *it creates the very condition that we are also trying to get out of.* In the example of someone developing an illness because they need time for themselves, their symptoms give them time to themselves on the one hand, but, on the other hand, that time is spent dealing with the illness rather than what they might have wished to have time to do.

Sigmund Freud argued that symptoms are signs of unconscious wishes seeking fulfillment through a physical avenue. Specifically, he viewed *symptoms as a compromise between an unconscious need and an unconscious defense against that need.*

Take Alzheimer's, for example. Some biological psychologists view *Alzheimer's as the ultimate loss of control.* Someone who is not willing to consciously give up control likely has an unconscious need for the opposite (remember our disowned selves who are the opposite of our upper-world selves): to let go of control.

That person likely also has an unconscious defense against the need to relinquish control, for example, an intense, ego-based self-monitoring that makes sure that he or she stays in control. Alzheimer's takes away both the control itself and our ego's ability to monitor ourselves and recognize what is happening to us.

Thinking about Alzheimer's in this way, we could say that the *freedom* that the disease produces is that a person living with Alzheimer's is completely free of any expectations or demands because she is completely unable to maintain control over her life: the freedom addresses the unconscious need to surrender control. At the same time, Alzheimer's creates *the very thing that a control-focused person fears most*: a total loss of control. For the person diagnosed with Alzheimer's, the part that wants to be free of control has its need satisfied because the person loses all control. At the same time, the ego, which is all about control, gets its needs satisfied because it does not have to experience this loss; with the loss of memory, there is no longer anyone home to register the loss of control.

Every physical symptom has a psychic aspect as well as a somatic component. In this example, we looked at how the somatic components – the physical disease of Alzheimer's – can be interwoven with psychic issues of control. NOTE: This example is only one way of looking at Alzheimer's and should not be generalized to all who are suffering with this disease.

Self-Inquiry

Pick a physical symptom you are experiencing and contemplate the ways that this symptom has two faces: What freedom does the symptom create for you, and what condition does it create that you don't want?

A body symptom is a doorknob to our sacred gate in the same way that a charged dream image is. To have a conversation with our symptoms and hear what the Greek chorus is telling us through an illness, we must open to a less mechanical view of our bodies than prevails in conventional medicine and instead *allow the symptoms to be symbols*. Viewed in this way, a disease becomes the initiation of a dialogue rather than an imperative that we immediately act to subdue its symptoms.

A Soul-Centering, Process Approach to Somatic Symptoms

Like dreams that repeat, chronic symptoms sometimes have the most pressing information for us and promise the most profound rewards, evolutionarily speaking, for our midlife rebirths. When the soul expresses an important message through a symptom or illness, the signal may either repeat or amplify until the message is received.

Arnold Mindell, founder of process-oriented psychology, noticed in his work with clients that, contrary to what one might expect, we have a tendency to make our bodily symptoms worse. If we get poison oak, we tend to scratch ourselves, which increases the itching and intensifies the rash. If we feel a pain in our necks, we tend to press on the spot, which makes us feel the pain more.

Mindell concluded that the body's natural reaction to disturbance is to amplify the condition. He wondered whether his patients unconsciously understood that their psyches were attempting to communicate through symptoms and whether, by doing things that intensified the symptoms, his patients were unconsciously trying to engage with the process so that they could understand the message. He took this observation into his clinical work and encouraged his clients to "amplify" their conditions: to consciously make the conditions worse. The results were amazingly effective in terms of both relieving the symptoms and harvesting vital connections and insights in the clients' dialogues with their deeper selves.

Mindell's approach has four parts. Before you read the steps, can you identify a physical condition that is currently disturbing? If so, follow the steps below using the symptom you've identified. If you don't have a symptom you can identify, read through the steps now, for use at a later date.

Part I: Self-Exploration: Begin by lying still. Feel the symptom, but do not think about it, judge it, or try to come up with an explanation about why it is there. In particular, notice and feel the sensations associated with the symptom: is there a temperature? do the sensations radiate? is there pain, pressure? etc. The aim is simply to observe what *is*. If we talk *about* the experience, or try to explain it, we are not fully *in* the experience, which is our goal. (If the symptom is a tumor or other condition that you know about but cannot feel, then pretend you can feel it and continue with this process on an imaginary plane.)

Part II: Amplification: After you have noticed and felt in some detail the sensations related to the symptom, without thinking about them, amplify or intensify the sensations. For example, if you experience pressure on your chest, you might press your hands against your chest to intensify that specific sensory experience. Exercise judgment – do not hurt yourself – but do not try to reduce the emotional or physical discomfort that results. Amplification increases our awareness and helps move the condition from a static to a fluid state.

Part III: Channel Switching: At some point you will come to an edge or a limit of tolerance. At that point, according to Mindell, you will "change channels." What this means is that a physical sensation of pain will turn into an image such as a knife behind the eye in a sinus infection, someone strangling you as you feel the pain from a sore throat, or the image of a black rock at the site of a tumor. The channel may switch in different ways, such as from hearing to feeling, from sensory to visualization, from seeing to moving, etc. Try to go with the flow, and notice where the process leads you.

Amplify each aspect that arises in turn. For example, if the channel switches from body sensation to an image, amplify or activate the image and see how the process wants to move next. Perhaps you will shift from a static image to one that moves, unfolding a short story line. Or, you might notice that the image becomes a series of images that may or may not appear to lead anywhere.

Part IV: Completion: At some point you will feel as though you have gone as far as you are able to go, or you will experience some space, greater openness, or peace. Often an insight or connection will complete the process. As you integrate the experience, either the conversation will continue, or the symptoms will subside or clear.

I used these four steps in working with a client in her late 50s who was losing her hearing due to a genetic condition. She began the process by lying down and feeling the sensations in her ears. At first she felt confused because she said it was hard to describe the absence of something. Then she realized that when she paid closer attention, she could describe the presence of some sensations she hadn't noticed in her habitual tendency to compare the loss of hearing state with what she had known all her life as the state of full hearing. She noticed a viscous, thick, full kind of sensation in her ears and the space around them. She also felt pressure, similar to what one might experience when landing in an airplane or diving underwater. She felt as though she was hearing a kind of white noise as well.

Without being directed to amplify, she spontaneously placed her hands over her ears and appeared to apply pressure; she reported that the sensations intensified. She began to feel afraid and said she felt totally alone and isolated. She remained silent for quite a while and then she began to moan. The moans built into a scream and as she screamed she pressed two pillows against her ears with all her might.

She stopped as suddenly as she began. The room was very silent. At some point she began crying softly. After a long silence, I asked her what happened. She reported that she suddenly had an insight: her entire life she had wanted to feel heard – by her parents, her siblings, her husband, and friends. But she could never feel heard in the way that she felt she needed.

The epiphany that came to her felt almost too deep to share. She hesitated, and I waited. When she spoke again it sounded as though she was speaking from inside a dream state. She told me that she realized that her body was blocking the possibility of listening to others because her pattern to be overly focused on others did not allow her to focus on herself. By blocking the sounds outside of her, the hearing loss was enabling her to begin to listen more deeply to *herself.* An inner voice deep inside of her was screaming at herself: "hear *me!*" She had always felt that she wanted others to hear her, but, in this moment, she real-ized that for most of her life she had turned a deaf ear toward herself. She didn't know what to do with the insight but intuitively knew she had stepped onto a new track. She looked as though she had been relieved of a substantial burden as she left the office.

Whatever problems, symptoms, or conditions we have, our soul will always encourage us to consciously take over the function that the symptom or problem is serving. To cooperate with this process, we must be willing to consciously take over the "service" that the disease or symptom provides and to provide it for our-selves. In my client's case, that might mean consciously interrupting her habit to overly attend to others and beginning to deeply listen to herself instead. Perhaps her hearing loss is asking her to destroy the part of her life – her need to be heard – that is destroying her hearing. Perhaps her soul is forcing her into an extended practice of silence, building cloister walls around her so that she can immerse her-self entirely in soulful waters.

As is the case with night dreams, although many dictionaries of symptom interpretation have been written, there is no comprehensive resource. Carolyn Myss' book *The Anatomy of the Spirit*, for example, suggests underlying dialogues that might be present in various illnesses. But we must not turn to this or other books alone to decode our processes; each person's process is individual, and no two people experience the same diagnosis in the same way. Books like this one by Myss are useful for stimulating the conversation, but, as we have learned in our spirit door passage, sometimes it is valuable to allow a situation to defy definition and resolution. The second half of life is often more about acceptance and loss than ambition and accomplishment. As we have learned over and over again, it is our failures and limitations that force us (our ego more specifically) to surrender, reducing us to what is elemental and authentic going forward.

The Symptom Is a Solution

When we experience an illness or somatic symptom, it is natural to want to alleviate our suffering; however, from a soul-centering vantage point, an intention to heal ourselves can sometimes get in the way of really seeing and understanding what is going on. We need to befriend our symptoms first rather than setting out to cure or ease them. Often when we do less initially, we accomplish more in the long term (this does not mean that if we are bleeding to death we don't act quickly but rather that we slow down our survival reflex with symptoms that don't, in fact, threaten our existence).

When we experience pain, our reflex is to contract. But a symptom is usually already a contraction. If we administer a cure that subdues the symptom, our soul will have to resort to expressing itself through other, usually more tenacious or "louder," symptoms. A symptom is not inviting us to take corrective action but rather to listen to the voice of our soul as it is speaking through that symptom.

A very effective, soul-centering perspective is to view *the symptom as a solution to a problem, not as a problem itself.* This ensouled vantage point will create an immediate spiritual chiropractic adjustment, aligning us to look for the deeper narrative.

What if a tumor were the solution to a problem? What if we have done a lot of inner work to address a particularly toxic relationship in our lives, and our bodies could clear the effects of that relationship, for example by producing a fully encapsulated tumor that could be removed surgically to eliminate the residue of the poison? Or, what if a disabled shoulder arises to help us stop carrying a burden that is too heavy?

The task in this approach is to discover the deeper narrative, the invisible conversation under the visible symptom. One way to do this is to select a physical (or emotional) symptom. Let's say that our lower back is in pain. We ask ourselves this question: "If we look at the pain in our lower back as the solution, what is the problem?" In other words, if we look at the lower back pain as *helping* us deal with something, what is it helping us handle?

Self-Inquiry

Pick a physical symptom you are experiencing currently and wonder how this symptom might be a *solution* instead of a *problem*. In what ways might this affliction be helping you handle something? What is it helping you deal with?

As mentioned earlier, the usual response to pain is to contract. Seeing a symptom as a solution instead of a problem expands our consciousness. When we ask ourselves to look at the symptom in the best possible light – as a message from our soul – we see that the symptom is drawing our attention to a condition that needs awareness and conversation. Or perhaps it is protecting us from something that might be worse than what we are currently experiencing. For example, a mother whose son is repeatedly getting sick and having to stay home from school would likely contemplate the possibility that this pattern might have more to do with wanting to avoid a problem he is having in school than with having a compromised immune system. When we honor our symptoms by seeing them as invitations to deeper conversations, we align ourselves with the aims of the soul, which are for the whole of our beings, including our bodies, to live harmoniously with the pulse and flow of life.

The Domain of the Sacred

When we enter the invisible world of our soul, we catch glimpses of things outside our normal boundaries and perceptions. These glimpses come with the deep kind of silence we can feel when we step into a cathedral or when we stumble upon the sacred and surprise ourselves. Perhaps at these times we catch the sacred unawares as well, and the surprise is mutual.

When we take these steps into a new dimension, a strange and foreign land, we might feel momentary shock. This land lies beyond and before anything we are able to inhabit full-time in present reality. It is a place we visit where perception is unmediated by rational thought, conditioning, expectation, or analysis. Here, hidden blessings reveal themselves to us as new experiences or insights embed themselves into our consciousness. We often reflexively pull away from these experiences because the intimacy can feel too great. But the seeds of that other world will be sown in us, in the form of a realization or an experience of the unexpected. From these seeds grows an expanded capacity to perceive and understand ourselves, and, as we will see in the next stage, out of this expanded capacity, the world is born anew. It's as if a new current of meaning carries us out of our old perspectives and into entirely new states of being.

Although dreams and symptoms are two of the most familiar forms in which the soul invites us to pass through the sacred gate and discover soul wisdom, anything can become a sacred gate into the invisible world: reading a poem, participating in a tea ceremony, standing before a painting, watching a play, listening to music, performing sacred practices, taking a walk, or reading a book. A connection to the invisible stream of life can be made when gazing into the eye of a horse or watching the synchronized movements of a flock of starlings. The respectful and conscious use of entheogens and psychoactive substances also takes us beyond ordinary consciousness. Meditation and prayer are direct routes to opening to the sacred. Sacred singing and dancing can bring us to meetings with the mystery. The doorknobs are infinite in number.

Personally encountering a reality that is hidden from normal awareness, like the sun behind clouds, pushes us beyond the usual boundaries of human thought, logic, rationality, and knowing. Each contact we make with the invisible world expands our perspectives to reveal hidden blessings and tunes us to the soul's key.

The central point to remember about connecting to the invisible world of the soul in the ways discussed in this chapter is that we are *entering conversations, not managing outcomes.* As the Buddhist precept reminds us, the process (or the journey) is what is important, not the outcome (or the arrival). As each invisible message becomes known, it ceases to be a mystery, and another invisible layer awaits, drawing us both toward ourselves and more deeply into the world within which we are inexorably embedded.

With each small and large step away from our known worlds into unknown landscapes, we become a little less tethered to the conventional, the visible, and the understandable. As the gravitational pull exerted by old forms and constructs weakens, we step closer to what Rumi was describing when he wrote, "Lovers don't finally meet somewhere. They're in each other all along." This epiphany is the topic of the next stage.

STAGE 11

The Pulse of Love

⥹⥺⥹

In Stage 10, we became more accustomed to detecting the soul's not-so-subtle messages and allowing those messages to draw us through the sacred gate to experience the soul's invisible world. There, we discovered a realm beyond what we have been accustomed to inhabiting and began developing our capacity to attend to our souls' guidance about what life brings to each of us that is part of our unique journey.

Entering the soul's realm will also bring us into contact with perhaps the greatest blessing of the midlife journey: the unifying love that is in the divine spark or center of each of our souls and that unites us with all of life. The more we pass through the sacred gate and touch the energy of life unfolding, the more our hearts open. In Stage 11, we explore the ways our hearts open and the nature of the unifying love we experience when they do.

I am not talking here about the physical organ of the heart but about the non-physical center in our beings, *the magnetic sensing organ of the soul*, which lies in the innermost chambers of who we are. We might call this our "heart of hearts." This is the energetic blueprint of which our physical hearts are one manifestation.

Love is the soul's activating energy and the ultimate synthetic force, integrating us into the weave of life. Love exposes, intensifies, and amplifies our aliveness. When the kind of love I am talking about grabs hold of us – or we grab hold of it – it becomes the basis for all of our choices. This love catalyzes us to evolve into new forms that are committed to the whole of life.

The love we experience during this period of midlife gives us direct experience that all forms are manifestations of one, unified consciousness. This is the state where there is no separation between us and others, or, in the words found in both Christian and Buddhist texts and prayers, "I am in you and you are in me." *It is the love for the soul within the other and the ability to see the soul of the other as the soul within ourselves.* The soul guides us to this experience of love, enabling us to love and accept all beings as they are and delight in the diversity of this one life. This love of the sameness lying at the heart of all creation extends to all living beings, as well as those we might have formerly seen as nonliving beings.

In this chapter we will look first at what I call "astonishing" love, the kind that can come all of a sudden and grab us. This unexpected love has the power to transport us into new landscapes or to entirely change the landscapes we currently inhabit. After we look at an example of astonishing love, we'll explore a more gradual way in which soul-based love unfolds, through a process I call "following the pulse" of love, heartbeat by heartbeat.

Both forms of love exert a powerful gravitational pull. A known or unknown longing in our hearts draws us in, and we become enraptured, unable to break away from its magnetic invitation. This love often arises in places where we weren't aware there was an attraction in the first place. Although on the outside it might appear that nothing has changed in our lives, on the inside everything changes as a result of this love, as we will see in the stories that follow.

Astonishing Love

When love comes as a sudden surprise, it can be reminiscent of what some of us experienced when our spirit doors opened – feeling overwhelmed by a force greater than ourselves. By now we have had some experience of willingly travel-ing back and forth through the sacred gate, so we are more able to let forces from the soul's invisible world "work" on us than we were when the spirit door opened for us in Stage 5. As a result, in Stage 11, love does not have to blast through obstacles or knock us out of orbit to get our attention. The love we will be talking about shortly invites us into larger spheres of existence and relatedness, often so far-reaching that we know we can never own, have, or hold what we are experi-encing; we can only surrender to its enormity and bow in gratitude for its gift.

Our spirit door openings in Stage 5 were primarily about *integration*: metabo-lizing, assimilating, and incorporating into us that which is experienced as "other" or a force larger than us. The movement in Stage 10 was about using charged dream images and somatic symptoms to over-spill the boundaries of our rational minds, surrender our local sense of "I," and cross through the sacred gate into our soul's home base, which is the larger field of life energy from which we draw our individual life force. Now that we have some familiarity with contacting this life energy, we are able to surrender to it: in Stage 11, *we allow ourselves to be absorbed into the field of life energy on the other side of the sacred gate.* Not only that, *we meet that same shared life force as it is manifesting through other ensouled beings!*

The experience of our core selves merging and harmonizing with this field of life energy has a deeply spiritual feel. There is a sense of having entered a sacred space – another circle of existence as D. H. Lawrence writes – like one might experience in the presence a majestic mountain or beneath a star-studded sky. We feel small (in size, not age) in the presence of something large; as a result, we become less attached or referenced to our sense of "I."

Self-Inquiry

Reflecting on your own life, has love ever ignited your soul, opened your heart, and expanded your perspective? If yes, explain in what ways, and include your feelings as you explore. Be careful not to focus your attention on the object of your love; focus on the experience of yourself.

What follows is a client's story that exemplifies one shape that sudden love can take and the alignment with something larger than ourselves that comes with this kind of love. In my private practice, approximately one-third of my midlife clients experience a sudden astonishing love contact such as is described in the story that follows.

Adam's Love Apple

A client whom I'll call Adam enlisted me as a guide during his midlife passage. Adam is the founder of a midsize company that distributes American produce. During a yearly business trip to seed trials in Spain, he came upon a tomato that rocked his world. "It was love at first sight," he tells me enthusiastically in our initial session together.

"On first appearance it looked like a regular Roma tomato, but when we cut into it, we saw that it had full flesh and no gel." He continues: "While full-flesh Roma types are very common in California's San Joaquin Valley, they can only be used for making soup or ketchup because they are very mealy in texture and are uneatable raw; and they are horrible for any kind of fresh application" (when people fall in love, their passion overflows; they tend to speak at length in a riveted trance-like state that is equally captivating for the listener, who is carried by their passion across the threshold between the mundane and the sublime). Adam went on, "We tasted the tomato, and, to our surprise, it was delicious! The texture was wonderful, and the rich, deep tomato flavor really got our attention."

Botanically speaking, the tomato is a fruit (technically a berry) although most of us in North America think of it as a vegetable. The French call it *pomme d'amour* (love apple). From the beginning, Adam was surprised by the force of his feelings for this new tomato. He had come across a lot of produce during his 40 years in the business, and, although he tended toward high levels of enthusiasm in general, he told me "this was different." He spoke about the way his love apple "startled his senses." "The tomato solicited me, not the other way around," he said to me as if confiding a secret. He felt that the tomato had called to him at the seed trials, and they had "constellated a profound and mysterious rapport."

In between long monologues, in which Adam would wax eloquent about the rich red color of the fruit and its luscious, indescribable flavor, he would share tender anecdotes about the deeper teachings the fruit was transmitting to him. "I don't know why or how – and I sometimes think I've gone crazy – but this little love apple is forcing me out of static thinking and feeling patterns. The more I allow this tomato into my life and into my heart, the more I see that my entire life is deeply interwoven with the plant kingdom. I am beginning to see this plant as a powerful spiritual teacher."

Even though Adam is a consummate businessman experienced in bringing new products to market, he found that the journey from the tasting to making this particular tomato available in U.S. grocery stores was something different. The process was driven by love rather than business considerations: "It took us four years of trial and tribulation to learn how to grow this very challenging variety in a way that we could produce a consistent, predictable crop. The investment in time and money didn't make any sense."

Adam's surprising connection with this tomato evoked very intense feelings that opened up deep undercurrents of intuitive guidance in him. One lesson he shared was about the direct experience that everything is alive and has its own consciousness. "I am learning that plants are sentient life forms. Up until now I thought they were just here for my use and pleasure," he acknowledged with remorse. Adam felt like he had taken a bite of the biblical apple; his engagement with this plant did not allow him to return to his former levels of denial and unconsciousness, specifically about his place in the world of living creatures.

"My relationship with my love apple has brought me so much closer to the idea of oneness I have read about but never before experienced. The reality that I am not alone and not meant to go it alone, and that I am supported all the time, is no longer just an idea. What once was a place of inconsolable loneliness is now a world of interrelatedness."

Because the tomato is deeply embedded in the ecology of place, Adam began learning the importance of place for himself as well. Swept up in the new world that the tomato opened for him, he decided to invest in several farms to encourage them to grow this particular tomato in the United States. As he dove into the farming practices that would best support his new love, he discovered things about current farming methods that broke his heart. "Our topsoil is disappearing, and the topsoil we have left is tremendously impoverished of nutrients" he shared from a place of deep anguish. "We are looking up at the weakening ozone layer but not looking down on the ground we are standing on. It's crazy!"

His love for this tomato made him "want to do the right thing," he told me. The task was daunting but he felt chosen – *called by the life force within this tomato* – to engage, "like the blossom calls to the honeybee." It made him feel more connected to life, and in addition to bringing up challenging questions about the practices of the farms he invested in, his relationship with the tomato brought up questions about fundamentals of his business practices as well. He began to recognize that many of these practices are part of systems that don't support the sanctity of life. This exposed him to challenging environmental, ethical, and moral concerns that were new to him. In his old paradigm, the world was divided into opposing forces: "us or them" and "me or you." Now he wonders how we can all live together in peace. The first challenge to this peace that he wishes to seek was that the dictates of his heart guided him to modify his business significantly, causing more than a little upset among the other owners who were fixated on self-preservation; their reactions in turn stimulated old fears of scarcity in Adam.

"My little love apple has cast a spell on me, and I feel inexorably drawn more deeply into the world I've been turning away from most of my life," Adam told me. He never expected to enter into such an alliance, and he quickly realized that he couldn't participate in this relationship without up-ending his entire world of assumptions and beliefs. "This is not the kind of thing I could have sought out; I didn't know it existed." He still doubts its existence from time to time. *"My love apple filled a place in my heart and soul I never knew was empty. It also paved a way into a world I never knew existed.* I feel as though a great responsibility has been bestowed upon me; I feel the burden and the gift of it."

Self-Inquiry

* Do you feel available/receptive to a love so fierce it could change your life, or are you experiencing such an astonishing love currently?

* What might be some barriers that prevent you from opening to a love contact that can transform you?

Adam's story illustrates a sudden, irresistible pull into an enraptured connection with something larger than who he knew himself to be prior to the meeting. Through the tomato, Adam came into relationship with plants and the Earth and a desire to be of service to the health of the soil and the planet. That contact was powerful enough to pull Adam out of his small world of self-preservation into a much larger one interested in the well-being of the whole. He experienced a kind of ecstasy in the connection to something larger than he had known before. Love binds us together, and, through our openness to its force, we contact the eternal aliveness that underlies the existence of all things, the original nature of life. In the late stages of our midlife journey, when our egos have less hold on us, our identities are more open and fluid, and we have crossed through the sacred gate into the domain of soul, we are open to experience this transformative love – either in the sudden, astonishing way that Adam did, or in less dramatic ways as we will see shortly.

Self-Inquiry

In this story an experience of **AWE** or **AMAZEMENT** is present. This story illustrates the place where we come into contact with or are witnessing the **BEAUTY OF EXISTENCE**. It's often a **HOLY EXPERIENCE** and a kind of **REVERENCE** is felt.

Oh my god, that hummingbird! Oh my god, that sunset! Oh my god, that newborn's face!

Name a breathtaking moment you have experienced recently. Does this breathtaking moment feel like contact with the mystery, the sacred, or the divine for you?

Following the Pulse

In contrast to the sudden and surprising love in the preceding story, a more common form of the love that draws us into connection with the whole of life is experienced in the form of *pulses*. We had some experience with pulses when we were learning to detect subtle soul energies within us in Stage 9. The pulses we are speaking about now are magnetic attractions that we feel as we resonate or vibrate in response to, or with, the world around us. In these experiences, we tune in, through the perceptual field of our hearts, to a deep connection, a subtle love vibration. We resonate like tuning forks in response to vibrations emanating from another being or entity in the field of energy around us. Feeling these vibrations draws our attention to the "other" that is emitting them; this "other" can be a living being or a subject or a work of art or, really, anything outside of or even within ourselves.

Expanding our capacity to be enraptured by all of life means learning to follow these vibrations or pulses, which are inviting us to engage. Most of us will experience these invitations by simply noticing something that touches, compels, or invites us to pay attention. Something subtle urges us to go this way instead of that way, to stop and look, to pay attention. The first contact can be as light and gentle as a butterfly landing on our hands. We learn to become interested in seeing where the connection will lead us.

Our ability to notice, cultivate, and respond to pulses has been growing. In Stage 11 we focus our attention on an ever-broadening array of pulses that make up our uniquely individual attractions and fascinations. As we continue to cultivate our perceptual capacities, these attractions are revealed to be resonances with the living soulfulness of the world. They develop into reliable markers that guide us on the true path of the soul's unfolding.

A note about the words "attractions" and "fascinations": these words, which I have just used above, are usually used to refer to a positive experience; we generally think of ourselves as attracted to or fascinated by things that appeal or are pleasing. However, by the time we arrive in Stage 11 in our midlife journeys, the more soul-centered we are, the less likely we are to make either-or distinctions between good/bad, right/wrong, positive/negative. What attracts or fascinates us is the fact that *energy – or life-force – is present*. The energy attracts our attention, regardless of whether the outer appearance attracts or repels.

In other words, following the pulse means keeping a close eye on flutters of energy. It means staying in touch with the rhythmic movement of the ever-evolving web of life that is experienced both within and outside of us. The key to doing this is to notice what we feel in a given moment and allow ourselves to sit with our experience.

When I use the word "feel" here, I am not talking about physical sensation, as in when we pick up a stone and feel, using our sense of touch, how hard it is. Nor am I talking about feeling emotions, like happiness, sadness, or anger. I am talking about awareness of vibration or energy; we *tune into* the energetic vibrations present. We do this with the non-physical sensing part of us. And, what we sense is hard to put into words but is close to what we sometimes called "vibe." It is the kind of hard-to-describe experience we have when we walk into a restaurant, and something about the place doesn't feel good to us, so we decide to walk out. Or, the subtle experience we notice when we are talking to someone at a party, and we sense that something is "off," so we make an excuse and leave.

Sometimes vibe is called intuition; intuition may be a part of the mix along with subtle energy or vibration. As we tune into the vibrations of the larger field around us, our capacity for attunement to ourselves and to the world increases. A little later in this chapter, we'll explore a practice for cultivating this capacity. But first, let's explore an extended example of what can happen when we follow the pulse.

Grace: Sewing a New Self

A client I have worked with for many years, whom I'll call Grace, first came to see me toward the beginning of her midlife passage. She had had a disturbing dream in which she saw herself as a baby lying alone in the center of a field of unmowed wheat; she was crying. The baby had no arms and hands. Her son (who in waking reality was about to leave for college for the first time) was riding a horse, protectively circling her but not getting close.

The image of herself as a baby without arms and hands was very disturbing for Grace. It unsettled her emotionally so much that she was having difficulty concentrating on her daily tasks. She was experiencing a sense of dread in the pit of her stomach, a constriction in her throat, and feeling that her life had taken a disastrous wrong turn at some point without her noticing.

When trying to explain what the feeling of dread was like, she told me the boiling frog story. This is a widespread teaching story that says that if we put a frog in a pot of boiling water, it will jump out right away to escape death. But if we put a frog in a pot of water that is cool and comfortable, and then *gradually* heat the water until it starts boiling, the frog will not be aware it is in danger until it is too late. Grace said, "The dread I feel is like what I imagine the frog might feel just before realizing that it is too late to save himself. In the middle of my life I find myself lying alone – without arms or hands – helpless in a field. How did I get here?"

Grace was well aware that, with her son's imminent departure for college, her role as a mother was coming to a close. "It's as if I'm coming out of an 18-year dream; who will I be if I am not a mother, I wonder?" She interpreted her dream's Greek chorus to be telling her that she had stepped so far away from her artistic nature that her artistic instruments – her hands – had atrophied from non-use. The truth of this insight and the grief she experienced felt life-altering. Grace had this dream when she was 46 years old and sees it as a key midlife entry point.

Before we continue, a little back story is necessary to help illustrate the way Grace had already begun following pulses that ripened during her midlife. Many years before midlife, when Grace supported herself with a job in a graphics design firm while pursuing her love of creating by designing artworks out of mosaic tiles, she purchased a four-foot-high fabric relief depicting a woman; the piece had been made by a Hawaiian artist. Grace herself is barely 5 feet tall, so the wall hanging was close to life size for her. This purchase was well outside Grace's financial comfort zone, but she felt a deep, irrational need to have the wall hanging. She has hung it in the bedroom of every home in which she has lived since. Being drawn to and purchasing the wall hanging was the initial pulse to which Grace responded, long before she was ready to engage further with the life energy that waited for her there.

Some time after the dream about herself as a baby lying in a field, in what would have been Stage 1 or 2 of Grace's midlife, she noticed that the fabric on the wall hanging had started to come undone, to the point of looking almost tattered. She had been aware of some unraveling over the years and had thought many times that she needed to do something about it but never had. Loose threads, faded colors, and several places where the frame had cracked during an earthquake made Grace feel as though she needed to take the piece down at long last. Meanwhile, in her outer life, the company where Grace worked lost its largest account, threatening her income and throwing her into a panic about how she was going to support herself financially. The next few years were spent scrambling to hold her outer life together, a familiar early-midlife experience of unraveling.

Grace couldn't bear the thought of getting rid of the wall hanging or giving it away, so she decided to store it in the garage. Years later, Grace would observe that the wall hanging's time in the garage roughly corresponded with her own time down under (Stage 4), during which she experienced anxious depression.

The parallel process between the wall hanging and Grace's midlife journey continued. As she progressed to Stages 8 and 9, Grace began to notice a subtle energy that she couldn't name at first; she felt it in her heart, first as a spark, then an ache, and later as a warm, friendly glow. Over time, it grew into what she recognized at first to be self-pity – an authentic response to the losses she was experiencing – and later it developed into self-love.

During this time, she also began to suffer from arthritis in her hands and remembered several dreams about reaching for the wall hanging but her arthritic hands not allowing her to grab hold of it.

One day, without forethought, she moved the fabric image back to her bedroom. What happened next was surprising: she began to talk to the woman in the wall hanging. Who was she? What relationship did Grace have to her? Could Grace help her? Could they help each other?

The questions kept coming. Was the woman in the wall hanging real? *Was Grace real?* Grace became aware of a deep yearning to feel real. She identified strongly with the story of Pinocchio, reading and rereading it several times during this period.

At the same time, without conscious thought or connecting the dots but feeling her way impulse by impulse, Grace began searching for and frequenting textile shops. She began buying fabric and yarn, not knowing why until one day she brought the accumulated bundle to the woman in the wall hanging and offered it to her as a gift.

Grace found herself talking to the woman on the wall every day and eventually would admit to herself and close friends that she had fallen in love with the woman. Her husband good-naturedly joked that he felt jealous. But it was not that kind of love. She felt a *deep and mysterious rapport* with this woman and sensed that some part of her salvation lay in following her passion to interact with the woman. "I believe we are in each other's lives to help each other, as insane as that may sound," she told me.

One day Grace began the process of repairing the wall hanging's cracked frame, renovating the female figure's dress and re-stuffing the arms that had become the target of mice during the artwork's time in the garage. "The challenge in re-creating her is that I have to stitch every thread blindly. The piece is so large I have to stretch to even reach certain parts of her body. I feel as though I am holding her, but I also feel held by her.

"My arms can barely reach the back so I have to place myself to the side, not able to see the back or the front. I can only do the stitching by feel. My fingers have become my eyes; my heart guides the needle, my life force flows through the flesh-colored thread. The wall hanging is not me, but somehow her presence makes me feel more complete. I notice I want to sew tightly even though it takes much longer. I do not want her to unravel and lose herself again. I do not feel as though I am sewing myself back together as much as that I am creating something fresh and new."

Later Grace observed, "I remember when working with mosaics all those years ago that I loved taking broken pieces and creating something new and whole from them. As I painstakingly worked on bringing the wall woman into a fresh new expression, I felt like the artist of my own life reshaping myself out of the materials at hand. Each stitch becomes a further refinement."

Grace's repairing of the wall hanging was a way of stitching her self into the weave of the world. "From this process I am beginning to really know what it is to find beauty in a broken world. I am connecting to the suffering in the world in a new and astonishing way. I feel as though I have a way to hold all the pain I see around me for the first time in my life. I hold it in the same way I hold the woman on the wall and myself: with love, with compassion, and with an eye on how I might be of service."

I smile to this day as I recall the last sentence of Grace's midlife memoir, and its inadvertent typo: I have *sown* [sic] a new self – a fresh new weave – out of the corpse of my old self."

By the end of this renovation work, which took a full year, Grace realized, in retrospect only, that it was her creative self that had gotten broken, frayed, and faded many years earlier and that through the slow and tedious process of sewing the wall hanging and herself together, one stitch at a time, she had come back to life. "Love brought me back to life. Love for the woman in the wall hanging, love for myself, and love for this life that has allowed me to be reborn within it. I am so grateful."

The last dream Grace shared with me was of standing in front of the woman in the wall hanging, talking to her. In the dream, the woman's arms separated from her body and reached out for Grace. Grace walked into the embrace and then through the wall to the other side. Grace felt that something changed after that dream though she did not yet understand the lived experience of the change. She felt as though she had walked through a doorway into the mystery and was excited to see what would come next.

Self-Inquiry

What love pulses have you been tracking in your midlife journey thus far? Sometimes it is only when looking back that we can connect the dots that have accumulated.

Everything has soul. When a relationship shows up – with a wall hanging as it did for Grace, with a tomato for Adam – it has the potential for soul deepening as long as we do not subject the relationship to our rational minds but instead follow the impulses in our hearts. In Adam's story, the transforming experience of love struck him like a bolt of lightning; in Grace's case, the process was a long slow one, initiated many years earlier with her impulse to purchase the artwork and then manifested over a lengthy period during her midlife journey. In both cases, the path was the same: *If we open to the love that underlies and infuses all things, we will find the path to the epicenter of our being and the wellspring of life itself.*

Following the love pulse – through the process of noticing small and large attractions, whether they come in the form of vibrations, insights, feelings, knowings, intuitions, etc. – we come to know what our hearts have known all along: that our lives intersect with an infinite number of seen and unseen beings and energies. This knowledge ultimately allows us to be more open, available, and ready when our soul, which feels the pulses and vibrations of the life force long before our conscious mind recognizes them, orchestrates direct relations with the souls of other – and ultimately all – beings. We are becoming able to follow the individual sparks of divinity within us toward the infinite light and life of the mystery of which those sparks are a part. When we do this, we are creating the world over and over, merging with it, joining life to life, and igniting our passions, connecting us to the underlying unity.

Following the pulse (and, as a reminder, I am not talking about addictive impulses here) is about responding to the impulses of life as they are being born in us and allowing our hearts to be what they are intended to be: channels to connect with the world around us. Following the pulse means allowing our hearts to open to and beat in harmony with the pulse of all creation. That pulse is love.

Becoming Love in Human Form

As we've seen through the stories in this stage, love is a felt experience that stretches us from the deeply personal to the mystery that is beyond time and space and, as such, beyond comprehension. This love is intangible but not insubstantial. Like soul, love can be perceived through the effects it creates. Like the wind that we cannot see but whose presence we know through the rustling leaves and swaying branches, love creates things that can be seen and felt: joy, warmth, a sense of connection, interest in the well-being of self and others, and awe, to name a few.

Our basic nature is love. The basic nature of everything is love. "Profound love demands a deep conception and out of this develops reverence for the mystery of life. It brings us close to all beings," wrote theologian and physician Albert Schweitzer. This newly born reverence for the mystery of life is clear in the stories of Adam and Grace.

What these two stories also have in common is that no one had a precedent for what transpired. Often, our experiences of love in Stage 11 are not only outside our frameworks but outside anything we could imagine. The idea of falling in love with a tomato or a wall hanging never crossed either of the storytellers' minds. But all of a sudden, there they were, fully engaged with something far outside the realm of ordinary experience.

Often an experience like this never normalizes completely. Some part of the experience always remains just out of reach because it is located partially in the mystery itself. We can only open further and further into that mystery.

These are new events on a soul level. In our pasts, if something new arrived, our egos would acclimate, adapt, and adjust until the new experience became a part of our worlds. For example, although most of us who move a long distance to a new environment experience the move as a big change, if we remain in the new place, we will, many years later, feel ourselves as native there.

But talking to an ensouled wall hanging or a tomato? These are windows into worlds we can never completely know; these experiences take us to continents without coastlines. We are engaging with the mystery itself and bridging our way into that world through the medium of love, which has called to us, and called on us, in a way that we will likely never fully comprehend.

Many writers, artists, and thinkers have attempted to describe or frame the mystery. If we don't put frames around it but instead just remain present to the experience, we feel awe and wonderment. "All I know is that I am hanging out with something really big, and I can try to be as present as possible," Grace says. "I am looking through a window into a much larger field of life, existence, soul, and being than I had ever anticipated was there."

The Practice of Feeling the Relationship

In this section, we explore a practice of opening to and coming into relationship with the currents of life force that surround us. We begin by taking a walk, preferably in a natural setting. We don't have to have a redwood forest or some great natural wonder for this exploration; any natural setting will do. We allow ourselves to wander without time constraints for an hour, or more if possible (the more time the better). Taking this amount of time helps us interrupt the habit of feeling besieged by life necessities that remove us from the present moment. If we are able to give ourselves an afternoon or a full day away from everything except our unfolding relationship with ourselves and life, that creates an optimal opportunity for the practice I am about to describe. But if we can only spare an hour, we use the hour we have available instead of waiting for some future opportunity when there might be more time.

As we walk, we look around us in a fresh way until something catches our attention. We are alert to the first few moments of the encounter (as we might be if a honeybee landed on our hand). We might see a spark or flash, experience some curiosity, feel enamored, or be drawn into an invisible web of fascination. We might sense a subtle – or not-so-subtle – resonance, as if a chord has been struck. In this instant, we are being contacted by another life energy.

This is the "external" version of cultivating subtle energetic soul pulses discussed in Stage 9; as we learned there, it is essential that we not push to create something. We allow ourselves plenty of space and time. When we feel the touch of something – a tug, a hello, or "look over here" – we stop. It might be a shape, a sound, a vibration, intuition, or a feeling. We look, really look, and tap into sensory awareness so that we can open to and allow ourselves to be with whatever has called us. We might listen, smell, or feel the sensations on our skin. Subtle vibrations require subtle sensitivities.

For example, let's say a large web with a spider enthroned at its center catches our attention. We allow ourselves to stop and stare. We look, without filters or expectations, and see what is there. We sense any small impulse in the moment of first contact. We take in all the sensory information before us. We stay out of our minds and allow the perceptual field of our heart to open.

The "perceptual field of our heart" may be an unfamiliar concept, so let me explain what I mean through a quick exercise:

In your mind's eye, imagine that you have asked a friend to stand 12 feet away from you and remain in place. Then imagine yourself beginning to walk toward your friend. At some point you will experience a palpable "feeling" that you have entered your friend's personal, or energetic, space, which extends beyond the space that your friend's physical body occupies. In similar fashion, the person standing still also "feels" you entering his or her space. The first time we do this exercise in my workshops on undefended love, this feeling usually arises when the person walking gets within 1 foot of the person standing still. As we successively repeat the practice, people become more attuned to the borders of each other's personal space and begin sensing the contact at greater and greater distances from each other's actual physical positions.

The point when we feel each other's space is the point when the perceptual fields of our hearts touch.

In the practice I am describing here, of feeling the relationship with another by using the example of the spider, we are opening our heart's perceptual field to be sensitive and receptive to the world around us by walking with alertness for something to catch our attention. (The truth is, even if our heart field is closed, the power of another being's presence can shake us awake and we will notice – especially when in the presence of something essentially moving like a newborn, a harvest moon, or an act of kindness.) Once we feel the spider's energetic "hello," we consciously open to sensing that hello. That opens us to the spider's heart field.

Returning to the example of meeting a spider in her web, having made initial contact, we might visualize ourselves "reach out," as if our heart had hands and fingers, toward the life force underlying the appearance and form of the spider (or whatever has drawn our attention). This reaching out is not aggressive, as in grabbing, nor is it probing; rather, it is a *receptive, curious,* and *respectful* moving toward another being as a subtle expression of our seeking to contact and know that being's life force.

As we open to the meeting of our perceptual field and that of the spider's, we ask ourselves, *how does it feel?* Not what do we think, but *how does it feel to be in the presence of this spider in her web in this moment in time?* We surrender to the direct experience, paying attention to what *is*. We have to avoid using this moment to look at what is in our minds. This moment is a sacred moment of contact between us as an individual and another inhabited life form, the spider, who has called to us. If we were standing before a bull elephant with no barrier between us and him, we'd be on full alert; we offer the same respect to life's tiniest creatures as we would to one of life's largest, but, here, we are not anticipating any particular thing to happen next. We are simply taking in the spider's energetic presence and extending ourselves to meet it. If a revelation arises, that is fine as long as it deepens the intimacy of the moment.

E. E. Cummings wrote, "...whenever you think or you believe or you know, you're a lot of people: but the moment you feel, you're nobody-but-yourself." The meeting with the spider is one self's personal soul reaching for another's, and through this meeting, both parties touch their shared life force.

In this brief moment in time as we surrender to the direct experience of whatever we are called by, a feeling quality might flood or seep into our awareness. We might experience this as a small shock of understanding or a singular moment of insight. The unique feeling tone we are experiencing lies below the appearance of the spider in its web, bringing us in contact with the consciousness animating the spider and web. We are on the threshold of the ensouled or inner life of this living being. *By reaching out with our non-physical being toward the spider in its web, we are reaching out to its life force, the animating source of love and vitality that underlies the spider's form, our form, and all forms.* By making contact with the animating vitality that lies within the form of the spider, we are making contact with the oneness that unites all creation.

When the energy of the encounter subsides, we continue our aimless walk until our attention is drawn to something else. Perhaps this time we notice an old tree. We look, really look. We sense the tree; we take it in with all of our senses – sound, touch, smell, taste, and feeling. The sensuous realms offer us the opportunity to open up fully to a given moment.

As our senses open, we ask: "*How does it feel?*" To be precise, the question here is not exactly about how *we* feel although that is a good starting place. It is more accurately, *how does the energy between my self and the tree feel?* How does the *relationship* feel?

Once again we might notice a vibe, a feeling, a mood, a quality that is different from the one we experienced in the presence of the spider. Often a current of meaning will follow. We allow the new feelings, sensations, tone, or quality of experience to bring us to the invisible connection below the outer appearances. Faint but perceptible stirrings of soul will emerge as we touch the aliveness of what has called our attention and touched our heart. We try to remain open until *saturation* occurs. Saturation does not mean *making meaning*; it means *being with something to the point at which no more can be absorbed or added.*

For example, if you are a woodcarver and have a block of wood, you could carve anything out of it with a few good tools. We do this all the time; we bend things to our will when we create meaning out of reality. But when we bend life to our will, it lacks something. Despite our mechanical skill, the final piece does not feel alive.

A woodcarver who is a true artist studies the shape, grain, and texture of the chunk of wood. He or she listens to the material and opens up to moment after moment of shared feeling, all the while asking what that wood wants to be. And then he or she carves that. The wood is still carved, but what comes out is drenched in life force; the artist helped the raw material to realize itself.

All of us are the artisans of our own lives, and the final creation results from the accumulation of moments. When we are saturated – when we no longer make meaning or figure things out but instead relate in a way that draws out the truth or beauty of what is there and sculpt that – then we are alive in life.

Returning to the practice I have just described, if we notice nothing on our first walk, we set a date for another walk. We need to give the practice – and ourselves – time. If we find we are having difficulty with this practice, and if we live or can visit someplace where we can safely walk outside at dusk, dawn, or in the middle of the night under moonlight, we can try the practice then. At these more mystical times, appearance and form are less obstructive, which might make it easier to sense the contact with another life energy.

In *The Pure Soul Mantra*, Rabbi David Cooper writes about Judaism's idea of the soul: "it is not a little character that has a separate identity within us. Rather, the soul is related to the mystical appreciation that every created thing is embodied with its source in some special way. A rock, a grain of sand, a molecule of water, an ant, a spider, a leaf – each is imbued with various levels of a soul force." And, in the largest sense, Cooper says, the soul in Judaism is "a mystical foundation out of which all of creation and all of life unfold."

Soul-Making

When love contacts ignite, a new life and love is born out of the rapport between the two lovers; this third thing is something greater than the parts and has a life of its own. It is formed by the relationship between the two, but it has its own living essence. This third presence can feel ancient, as though it is deeply rooted in the universe.

A love connection, as we've seen, can be with plants, trees, a wall hanging, or our deeper selves. It can also be with a language, like the Irish language is for a close friend of mine. It can happen in relationship to a teacher, as it did with a former client who discovered her guru and followed him to India. It can take place with a creative form, as it has with several clients whose self-petals unfolded in sympathetic resonance to jazz, salsa, and soulful poetry. It can happen with animals, as was the case for one client with salmon and another with raptors. It can ignite in relationship to water, as a client discovered when she took a series of swimming classes to overcome her fear of water and fell in love with the essence of water as a living being.

The key characteristic is that form and appearance – ours and that of the being or thing we love – become mutual portals to the soul-centers within each of us. We pass through this doorway over and over again, mostly oblivious to the threshold and more in touch with the communication occurring from sacred core to sacred core.

The act of deeply relating to something creates a field. The act of bringing love to that field, through caring about the relationship, builds soul. Soul allows us to contact the part of our natures that is constantly creative and uniquely alive in the face of experience. Soul creates newness, freshness, and vitality. We long for soul because that is where the life force is, and it is deeply imprinted in our natures to long for life itself.

Soul-making is about our active relationship with life and takes place whenever a connection is alive and matters to us. Although we might not understand it, as Adam and Grace did not fully understand their experiences of vital connection, we know it is meaningful. The way we can tell that we are on the soul-making track is that there is energy present. It is hot. It is all about the encounter and what it means to be open in the encounter because the soul is always inviting us to open more deeply to the relatedness, the contact, the connection, and the love that exists in our beings. By attending to and following our attractions, the energy present, or the pulse, we are being organized by love into vehicles of soul expression. And, at the same time, although we feel the blessing of love and soul when we experience them, it is also true that, for the many reasons we encounter every day and throughout our lives, being open, connected, and available in the present moment is challenging for all of us.

Despite the challenges of making soul connections, we are at this point in our midlife journeys feeling lighter, more joyful, more content, more grateful, more soulful, and even enraptured with the great blessing of being alive. We are learning that love is a force that ushers us into the infinite realm, not disturbingly as we may have experienced when our spirit doors opened, but in a way that exposes us to the infinite holding environment within which we are supported in every step. This awareness and the hidden blessings we have uncovered during our journeys so far give us the strength and capacity to reckon with increasingly complex concerns when we encounter them, to be undone by them and renewed in the wake of that undoing. The positive changes we have seen so far in our journeys are reminders of the power of engaging with experiences that undo us as we cycle repeatedly through all the stages being described in this book, from unraveling to feeling the pulse of love and beyond as we will see in Stage 12.

As we cooperate with the process of being recycled in this way, we learn over and over the power of love's alchemy, which takes place in our souls. That power conducts us to an inner secret whose freshness is constantly being renewed: *that we were born within an unbroken wholeness, have always been part of that oneness and can never be separate from that.* In the next and final stage we will explore the transformation from the local heart of our soul into the shared heart of the world.

Becoming
Revolutionary

༖

From my vantage point, the midlife journey is as much about fully inhabiting our vulnerable humanness as it is about awakening and embodying divinity in human form. On the personal, physical level, we cannot help feeling vulnerable, open as we are to pain, sorrow, and death. But at the level of the divine, immortal essence that animates us – our soul-fullness – we are endlessly durable.

If we try to deny our vulnerability, we lose touch with our tender heart. If we forfeit awareness of our divine essence, we are deprived of the knowledge that we share our nature with all of life. *At midlife we are being stretched, prodded, pummeled, coaxed, guided, and loved into an awareness of the full spectrum of ourselves and our place in the larger network of life.* This awareness is, perhaps, the ultimate hidden blessing of the midlife journey.

To bring us to this ripening awareness, the events of midlife have been urging us to *enliven all of the levels of our beings*: to know ourselves both on the visible, divisible planes of existence – the physical, emotional, and mental – and on the formless, invisible plane where we are connected to all of life. The soul's emergence from the chrysalis of ego during midlife enables us to express the divine within our unique, personal, finite, physical existence. And, as we've learned, the soul is the energetic force that integrates and synthesizes all planes of existence into one by means of its essential quality, love.

The more open we are to the soul's vantage point and the magnetism of its binding force, love, the more we identify with all of life and lose our egocentric fixation on self-preservation and separation, my well-being over your well-being, "what I am" versus "what I am not." Living more and more of the time with an open, inclusive identity center, we recognize parts of ourselves in all forms of life until our expanding consciousness overspills the concept of individuality. Even as we still have the ability to experience things in a very personal and embodied way, our consciousness increasingly rests in the awareness of the inseparability of all life. In more colloquial terms, our consciousness is centered globally – in our shared soul-essence – while capable of acting locally as unique beings.

A New Natural Order

We begin our exploration of Stage 12 by looking at three characteristics that I have observed are widely shared during the final stage of midlife. These elements – right alignment, right placement, and right element – can be thought of as the spokes of a wheel with our new, intent focus on the soul and its guidance at the hub. As we continue to experience the internal and external pressures of life's complex interactions, these spokes will constantly be aligned and realigned, just as a bicycle wheel's spokes must be trued for the wheel to continue traveling over new ground. In the truing process, we lose and re-establish balance over and over, creating a new, evolving natural order that carries us into and through our second adult life.

Right Alignment

By Stage 12, most of us are becoming increasingly aware that the energetic current of our life is shifting. At the outer level, we might experience this as a decrease in physical, emotional, and intellectual energy. On the inner level, we might experience this as an uprush of energy in the form of intuitions, knowings, dreams, synchronicities, feelings of gratitude, and other more subtle energetic movements.

In response, we begin to shift naturally away from raw strength and athleticism toward soul-based stamina and perseverance. Rather than being stimulated by an adrenaline rush of conquest or challenge, we are increasingly interested in feeling deeply touched and connected. Sensing that the next chapters of our lives will thrive with less outer stimulation and activity, many of us seek longer periods of silence and solitude (I am speaking in generalities here; each individual will experience the later phases of the midlife journey in a unique way).

In response, we might begin to consciously "time" our activities, leaving space to recover between outlays of energy, and guarding our physical expenditures so that we build up energy reserves to be used in ways that are in alignment with what matters most to us. Yesterday, an author friend mentioned a symposium in Europe scheduled for the fall. He said, "At an earlier time in my life, a conference in Europe would have been an exciting prospect for new experiences; but now, I don't want to miss my walks in the woods near my home as the season changes and the colorful displays of fall foliage explode."

After speaking with him, I realized that at this stage of midlife we are finding the intersection point between the effort of this life and the Tao, which is the natural, effortless flow of the river of life. We are seeking to align ourselves with life's flow rather than trying to "push the river."

Self-Inquiry

In what ways are you more consciously adjusting and allocating your life force – your energy, time, and resources – in *right alignment* with what matters most to you?

When we live in harmony with the laws of nature, as appropriate to our life stage, we replace willfulness with willingness, and a lot gets done that way, which our egos would not have believed or expected earlier in our lives. At this point in our journeys, stillness and open receptivity to our natural capacity to feel and follow the thread or pulse of what is alive and right for us guide us in knowing when and how to act. When we feel we have lost our sense of right alignment, we return to truing our wheels, checking whether we are aligned with what matters most so that we roll more effortlessly over the ground, including the potholes and barriers, before us. At first this is an intentional practice; over time it becomes second nature, like sensing and responding to the water and air currents while wind-surfing.

Right Placement

At the same time that we are learning to move in right alignment with what matters most, we begin to position ourselves strategically so that our contributions have maximum impact. In characteristically colorful terms, David Whyte tells a story illustrating what it might look like to position ourselves so that we deploy our energy strategically and most effectively.

Whyte describes an old sheepdog, one of the best in Northern Wales. This elder collie had lost an ear, was blind in one eye, and walked with a pronounced limp, evidence that he had lived a full life.

Whyte contrasts this senior citizen with the younger collies racing up one side of the hill and down another in dramatic arcs, enthusiastically moving sheep from one field to the next. The sheer force of their youthful, boundless enthusiasm sounds joyful to witness.

However, when the shepherd could not get the young collies to move the sheep where he needed them to go, he would summon the old dog. When called, this seasoned collie would walk purposefully to a strategic position and, with an economy of movement, would get the entire flock to go precisely through a gap in a wall or into a holding pen.

Whyte says about this master sheepdog, "He had an astonishing ability to place himself at exactly the pivotal fulcrum that would move this living body of sheep in whichever direction he wanted." Whyte identified this fulcrum as the place of greatest leverage. He goes on to say, "As we get older we become fiercer and more concentrated around the fulcrum on which our lives turn."

I work with a large number of men and women who, toward the end of their midlife transitions, find themselves "competing" with younger co-workers and associates. These clients feel disheartened and demoralized, afraid they will lose their jobs because they cannot keep up, or they feel troubled by an old fear of being ostracized by younger members of their clubs and social groups who are interested in topics and activities that my clients find less compelling.

I tell them the story of the old sheepdog. I suggest that perhaps they should no longer expect themselves to churn out large volumes of work or take the lead in day-to-day activities. More likely, their role now is to come in at just the right time – to position themselves with economy – and give the critical input that will guide a project in the optimal direction. If they try to compete on the basis of energy (physical, emotional, or intellectual), chances are they will not contribute as they wish to, nor will they feel the satisfaction that comes from being in the right place at the right time, not by chance but by design.

Life experience produces the focus and durability needed to meet challenges. Recall the opening story of the fishing nets in Stage 1: the mother dolphins reassure the frantic baby dolphins *with their presence and companionship*. At this stage, we are the ones who now know how to jump in and out of the nets and how to reassure those around us with our presence, wisdom, experience, and love.

When allocating energy for projects, social groups, families, or ourselves, we can position ourselves consciously. Our guiding focus – our wheel's hub – is the soul with its inclination toward the things that call to us with vibrant life energy.

By this point in our journeys, we have likely developed more humility and less hubris. In place of youth's naïve expectations that things will turn out as we wish or envision, we have learned to expect the unexpected. We know that instability is indispensable for our continued growth and expansion of consciousness, and we have learned to use the gift of instability to make the constant adjustments necessary to keep our wheels aligned.

We have come to understand the precariousness of our situation – that outcomes might not be comfortable – and that the key is to dwell in the position that belongs to us and no one else. This position is our humble throne, a simple seat that is naturally ours, which we attain independent of our outer accomplishments.

Like Frodo in Tolkien's *Fellowship of the Ring*, from this position we see what must be done, and, if it falls to us to do it, so be it. "I will take the Ring, though I do not know the way," Frodo says with utmost humility. The largest task in Tolkien's trilogy falls to its seemingly smallest member. By now we know we might end up on paths we did not consciously choose, with burdens that feel like too much to bear, yet we move forward one step at a time. Like Frodo, we step into the larger journeys that are ours to walk as we move forward into life after midlife. Our assignment is to become who the gods intended us to be, in the face of – and assisted by – the obstacles they have placed in our paths.

Self-Inquiry

Where in your life might you be better *placed for greater effect*? Like Frodo, what is your task to bear now? Can you more consciously position yourself in relationship to this task?

Right Element

Truing our wheels by aligning with what matters most and positioning ourselves for greatest effect, we naturally begin to notice, or long for, an experience of being in the right element for us. For ducks, the right element is water, and for other birds the sky. When we are in our right element it means that the context or environment that we are in fits or complements us in some deep way.

Years ago I frequented events held at the local Scottish Rite Center, an enormous, unique structure boasting grand staircases, opulent furnishings, and a hand-carved ceiling. It is a popular venue for weddings, musical performances, theatre, seminars, etc. However, the parts of the building not showcased are old, tired, and gloomy.

In one of the darkened corners of this historic building was an old-fashioned elevator, complete with a brass-plated elevator cage and a throw-back from times long forgotten: a full-time elevator operator. An African-American man, perhaps in his early 60s, lived much of his week in this dimly lit box, shuttling people from the basement to the upper floors and back. Although his attire was as old and tired as the part of the building where the elevator was located, his uniform was pressed to perfection, and his shoes polished until they shone like black volcanic glass. His gloves, which were the kind of eggshell white that comes from too many washings, put the finishing touches on his time-out-of-time outfit.

This man's smile was extraordinary. He had the twinkling eyes of someone always on the edge of falling into a warm memory. His kindness and interest made this otherwise dark and dreary elevator a bright, magical place. He instinctively knew when to say something, when not to, and what to say to make each visitor feel welcome. As unlikely a place as it might seem, the elevator was this man's element.

Just like any plant or animal, we need to navigate toward environments where we truly belong. To arrive where we belong, we might have to surrender our prejudices that make one activity or place better or more important than another. If our assignment during this lifetime is to be a spiritual teacher, this is not a better or more important role than the one filled by the elevator operator at the Scottish Rite Center. If what we love is building ships in bottles, that is no better or worse than volunteering at the local hospice.

When we are in our element, we feel it like the rightness of an eagle soaring, dolphins breaching the surf, or a caravan of camels traversing sand dunes in a long line, nose to tail. It's as if a round peg found its round hole, and everything is just right with the world. We enhance the element, and it enhances us.

The title of one of Alice Walker's books tells us, *Horses Make a Landscape More Beautiful.* And they do. What is equally true is that the landscape makes horses more beautiful. In the same way that a diamond is best displayed on a black velvet cloth, the bright light of the elevator operator was best placed in the darkened space of that elevator; they belonged together.

This is not to say that we will be without conflict when we are in our elements. We might still struggle because being there can demand a great deal of us. Many reading this passage have probably seen the famous movie *The March of the Penguins*, which documents the migration and mating patterns of penguins, in which the challenge and suffering are extreme.

Writers face a blank page, painters a blank canvas, and musicians a blank score. But if the activity feels like an immensely satisfying and meaningful way to spend a life, we choose it despite its challenges. When we are in our element, we feel the presence of soul. It's not unlike when we fall in love; or are in the zone; or sing a high C without fear, effort, or restraint. These are the places where our hearts, feelings, thoughts, and senses are moved in ways that take us outside ourselves into the joyful and seamless flow of life, and we feel a part of something larger than us. We are actually contained in that larger presence rather than the other way around, just as a bird flies through the air, the moon hangs in space, or we feel immersed in love during the opening phase of a powerful connection.

To know our element, we must know what we love. Rumi writes, "This is a subtle truth: Whatever you love, you are." Knowing what we love tells us who we are; living in that love places us in our elements, the fields where we come to life.

Self-Inquiry

* What locations or spaces bring you alive?

* What conversations awaken you?

* Who do you feel intimate with, in a soulful way?

* What are the activities that move you more deeply into yourself?

* What are you compelled to do just for the love of it?

Exploring these answers to the self-inquiry questions above brings us closer to our element, and we become more *elemental*, more essential, and more truly the self we were born to be.

A Calling Forth

One thing that can impede developing these three qualities of our new natural order – right alignment, placement, and element – is the persecuting thought that we have to wait for or find a "calling." We cannot move forward on our path of understanding and expressing our core natures – both the vulnerable, warm animal-body, human side and the eternal, mystery-infused, divine side – if we become fixated on what we perceive to be a lack of a calling.

Perhaps many of us don't hear the universe calling to us because a calling is often conceptualized as a monologue, as god or some other powerful force beckoning to or directing us. Those of us longing for a calling need only notice that we are being called *all the time*. Far from a dearth of possibility, there is a din of invitation. We are being called through the failure of our expectations, when relationships come together and fall apart, when a deer unexpectedly darts in front of our cars, when a familiar song or the sight of a dog or a brand of chewing gum brings us back to another time and place, and every time we feel interrupted whether in a small or large way.

We are being called when we fall in love, when we hear a sermon that feels as if it was written specifically for us, and when we read a poem that makes time stand still. We are called when our partner shows up for dinner in that same irritating way he showed up for breakfast and when we feel the sense of defeat that he will probably show up in that same way tomorrow. We are called when our tennis racket's sweet spot is blessed with the ball in a perfect, momentary meeting. We are called when we have a heart attack.

We are called through sneaking suspicions, through gut reactions, and the narratives that keep repeating in our minds. We are called when we walk without forethought to a certain aisle in a bookstore or perk up when a familiar theme is heard in a song. We are called when we feel drawn to pick up a cute kitten or repulsed by vultures eating the body of a dead dog.

When we see through the lens that our human lives are sacred journeys of the soul, everything is a calling. However, until there is a response – *from us* – we cannot have the dialogue that is necessary for our callings to unfold and move us along our paths.

Even though we are called to our personal journeys each and every moment of each and every day, many of us miss the call because it does not come in an archetypal form or the form in which we expect it. We compare ourselves to famous people, who appear to have been called to larger-than-life missions or achievements, or to individuals who appear passionate about their paths and sense of purpose in a way we feel we lack.

The truth is, we are all called to be in conversation with ourselves and the world in our own unique ways. Feeling professionally stifled can be a calling, as can insomnia, chronic anxiety, depression, illness, divorce, weight gain, or addiction. But when these kinds of callings beckon to us, most of us quickly mumble "wrong number" and hang up the phone. As my client whose call came in the form of bankruptcy said, "I'm waiting for a better offer."

Because we do not recognize the call, we go at things backwards. We try to think up a calling and then complain when we don't feel the energy, inspiration, support, and desire to fulfill it. Then we return to waiting for our call, all the while missing the conversations that are beckoning to us.

Our invitations to dialogue can be identified by paying attention to whatever solicits, captures, or commands our attention. We can find conversations that are calling to us by noticing the themes in the songs we listen to, the novels we read, the articles that attract our attention, the movies we watch, and the books we are drawn to. What are the themes that touch and move us? Do they have to do with overcoming adversity? loss? betrayal? love? fairness and justice? health? ethics? technology? making money? spiritual understandings?

Self-Inquiry

Can you identify something that is calling to you – an interaction you had with someone that is stuck in your head, a series of repeated occurrences or images, a theme that weaves through the books and movies you are drawn to? Spend a few minutes writing about the details – what you remember, what you felt, what the experience evoked – and see whether anything emerges that feels compelling, a thread you might want to follow further.

Seen from the largest perspective, when we work with the midlife passage in the ways that this book describes, that passage is, itself, a long conversation of the kind I am talking about. As we have been examining the specifics of the structure and unfolding of our human souls within the midlife framework, each of us has been engaged in conversations specific to us. Perhaps we have been having a conversation about relinquishing ideals or our habit to idealize, or about becoming less attached or learning to bond, or about using truth as a path to our deeper selves, or about the struggle to regain one's voice, sobriety, humility, or innocence. No matter what the topic, we all have deep conversations going on all the time, whether we are conscious of them or not.

We can be who we are consciously or unconsciously. To live consciously, we must converse with ourselves as well as with that which lies beyond our understanding. If the conversation evolves into a visible calling, that is fine. Those who are truly called know that they are in a lifelong conversation and have no need to dramatize or inflate their roles or their journeys.

We need not judge the conversations that are ours, or find them lacking in comparison to the heroic conversations we might have admired or aspired to in the past – the conversations we imagine belong to the impassioned few whose callings have grand stature in our eyes, such as helping the poor, making millions from investments, winning Academy Awards, or saving forests from being decimated. All conversations do not look the same. Some of us have, as our conversation, to be quiet, to garden, to be kind to our neighbors. Some of us will be called to a long nap, or exploring the Zen of golf, or the dreaded role of being the one lost in the desert for a very long time. Some, like Joan of Arc, are given their conversations verbally while others have to seek out the conversation through a variety of intuited or symbolic channels.

Our personal conversation might lack pizzazz in our eyes, but if it is truly the dialogue that belongs to us, then only we can have it. In the moment of owning and engaging with our life as it is, not as our minds wish it would be, we find ourselves dropping into the new natural order again: right alignment, placement, and element. From this soul-centered position, we evolve.

Invitation to a Larger Matrix

At the same time that we are settling into our deeply human place in a new natural order – and using the thread of conversations and callings to stitch closed the gaps between us and all of life – we are also discovering our place within the collective heartbeat, the group soul.

Below is the map of the relationship between the ego, the personal soul, and the group soul that I introduced in Stage 8. It reads from the bottom up:

4 GROUP SOUL

⬆

3 PERSONAL SOUL

⬆

2 INTEGRATED EGO

⬆

1 UNITEGRATED EGO

As you can see, *group soul* is the highest level of consciousness gained during our midlife transition years and, at best, it is usually only glimpsed. Our inner work in the second half of our adult life may become about embodying this realization.

My own awareness of group soul was ignited through an astonishing love story with honeybees, which is why I include my story here, instead of with Adam's astonishing love story in Stage 11. Similar to the story of Grace, whose engagement with her wall hanging lasted throughout her midlife period, my story also had threads that wove throughout my midlife passage. However, here I pick up the story toward the end, when a swarm of bees was installed in its hive on my property, so that I can focus on the epiphany that came to me on that special day.

Without any protective clothing, I sat inside a swirling mass of honeybees, listening to an ancient medley of sound I had never heard before. Thousands of bees filled the air around me while many more crawled along my bare arms and legs, and, very much to my surprise, I felt no fear. That afternoon I had one of the most astonishing and magical experiences of my life as *I fell in love with 10,000 stinging insects.*

To be allowed to be with the colony as the bees were settling into their new nest was honor and blessing enough, but even more amazing was when the experience changed, and I was no longer surrounded by them but felt as though I was *inside* the colony. I felt like one of them, and I felt them – their hum – inside of me. I experienced myself spontaneously overflowing what had previously felt like the solid boundaries of my physical form. It felt like they enveloped me, took me into themselves, and liquid sunshine – love – was pouring into every cell of my being. It was extraordinarily intimate.

I felt an overwhelming desire to know the honeybees, not in the abstract as a thought or concept, but deeply, soul to soul. My life force rose up to meet their life force, and *I felt the colony as one whole – one consciousness – made up of thousands of parts.*

Later I learned that others have arrived at a similar insight about bees, but, in that glorious moment, it felt as though an invisible gate to an invisible kingdom opened, and I walked through, much like Grace walked into and through the arms of her wall hanging in her dream. My consciousness permanently shifted, and the concept of group soul came to life inside of me.

In the 19th century, German beekeeper Johannes Mehring realized that *a colony of bees is one organism with a unified consciousness, one animal consisting of many bodies*. That is, the colony is an indivisible whole, a single integrated living being made up of all the individual bees who live in it. The old German word *bien* (pronounced "bean" as in "lima bean") refers to this sense of one being in countless bodies. A bee colony is both a society of thousands of individuals and a single super-organism; in a colony, the individual and the group consciousness merge and depend upon each other.

Our logical mind can find it very difficult at first to grasp the idea of inter-mixed individual and group consciousness. It took a while, after my initial epiphany, for the information to sink in that *the bee colony is a living example of one consciousness that has many bodies capable of moving around independently*. And, even beyond that, my consciousness had to really stretch to recognize that *each individual bee shares and has operating within it a piece of the colony's single unified consciousness*.

When I experienced the colony as a single consciousness composed of thousands of individuals, I realized that the honeybee colony has evolved to live what we are reaching for in Stage 12 of midlife. By the swarm's grace I was inducted, briefly, into *full-spectrum consciousness that spans from individual to group.* I realized that my personal soul, which operates within me as an individual, is connected to all of life, a cell in a larger cosmic order.

Adi Shankara, a well-known Hindu philosopher, teaches similarly that each of our souls contains a piece of god, life, or universal consciousness, and, at the same time, we are also contained within that larger divinity. That is, we are cells in the body of god, life, or universal consciousness. What is it like when this idea that we are contained within god, life, or universal consciousness becomes a perceptual reality? It can feel like a slow tide rising, like a whale emerging from shadowy depths and submerging back into the darkness, weaving a watery line between two previously unconnected worlds: boundlessness and individuality (like the phrase that came to me in a dream, of the soul as *a boundless singularity*).

Self-Inquiry

What if you knew that you are an individual cell within a larger body of consciousness, capable of operating independently but at the same time intricately part of something larger? How would that feel? If you believed this, how would you belong to this world differently?

With this realization we glimpse the reality of the group soul. We develop what paleontologist and philosopher Teilhard de Chardin calls our "collective eyes." Spiritual teacher Thich Nhat Hahn expresses his understanding of group or collective soul when he writes, "It is possible that the next Buddha will not take the form of an individual. The next Buddha may take the form of a community, a community practicing understanding and loving kindness, a community practicing mindful living."

The more we abide in this realization, the more we understand what is meant in the Bible by the phrase, *"the one in whom we move and have our being."* The Golden Rule, *do unto others what you would have them do unto you*, takes on a special meaning when we realize that *we are all one*.

As we stretch to embrace more and more of the continuum of what it means to be fully human, from the personal to the divine, we toggle between two states of consciousness that could be called "local" and "universal." The local is the great tenderness that resides at the core of our individual humanity, and the universal is the expanded state of "hive" consciousness that I met as I sat among the bees. We become aware that our individual humanness is a "localized wholeness" within the wholeness of all creation. Said in another way, *when we tenderly touch life from our individual mortal selves, we grow into our immortal, boundless natures.*

In the doorway between form and formlessness, if we are open, we can be instructed from many planes of existence; the bees just happened to be the teachers that chose me. Amazingly enough, as I listen to clients who are near the end of their midlife passages, their experience is very much the same even though their teachers are different and the ways they speak about their changes are infinite in variety. These clients are more relaxed, loving, humble, innocent, gentle, and open than before. It is as if a lifelong burden has been metabolized or put down at last.

One of my clients had a midlife passage that included one of the most grueling recovery processes I have seen (from a pornography addiction). For his 65th birthday, he went to the desert to celebrate what he felt was the beginning of a new life for himself. As he lay on his back in the middle of the night, the moonless sky particularly dark, he directly experienced himself as lying on a chunk of Earth floating in a universe of unimaginable size.

He went on to share the ways in which he felt so small in the universe yet so deeply a part of it as he lay on his small fragment of matter in a cosmos filled with other fragments of matter, like ice floes in an eternity of space. "At the intersection of the majestic and the miniscule, I felt a part of everything, no part of me left out." This came from a man who had, before now, always felt like the odd man out and never felt himself belonging to anything, let alone everything.

The ability to be absorbed into a larger body of consciousness – even for a moment or an hour – where we are united in purpose with no barriers between us and any other member of the group or life, is an evolutionary leap. Most of us take that leap gradually. It requires that we let go of our individualized agendas, plans, attitudes, and points of view at times. We can let these go as we would let go of a burden. It is a welcome gesture.

At first some of us will notice this movement toward group consciousness when we cultivate relationships with other individuals or groups of people who are sharing our evolving perspectives and insights. This book on midlife is an example. When you purchased the book, some part of you responded to and followed its keynote. By delving into and cultivating relationships with those resonating to the same vibration, you are participating in the creation of new worlds that begin with the new thought forms based in the expanded states of consciousness that we have been exploring. These new thought forms, in turn, produce a magnetic energy that attracts others to us, and us to others of like heart and mind, like steel shavings drawn to a magnet.

We must aim for a wide-open simplicity that is capable of registering new vibrations that lead to new truths. The more we are open to the full spectrum of experience, from the mundane to the sublime, the more our unique beings evolve into living expressions of the divine. It is only when we are open that we can be available for the revelation of more evolved states of consciousness, ultimately moving toward a state of shared consciousness, as is the lived experience of the honeybees.

A cautionary note: the developmental stage being discussed here is not a given and not a landing place; the gravitational pull toward expanded awareness waxes and wanes unless we bring a level of discipline and dedication to this path. At this stage in our journeys, we are being invited to commit to what spiritual teacher Cynthia Bourgeault calls a "participative knowing based on continuously renewed immediacy, not receding memory of the Divine Touch." In other words, unlike episodic epiphanies that are transitory in nature, the more long-lasting change in awareness being discussed here requires commitment, devotion, and effort to become a sustainable reality.

The Soul's Aperture Setting

In addition to right alignment, placement, and element discussed earlier, there is a fourth characteristic of our soul's natural order that appears to fall into place naturally for most of us in this final leg of the midlife transformation: a shift to taking a longer view of one's life. In my work with clients, I call this longer view the "soul's aperture setting." What would it be like if we experienced this entire lifetime as the equivalent of what we would do in one day, so that what we will do tomorrow, after this lifetime, remains totally unknown?

One life is but a short moment in the long cycle of the soul.
—Alice Bailey

For example, a mountain just sits there for centuries and centuries and maybe erodes a little bit but not a lot. From the viewpoint of a human lifespan, the mountain stays the same. But, from the perspective of the galaxy, a mountain such as Mount Everest looks fluid, a flow of a mountain coming into being and going out of being, a ripple on the surface of the water. How we view everything depends on the width of our aperture setting or the time scale over which we are viewing life. At a wide aperture setting, we see that things are constantly flowing and changing, coming into visible reality and moving out of visible reality. The Buddhists say: life is continuously arising and continuously being destroyed.

When we are in our boundless natures, or our perceptual fields are opened wider than usual (for example, with the help of deep meditation practices or entheogenic medicine), we enter into a much larger field where things that might normally appear static, dense, or deterministic instead appear fluid. One possibility in expanded states of awareness is to occupy a very large field in which lifetimes, or whole states of being or incarnations, come and go. Which, in fact, they do. We just mostly don't live at the scale where this is apparent to us. We have a thought that lasts for a few minutes and then it shifts. Entire lifetimes are like that for the soul – waves of perspective that occur at very fast speeds. And if the quantum physicists are right, consciousness itself is not determined. It has the capacity to occupy any scale. It is the ultimate field in which all of life is happening. Consciousness is a waveform filled with all possibilities all the time.

If we see ourselves as part of an evolutionary wave unfolding over millions of years, many of us experience relief from the chronic pressure to be someone, get somewhere, and do something. We can feel more interest in the larger picture, at least our entire lifetime, and less distress from an immediate, disturbing experience.

Self-Inquiry

If this lifetime were a single day in your soul's lifetime, would today's challenges be less disheartening and more interesting? Pick a current struggle and explore it from this perspective.

With this expanded view, we can explore whether and how we might pace ourselves differently going forward. Where might we place ourselves for best advantage? Would our chosen locations shift in some way? Where would this wide-angle perspective lead us? What new natural order will organically unfold in response to our expanding consciousness at this stage of our lives?

A postulate from esoteric philosophy might help us open our aperture settings. Consider this passage from Alice Bailey's *Esoteric Psychology* about what happens when we recognize the Law of Rebirth (reincarnation):

"All souls incarnate and re-incarnate…. Hence each life is not only a recapitulation of life experience, but an assuming of ancient obligations, a recovery of old relations, an opportunity for the paying of old indebtedness, a chance to make restitution and progress, an awaking of deep-seated qualities, the recognition of old friends and enemies, the solution of revolting injustices, and the explanation of that which conditions the man (woman) and makes him (her) what he (she) is."

This passage always gives me chills. The possibilities for connection, restitution, and evolution are infinite when we view our lives from this aperture setting. From this vantage point, it is difficult to blame anyone for anything because we have, at one time or another, been everyone and done everything. Loss, too, would be an out-of-date concept. (Although we do not make loss obsolete; we allow ourselves to remain deeply personal even as we widen our settings and allow all of life to pour in.)

In Closing

If you have read this far, you have journeyed through human limitation, fixation, and unconscious orientations, into incomprehensible but compelling realms on the way to embodying your humanity and your divinity as fully as possible.

The story of life is progress, but not in the way that the ego tells us during the first half of our lives. Now we recognize progress as *becoming, a perpetual and cyclic emergence of the new.* The human life story – and especially the midlife story – is the story of metamorphosis, the long and often painstaking creation of a vehicle through which our souls, when they emerge from the chrysalis of the ego, can express themselves in the visible world.

The metamorphosis that takes place in the individual going through his or her midlife journey is intertwined with the larger process of evolution. Both metamorphosis and evolution are processes of the building up and tearing down of form. In midlife, our individual egos and our bodies are transformed. Evolution transforms all of life. *The aim of evolution is the creation of increasingly more expansive and inclusive forms that are capable of embodying the vastness of the expanding universe itself.*

Having made the midlife crossing, at least as far as we could travel in the course of reading the material presented here, we are in the process of discovering the vast blessing of a new kind of immortality that is not based on a material legacy but on the depth and reality of what we live. As Martha Graham has written, "If you think about it seriously, all the questions about the soul and the immortality of the soul and paradise and hell are at the bottom only a way of seeing this very simple fact: that every action of ours is passed on to others according to its value, of good or evil; it passes from father to son, from one generation to the next, in perpetual movement." In other words, our immortality comes from the lived reality of who we touch, what we give, how fully we take on the challenge of being ourselves, and how deeply we enter into the dialogues and relationships that are ours to have.

The cycle of transformation we have learned in this book guides us through the stages of development necessary to become active participants in life. We have begun learning to extend our personal awareness beyond surface realities, and beyond where society and our conditioning tell us we can go, until every fiber of our being feels the pulsing and breathing weave of life. When we touch the interconnected web of life, we know ourselves as intimately woven within the cycles of the visible natural world – the revolutions of the days, the seasons, and the planets – as well as the mysteries of the invisible world. *We become citizens not only of this world but of all worlds and dimensions.* Whether we are bound fast to time and space or unbounded, we are open to all experience, to however life manifests.

As we move into life after midlife, the most powerful means we have of deepening the transformation that has taken place during midlife is to consciously engage with each experience that life sends our way and the process that unfolds in response. We have seen over and over that the experiences through which we evolve require breakdowns that are followed by expansions into new awareness. When we participate in, rather than resisting, these evolutions, we *consciously own the capacity to recycle ourselves.* That is, when we surrender to the cyclic experience of being dissolved or unraveled by life experiences – whether those are personal crises or encounters with the life force of spiders in their webs – and then re-integrate and emerge with a newly expanded consciousness, we meld with the natural cycles of death and rebirth. We live fully what life brings to us and are made more deeply human and at the same time bigger and more boundless by each experience.

No living system, however complex, can escape the fundamental cyclic nature of life: not you, not me, not the richest person in the world, not the poorest or the most spiritual. The more we allow for the inevitability of the cycle of aggregation, chaos, decay, and regeneration, the more we extend beyond physical realms into invisible worlds, slipping effortlessly from this side to the other side and back as the great wheel of life turns. Eventually there are fewer and fewer obstacles to where we can travel and who we can be. The fabricated worlds of logic and ego are gradually replaced by life teeming with aliveness. As this happens for us, we restore ourselves and the world to wholeness.

The lesson we take from midlife replaces the static model of Newtonian physics, which falsely promises that life can be measured accurately and made predictable. In its place, we have the new quantum physics, which complements our experiential knowing that life cannot be measured or arrested. Life emerges from the continuous interaction between chaos and order, destruction and the arising of the new. Both movements are required.

The idea of spiritual development no longer belongs selectively to the world of religion. Today we are the custodians of our own spiritual lives and of the expansions of consciousness that make up those lives. Moreover, as we have come to recognize our spiritual natures during the midlife journey, we have become able to see the divinity in others and in all forms of life. The more we think of each other as souls, the more we act out of love and respect for all beings. From this vantage point, no corrective paradigm is necessary – from our own ideals or standards, from a system of religious tenets, or from other rules – because everything is simply an expression of life and is, therefore, good just as it is. Our objective throughout our midlife journeys has been to align outer manifestations with inner realities so that all expressions are *whole-life* expressions. By the end, even the distinction of outer and inner falls away.

A Closing Zen Parable

> *A man walking across a field encountered a tiger. He fled, the tiger chasing after him. Coming to a cliff, he caught hold of a wild vine and swung himself over the edge. The tiger sniffed at him from above. Terrified, the man looked down to where, far below, another tiger had come, waiting to eat him. Two mice little by little began to gnaw away at the vine the man was holding onto. The man saw a luscious strawberry near him. Grasping the vine with one hand, he plucked the strawberry with the other. How sweet it tasted!*

Although this book has presented the midlife journey as a succession, ultimately the journey is neither rational nor methodical; rather, it is utterly irrational, unexplainable, and intuitive. *The only way to navigate midlife is to abandon the separate self and leap into the unknown at every opportunity.*

I thought the Zen parable would be an apt closing to our time together, the perfect complement to the opening story of the baby dolphins caught in the nets. We begin and end our journeys in the same condition: trapped in the unfathomable, irresolvable predicament called life. When we view life from a separate, ego-based sense of self, our prospects for handling the condition are not hopeful. But when we view it from the vantage point of the soul – which embraces our singular humanness and boundless divinity – the same condition offers a priceless opportunity, one we can take in with great joy.

In the parable above, some interpret the tiger above to be the past and the tiger below the future (certain death). The mice might be time and circumstances, chewing away at the fragile thread that connects our past and future as we dangle precariously between what has been and our inevitable conclusion.

Given that we are going to die, how are we going to live? Are we going to taste life (the strawberry) or spend our lives worrying about the circumstances that are chewing away at us (the mice)? Are we going to hold on tighter to what we know (the vine) or risk reaching for the moment (the strawberry)? Is the parable telling us that only by being in the moment can we truly appreciate life? Or that it is only when our situation feels the most precarious that we can open to the joy present in the moment?

Or is there a deeper message still?

In my mind, another reading of the parable is this: *The greater our capacity to be fully in the present moment, the larger that moment gets.* The more we can open to the largeness of a given moment, the more the past, future, and present are fused into one vast moment. Dangling from life's thread, to use the image from the parable, and tasting the strawberry that presents itself to us in the moment, our localized sense of self, our boundless sense of self, and our soulful point of interpenetration are fused into one. Death is like that: it is the moment at which one's entire life becomes a moment in the larger movement of the universe.

We can only fully be present for an experience if there is no one left to hold or capture it. If an "I" – a fixated ego or a conscious self-witness – is there to observe, then we are not in the moment. Children, the elderly, and really enlightened people don't have a lot of "I." The capacity to open to the moment is not about being awake in the sense that we usually think about it. It is about getting beyond the need to hold onto and possess what we think we need in order to understand, feel safe, be stable, or whatever else we clutch to feel okay. Being open to the moment means not needing any particular conditions to be met in order for us to feel okay.

"80-year-olds have given up the need to perfect themselves and 8-year-olds haven't learned it yet," says spiritual teacher Jonathan Tenney. Between 8 and 80, we think we have to protect ourselves. We imagine we are at risk from the loss of something. But, as we have seen throughout our midlife passage, the deepest teachings come from experiences that bring us into states of humility and loss, forcing us to let go of whatever we think we need in order to be who we are.

A key teaching of midlife is to enter the flow of life, to slip our canoes back into the water over and over. We can do this whenever we want to simply by meeting the psychological, emotional, or developmental edge present in any *mundane moment*. We don't have to wait for divorce or retirement or some other major event. The moment can be the littlest thing that happens when we are cooking dinner or driving to work. Moments that offer the opportunity to recollect us to ourselves happen all the time. They are small intersections; if we can stay in those intersections, the moments open up in mysterious and marvelous ways.

Many of us know how to focus on a moment when it comes in a big way – for example in the form of illness, a major relationship conflict, a lawsuit, or a challenging developmental issue – that grabs us and pulls us in. We know how to focus on moments of rapture in the form of sunsets, lovemaking, soul-stirring music, or other kinds of peak experience. We know how to focus on moments of physical and emotional pain, trauma, and drama.

But we mostly skip over the small, seemingly unremarkable moments. The little ordinary moments that make up the day-to-day life that we are living all the time don't necessarily grab us. *We have to consciously open to these moments and bring ourselves to them.* Instead of coming alive only at the big level, we need to come alive at the micro level too. There we will discover that there is something to do besides hold on, defend, and accumulate. There we will find the greatest joy of all on the path that returns us to the flow of life.

Every stage fully inhabited naturally prepares us for the next one. Life is a cycle; we cannot bypass any stage if we are to live fully. Although old behaviors and habits of thinking are not easily changed, stepping into new rhythms, such as the ones this book has offered, supports our unfolding and reveals that we are pliable and capable of unlimited expansion.

Everyone who writes about midlife quotes Dante's famous lines in *The Divine Comedy*, "Midway along the journey of our life, I found myself lost in a dark and treacherous wood," because the experience of loss and darkness that those lines describe is almost universal. But few quote his closing lines: "Yet, as a wheel moves smoothly, free from jars, my will and desire were turned by love, the love that moves the sun and other stars." I imagine that even as great a poet as Dante found it difficult to describe the final stages of midlife and the life beyond, in which love becomes the force that guides us. Perhaps the final stages are ultimately inexpressible even for poets. Or, perhaps the destination is, in fact, the journey itself after all.

We began our midlife journeys standing before a great unknown sea, one that we could not find a way around or across. We end, as is written in the Revelation of St. John the Divine, "And I saw a new heaven and a new earth: for the first heaven and the first earth were passed away; and there was no more sea."

From the moment of confronting that seemingly endless sea to this moment of ending our explorations together, we have traveled far, through challenging processes and dimensions of magic and mystery. We have arrived at a place where we recognize, as never before, how we are embedded in the fabric of the universe and the natural cycles of life, cycles we will live over and over as we meet each soul-expanding experience life sends to us.

We are now ready to become revolutionary in many senses of the word: to keep our wheels trued and revolving forward toward our next expansion of consciousness and the next after that; to live in harmony with the revolution of the Earth around the sun and on its axis, which creates the seasons and the days; to live the radical, soul-driven act of simply being and allowing life to unfold rather than trying to control it; to meet whatever life sends us with the transformative awareness that we are all connected, that there is no good vs. bad, no me vs. other – there is only love. From the perspective of our egos and the cultural conditioning that orchestrated the first half of our lives, directing us to strive and manage rather than allow, these are all revolutionary acts. We become revolutionaries in the service of life and the planet when, from a place of love and greater wholeness in ourselves, we knit together the fractured world.

As we stand on this next threshold and prepare to part onto our individual paths, I want to thank you from the deepest place in my heart, the place where there is only one of us, for your engagement and participation in this material and in life.

"Namaste" is the Sanskrit word that literally means "The spark of the divine in me bows to the spark of the divine in you." The soul and life force in me bow deeply to you and to the life force that brought us together for a time in this way.

I honor the place in you
in which the entire universe dwells.
I honor the place in you
which is of love, of truth, of light, and of peace.
I honor the place in you where,
if you are in that place in you,
and I am in that place in me,
there is only one of us.

May you be all that you are as you continue to unearth the hidden blessings that await you! Fare thee well.

—Jett Psaris

Acknowledgments

I am deeply grateful to the spiritually infused continent of India with its many generations of sages, who initiated my entry into midlife; to E, the doorknob to my spirit door; to the Green Goddess who instructed me in the multi-dimensionality of this one life we share; to the Honeybees who welcomed me into the heart of their honeycomb and shared their wisdom of group soul with me; to Cookie whose tragic loss broke open my heart; to the Camino de Santiago which showed me the way to my true home; to Mystic-Grace with whom I am enjoying the flowering of my open heart; and to Mary Busby and the Magdalene Order where the mystery is unveiled, in sacred ceremony, every week.

I also want to express my gratitude to Jonathan Tenney, Gay and Katie Hendricks, and Jennifer and John Welwood. Dear teachers, friends, brothers and sisters, I bow in gratitude to your love, wisdom, and generosity every day.

Special thanks to my editor, Nan Wishner, for her steadfast support and creativity. She is one part editor and one part clairvoyant, helping bring invisible insights into grounded and accessible concepts.

This magnum opus would not have been possible without the tireless inner work of countless friends, clients, students, group members, and workshop attendees who shared their lives and process openly and generously with me. Thank you all for your struggles to open, awaken, love, and care for the sanctity of life on your path to becoming who you truly are.

And saved for last but always first in my heart, words cannot express how grateful I am to my soul mate, partner, friend, and greatest blessing of this lifetime: Marlena Lyons. We have shared our life for 30 years, yet it would take more than 30 lifetimes to explore the tip of the iceberg that is you. Thank you for your depth, your wisdom, your humanity, your insight, your beauty, your joy, your laughter, your kindness, and your love. Every second is a blessing by your side.

About the Author

Jett Psaris, PhD, has spent the past 30 years inspiring others to embrace the full spectrum of their humanity through her writings, workshops, and private practice. She is a Nautilus Gold Award finalist for her first book, *Undefended Love*, coauthored with Marlena Lyons; and author of *Taking the Midlife Leap One Step at a Time*, the first online course dedicated to guiding seekers through an emotionally rigorous midlife transformation into the second half of life. Her books have been referred to as "sacred texts for modern times." For more information: www.jettpsaris.com.

Made in the USA
San Bernardino, CA
27 February 2017